An Introduction
to
African Civilizations

GEORGE W. WILLIAMS
Founder of African Studies in America.
First black member of the Ohio legislature.

An Introduction to African Civilizations

with
Main Currents in Ethiopian History

by

Willis N. Huggins
and
John G. Jackson

INPRINT EDITIONS
Baltimore

An Introduction to African Civilizations

First published 1937
Published 1999 by
INPRINT EDITIONS

Printed by BCP Digital Printing

ISBN-10- 1-58073-041-8
ISBN-13- 978-1-58073-041-9

ABOUT INPRINT EDITIONS

Our mission is to keep good books in print. We give life to books that might never be published or republished by making them available On Demand. Manuscripts and books are scanned, stored, and then printed as single or multiple copies from our digital library. When reprinting out-of-print books, we always use the best copy available.

INPRINT EDITIONS are especially useful to scholars, students, and general readers who have an interest in enjoying all that books have to offer. Our books are also a valuable resource for libraries in search of replacement copies.

Order INPRINT EDITIONS from:
Black Classic Press
P.O. Box 13414
Baltimore, MD 21203

CONTENTS

—3—

LIST OF ILLUSTRATIONS

An Introduction
to
African Civilizations

Preface

WITHIN recent years there has been a large and welcome accession of printed materials for the study of the civilizations, cultures, and social institutions of Africa. This has been due, chiefly to the partial publication of the findings in recent excavations, the willingness of many private collectors to make available more of their books on Africa, the wider use of the collections in the Boston Public Library, the New York Public Library, the Congressional Library, the Library at Howard University, Washington, D. C., and the Library at Fisk University, Nashville, Tennessee. Then, too, there is an increasing number of white historians and writers who are becoming fairer in dealing with data pertaining to Africa. Many white writers are in position to mold, or to help mold, opinion. They are not quite willing, however, to shelve old fallacies regarding Africa and the African upon which, apparently, they have directly or tacitly agreed. Some writers deplore the harm done to the cultural past of Africa and condemn other writers and scholars who have failed, with authentic data at hand, to interpret them aright. Most of the white writers are still too timid to enter the lists and help to make the proper adjustments.

The driving forces in the organization of a dependable body of information dealing with the African at home or abroad, have centered in the energies of a small group of black scholars, aided by a larger group of eminent white men.

As far back as 1881, the renowned Dr. Edward Wilmot Blyden, on the occasion of his inauguration as president of Liberia College, sounded the note for the organized teaching of the culture and civilization of Africa.

Contemporary with Dr. Blyden was the great Alexander Crummell, the dean, of the black scholarly and literary group, in the closing quarter of the Nineteenth Century. It was the magnanimity of Dr. Crummell that fired the imagination and re-doubled the vigor of Dr. W. E. B. DuBois, whose trenchant pen began to burn its trace, in national and international affairs, from the early nineties to this day.

Indeed in that period, Dr. DuBois wrote his "Suppression of the African Slave Trade," a model dissertation form, for writers in that field. Then followed, "The Atlanta University Studies," which set the pattern, for the scientific investigation of the status of black folk, in the Western World. At the opening of the present century he published his, "Souls of Black Folk," a work of the highest literary merit and a new form of racial expression. In 1915, the "Home University Library" brought out, "The Negro," in which Dr. DuBois outlined the program that must be followed, in order to deal properly with the whole field of African life and history.

Meanwhile, Dr. Carter G. Woodson came forward with his researches and publications which have blossomed forth into the widest popularization of the subject.

Quietly, Dr. J. E. Moorland and Mr. Arthur A. Schomburg led the field in gathering material. That of the former is now the "Moorland Collection," in the library at Howard University, Washington, D. C., and that of the latter is now the great "Schomburg Collection," in New York City, divided between the main library at Forty-second Street and Fifth Avenue and the branch library in Harlem.

Supplementing the work of these pioneers were the activities of the American Negro Academy and the more recent research and publications of men like Dr. Alain Locke, Dean Kelly Miller, Dr. Benjamin G. Brawley, Dr. James Weldon Johnson, Dr. Charles Wesley, Dr. Rayford Logan, Dr. William Pickens, Professor Charles S. Johnson, Professor John W. Cromwell, Sr., Dr. Otelia Cromwell, Honorable Marcus Garvey, Mr. Hubert Harrison, and Mr. J. A. Rogers.

An invaluable review of Ethiopian Source Material has been made by Dr. William L. Hansberry.

Outside the United States, the voice of the Honorable

Dantes Bellegarde was heard in Haiti and Geneva; the Honorable Blaise Diagne was heard in French West Africa and in the Chamber of Deputies in Paris; Dr. J. E. K. Aggrey and the Honorable Caseley Hayford were listened to in British West Africa and London; the great publicist John Tengo Jabavu was articulate in South Africa, assisted by Sol Plaatje and Clement Kadalie. Indeed the story of South Africa, cannot be told unless mention be made of the life and personality of King Khama, of Bechuanaland and his illustrious descendant, Chief Tschekedi, of the Bamangwato, whose recent conflict, with the British in Bechuanaland, is a memorable phase of South African life. Duse Mohammed, in his "African Times and Orient Review," laid down a program for Egypt and North Africa, while Paul Panda and Réné Maran lifted their voices, respectively, in the Belgian Congo and French Equatorial Africa.

In Ethiopia, the military genius of Menelek II in the best tradition of Pianhki and Sheshonk, rulers of ancient Egypt and Ethiopia, drove out the Italians in 1896 and maintained the liberties of that ancient free empire of black men. Hard by Ethiopia in the model state of Uganda, Sir Apolo Kagwa worked, in a statesmanlike way with His Majesty Daudi Chwa, King of the Bagandas, to preserve one of the finest culture-patterns that the world has ever known. The Uganda martyrs, saintly in devotion to their faith, represent a feat, in religious heroism, unsurpassed in the annals of the Catholic Church. The black world in South America, especially in Brazil, where racialism is not so tense, furnishes a theme for a separate story, and yet mention must be made here of Bishop Sylveria Gomez Pimentar, who rose to that high place in the Church in Brazil, in 1902, repeating the achievement of Bishop Luna Victoria, in Peru, back in the middle of the Eighteenth Century.

Significant among the recent contributions by white writers is, "The Negro," published in 1934 by Miss Nancy Cunard of the Cunard family in the British nobility. It is a volume (11 x 15) comprising 855 pages, profusely illustrated, in which Miss Cunard sets forth an anthology of Africans throughout the world.

Leo Frobenius, the great German scholar, completed, in 1934 his epic trilogy on Africa. In 1913 he published "Die Stimme Afrikas" (The Voice of Africa); in 1925, "Erlebte Erdteile" (Continents Where I Have Lived); and in 1934, "Kulturgeschichte Afrikas," (The Cultural History of Africa). In 1925, Frobenius published his "Das Unbekannte Afrika" (Unknown Africa), in which plates 134 to 194 portray the development of African Art. This work is complementary to "Erlebte Erdteile."

His latest work has an overwhelming wealth of pictures, legends, and accounts of religious and political institutions. His thesis, in general, is the same, namely, that cultural phases and their manifestations have sprung up throughout the world and among all peoples; that the noble fruits of civilization in Africa, like those in Asia and Europe, have been destroyed, again and again; that the present lack of cultural co-ordination in Africa flows, largely, from the fact that Africa's flourishing periods of art, political and religious institutions, commenced much earlier than those in other continents; that these periods came to an end, probably, suppressed by wars and strangled by slavery and the slave trade.

The records of that past are shown by crude drawings scratched on rocks, and the tissue of legend and religious symbolism that have survived to his day among the various native tribes.

Frobenius again makes a spirited attack upon those scoffers at Africa whose concept of fetischism has lowered the standing of Africans and has cruelly wronged their religious life. He offers something new, in that he divides the peoples of Africa into two major groups—Hamites and Ethiopians—and regards the Nubian as the finest example of the mixtures of these groups. The book closes, significantly, with an ancient Nubian sermon on, "The Life Pleasing to God," the thoughtfulness and humor of which is strikingly paralleled in many of the churches among the blacks today.

In order to bring the broader outlines of the subject as far down to date as possible, much data was personally checked

(1935) in the Bibliotheque Nationale and the Permanent Museum of the Colonies in Paris; the Brussells Museum at Tervueren and the Brussells Mondaneum; the British Museum, London; the Bodleian Library, Oxford University, England and the Berlin Museum. Spanish and Latin-American sources have been recently checked by Mr. A. A. Schomburg. The method developed for presenting the subject was worked out at the A. and M. College, Huntsville, Alabama, 1915-1917 and in later years with literary societies, selected student groups in the 135th Street Y.M.C.A. and the Ethiopian Students Club, West 117th Street, New York. It is now offered for wider use by teachers, entering this field for the first time, who have not followed its main lines of development in any definitely connected way. It is hoped that this book will prove valuable to students in secondary schools and colleges and especially so to independent study club groups and to the general reader.

Work in this field can be made attractive, inspiring, challenging, provided that one is armed at the outset, at least with the works of Dr. Woodson, Dr. DuBois, Dr. Brawley, the Cromwells and Professor Charles S. Johnson.

The Themes here set forth constitute a series of problems, which have sufficient elasticity, in the hands of the skillful and resourceful teacher, to cover assignments for the school year of 36 to 40 weeks, with ample provision for supplementary reading.

The crumbling of the "Aryan" theory has been brought down to date by grace of attacks on extreme racialism in Germany. This should be a matter of satisfaction to the black races who have been slapped in the face with those lines in Myers General History which read:—

> From time immemorial the negroes have been hewers of wood and drawers of water for their more favored brethren. (Aryans?)

More than that the way is clearing now for the crumbling of other fallacies which have persisted under the guise of racial classifications, migrations, gifts, and cultures.

A brief note on "International Relations" is included in order that the student may be enabled to keep his balance and have a sense of proportion in dealing with the world at large. The writer is under no illusion that there is a general history of Africa. Hence there will appear in this book many repetitions, consciously made, because of the belief that the study of superior performances among the indigenous African peoples or where they have met and mingled with other types, will help beginners, in this field, to form ideals and attitudes, and to acquire skill, in simple investigation.

Nor is the writer laboring under any impression that this book is in the least original except as to approach, method, and form. He is conscious of the fact that success, in realizing its full objectives will be incomplete.

Its final value lay in its possible power to induce reflection because of organized reading. This may urge the more ambitious to undertake the much needed real research.

A list of all those to whom especial thanks are due for suggestions, would be considerable in length. However, mention must be made of Mr. J. A. Rogers, who opened the way to private collections in Paris and to valuable material in Brussells and Berlin. Honorable Dantes Bellegarde, former Haitian Minister to the United States, opened his library in Washington, D. C., and made available important pages on Haiti. The author's recent visit to that country—August, 1934—gave him direct access to government documents and historical papers through the courtesy of President Stenio Vincent and the Members of his Cabinet.

Thanks are due also to Glen Visscher who kindly permitted me to use her library and read manuscripts which she has prepared on Africa.

Valuable suggestions and aids were received on West Africa from students here from that area, Mr. A. H. Vigo, Northern Nigeria; Mr. Samuel Ita, Southern Nigeria; Mr. A. E. Chinbush and Mr. A. N. deHeer, Accra, Gold Coast; Mr. Durodola Koli and Mr. Dousuma Johnson, Sierra Leone, and Mr. Lapido Solanke, who directs the publishing of "WASU" in London, in the interest of The West African Students Union. Thanks are due to Mr. Ernest Kalabala, of Uganda, East Africa, a graduate student in Education, Columbia University and also to Dr. M. E. Bayen, formerly a medical student at Howard University, from Ethiopia. Mr. Claude McKay, the novelist, recently returned from a long stay in North Africa, cleared up many points in regard to that area.

To two of my pupils, Miss Lorena Spicer, M. A., Columbia University and Mr. Wilhelm J. Halse, graduate student, New York University, I am indebted for checking the manuscript and reading proof.

WILLIS N. HUGGINS

NEW YORK CITY, JUNE 1, 1937.

EDWIN WILMOT BLYDEN
*Great West Indian Scholar and Benefactor of the
African West Coast*

MARCUS GARVEY
Seer and Organizer

Introductory Survey

LONG AGO DR. DUBOIS pictured the mind-set by which black men are distraught in western civilization.

The trouble is that few people have read what he had to say and those who did read it, probably missed its inner meaning.

Thus on page 3, in his, "Souls of Black Folk":

> After the Egyptian and Indian, the Greek and Roman, the Teuton and Mongolian, the Negro is a sort of seventh son, born with a veil, and gifted with second-sight in this American world,—a world which yields him no true self-consciousness but only lets him see himself through the revelations of the other world. It is a peculiar sensation, this double-consciousness, this sense of always looking at one's self through the eyes of others, of measuring one's soul by the tape of a world that looks on with amused contempt and pity. One ever feels his twoness,—an American, a Negro; two souls, two thoughts, two unreconciled strivings; two warring ideals in one dark body, whose dogged strength alone keeps it from being torn asunder.

Here is the quintescence of misgivings bidding the blacks to turn their attention upon themselves and into their own racial soul. In doing so they do not, necessarily, throw away whatever they may consider their American heritage.

One of the major difficulties, in the true alignment of the racial past of Africans, is the utter absence of a popular understanding of the proper ethnic labels for the peoples in Northern and Northeastern Africa. These mulatto groups may not know that the blacks in America exist. If so, then such lack of information, to our purposes, for the time being, is unimportant. If they do know of their kinsmen in the Western World and reject ethnic ties with them and the legions in Africa, then this is important and for the most part, only the pseudo-scientists are to blame. Men, whose forebears wrenched

Africans, body and soul from Africa, would not hesitate to commit further and more refined robbery, by filching from them spirit and culture. They must despoil them more in order to "justify" the sins of their fathers.

It is well at this point to remark that it is chiefly the blacks in the Continental United States that have made any appreciable ado about Means and Methods of Synthesizing racial culture. The tribal peoples in Africa have little feeling of "Nationalism," their patriotism and loyalty is narrow and rigid localism. Social cleavages, and even Color Caste among the upper classes in Liberia, Sierra Leone, Senegal and Ethiopia are as fixed as they were until recently among the blacks in the United States. Nor do the leaders and rulers in the African areas, just mentioned, seek any sort of culture or economic alignment which would lead to a broader understanding. Imperial Ethiopia and Republican Liberia took little note, the one of the other. This then is the triumph of forces within and without native Africans which are keeping them apart. Be that as it may, the job to be done is more and more intriguing and none the less challenging.

So long as the world veers to and accepts the American definition of "a negro," then wherever the "tar-brush" has veiled a people, even in the least degree, a claim to a share in that culture must be made. The pseudo-scientist cannot have it both ways. Either mulattoes in America and abroad should be taken into the white fold or they should be left alone. This, of course, would be too logical. Even mice can find many reasons, philanthropic and otherwise, for not belling the cat!

The great Hindu poet and savant, Tagore, was rudely treated when he visited California some time ago. Assurances to hotel owners that he was "not a negro," availed little if at all.

Perchance the saintly and swarthy Gandhi shies from American shores in order to avoid American mockery. Agha Khan, multi-millionaire sportsman and ruler of the province of Baroda in India, was once shamefully abused in a London night club. When assurances that he was "not a negro" were given to his attackers, they agreed that he could stay. They had thought that he was "a negro;" to him that was enough. Forthwith he left the place.

In 1919 an Ethiopian Mission came to America. Its members were officially received by the authorities in Washington. But when they came to New York they were refused entertainment at the Democratic Club albeit they were the guests of the nation then under a democratic administration. Thence they were carried to the Republican Club by their guide, Mr. Topokyan, Persian Consul in New York, only to find "nobody home." Presumably the latter club had been tipped off by telephone. These distinguished Ethiopians finally found themselves atop Hammerstein's Roof Garden, a place utterly different from what they had expected before they left Washington. They sailed next day. At sea they got a radiogram from the president of the United States regretting the incident. The members of the Mission were housed at the Old Waldorf Astoria. In 1933, a Prince Desta Demtou came to America from Ethiopia to repay the visit of the American official representative at the coronation of Haille Selassie as Emperor of Ethiopia. He and his compatriot, the Ethiopian Minister to Jersusalem, did not stop at the New Waldorf. This time the Hotel St. Moritz did the honors!

Turning sharply to the self-governing peoples of African descent in the new world, we get a close up view, akin to what has happened and is still happening in Northern and Northeastern Africa. The mulatto republic of Santo Domingo wends its way, probably, without a thought of Africa or of Africans in America. Except for some very definite historical incidents, the Dominicans would ignore their Haitian neighbors. Haiti, herself, only in a few exceptional cases, is all but guilty of the same indifference. However, twenty years under the American Occupation have elicited from the latter something of a gesture of amity and good will. The shadow of American bayonets may have to fall again upon the Dominicans before they feel the urge for mutual action with others of their kind. Indeed wherever black blood simmers throughout these isles, from Cuba and the Bahamas to the borders of South America, there should be an alignment among peoples of African descent, not merely for amity, but for active economic interests. This survey would fall, far short of its purpose, if attention were not called to three situations which affect the blacks immediately here in America. First, the rapid dwindling and crumbling of the status of "half-a-man," which the blacks, above the Mason-Dixon Line, have had up to now. Second, the blacks must stop that which should have never been, namely, sneers at the helplessness of their folk in Dixie and the underbreath whispers that they are cowards because they do not offer armed resistance. The blacks in the Southland are as brave a breed as ever lived. It takes courage for the upstanding man to live there. Of such as these, in the South, there are legion. Like other minority groups, similarly placed, they have not burst into futile, violent revolt, the end of which is easy to see. These same people, however, in Washington, Chicago and Omaha, acquitted themselves well in the face of tremendous odds during riot periods. If the blacks, North and South, really wish to resist oppression then more of them would "pay" for the instruments with which to fight. Were 10,000,000 of them to average ten cents each for civic defense and advancement, they could raise $1,000,000 a year and place it in the hands of one responsible organization; if they averaged one cent each they could raise the paltry sum of $100,000 per year for such defense. Neither of which have they done.

Third, there is the empty and destructive criticism of the total of what the blacks have been able to do in this country, in terms of the total of what other minority groups have been able to do. Often the expression is heard, "look at the Irish,— look at the Jews," when the poser has done little or nothing to develop within himself or others the springs of effective action shown by these groups. Since the Jews are supposed to have close analogies to the blacks in sorrow and oppression, let us look at them. In broad outlines, we see a people dispossessed of their land, broken, scattered, and harried everywhere in the centuries since their sorrows in Babylon, Egypt and Rome. Yet a people standing adamant against the crucifixion story and all other weapons used against them; a people highly and mightily represented in all the arts of peace, buttressed by finance (to be sure there are many pitifully poor Jews) and energized by strategic political vantage points; a people who have cleavages, in many respects, wider than those among the blacks and a provoking element among them which would throw over-board, much that is dear to the Jewish soul. Among them there are a few individuals who have dared, sometimes, at the risk of economic and social injury to themselves, to extend to the blacks counsel, fellowship, money. It would seem, utterly wide of the mark to compare, in toto, one people, less than 100 years from bondage, weighted with the color-bar, heedless that they were once great in the world's esteem and lacking in specialized training, in modern society, with a people centuries relatively free, flanked with accumulated honors and goods and quickened with a fierce pride in the glory of their cultural past. Yet with all their advantages the landless Jews in Germany find themselves well on the way to practically the same helplessness as that of black folk in the South. Black people have not risen, in armed, massed, resistance against their oppressors in the Southland, nor is it likely that the Jewish masses will rise, in armed resistance, against their oppressors in Germany. And no one should call them cowards because they do not seek that method of escape.

Some of the blacks still pin hope in a return of liberalism, forgetting to note how the march of events have qualified such action. Liberal forces have been sluggish in relation to the Irish, oppressed in their homeland; liberal forces did not rally to the Koreans when Japan was swallowing up that unhappy country. In defiance of the League of Nations, this same Japan plundered Manchuria, is entrenched there today, and liberal forces are practically silent. Except for the present economic boycott, liberal forces are "strangely" remiss in regard to the Jew in Germany nor are there signs that world opinion will call upon England to live up to the Balfour Declaration so that the Jew may enter, and be free in, Palestine. Only a hair's breadth is now keeping Liberia from being offered up as a sacrifice to the greed of the "Aryan" gods in Germany. Economic motives, not humanitarianism, have pulled the American marines out of Haiti. The economic forces, veneered with "humanitarianism," that once entered the Southland and freed the blacks, will go there again, nevermore, nor will they speak, effectively, for them in this hour of new world change and new reconstruction. The quickening of pace by the spur of "look at the Jews, —look at the Irish," is only momentary. In the long run it creates a defeatist psychology. If black men are willing to look at all, they should look, and teach their children to look, at themselves when they were equal, dominant, and ruling forces in the world; to look for and to get all they can, today, of the best that the modern world offers in educational, political, economic, and social development and at the same time to look around the world at the oppressed landless minorities of all peoples. This view will help gain a higher respect for themselves; a more assured position in the North and bring into clearer relief, the position of the blacks in the South.

Some of the American blacks have the assimilation complex; others are willing to hover around the fringes of their racial life, close enough to dash back to it when profitable, but far enough away to depart from it when expeditious. In general, these have no vision. They are neither fish, flesh nor fowl —mostly foul. The world of today and tomorrow is a narrow, nationalist, unsympathetic world. Implications show that no longer is patriotism enough. Yonder you must be a "pure" German, a "good" Frenchman or a "headless" Fascist and here you must be a "100 per cent American," with all its sinister import. Doubly foolhardy then will black men be if they do not bestir the soul that is within them, girding with courage and vision for the onslaught which they must meet.

Survey of Pre-Historic Man

AFRICA HAS been fertile in the production of human breeds. Whether the black type was indigenous there or entered from Asia does not seriously alter the equation. Even if it were granted that the blacks were not there first, indications are that they will remain in Africa after the Europeans there have perished.

Historians, dealing with Africa, have sought, almost as a first premise, to "prove" that given peoples and given types of historical relics are not indigenous. They follow this with assertions that the blacks have no history and that they have neither created nor contributed to culture and civilization. It would probably be as difficult to change this notion about the African as it would be to change the crucifixion label placed upon the Jew.

On this point, the reflections made, during the second quarter of the Nineteenth Century, by the great philosopher Wilhelm Friedrich Hegel, prove interesting:

> "It (Africa)" is no historical part of the World; it has no movement or development to exhibit. Historical movements in it—that is in it's northern part—belong to the Asiatic or European World. Egypt—does not belong to the African Spirit. What we properly understand by Africa, is the Unhistorical, Undeveloped Spirit, still—on the threshold of World History."

Such pronouncements were accepted at their face value in the great seats of learning in Europe and in America. Hegelianism, as far as African history is concerned, was not successfully challenged until the appearance since 1890 of works by W. E. B. DuBois, Leo Frobenius, Arthur F. Chamberlain, Franz Boas and Carter G. Woodson.

Paradoxical as it may seem, the black race is the world's oldest and youngest race. Youngest, because it gets joy out of laughter, turns sorrow into song and insists upon survival through its high procreative powers. Little can be gained by disputations as to the world's oldest race. Nature has attended to that. Life begins where there is heat. The great heat centers of the world are the Sudan in Central Africa, the Nile Valley and Ethiopia in Northeast Africa and the Kalahari Desert in South Africa. Paralleling these, but not quite co-ordinate, are heat areas in Central and South America, the Gobi Desert in Asia, the sub-continent of India and distant Australia. Whether we conclude that waves of black men entered Africa from Asia or that hordes of peoples from the Nile Valley moved southward to the Cape, the results would be the same, namely, a reverse migration of blacks who had earlier moved north, east and southeast. Evidence that the blacks spread into these distant areas is seen in the Elephanta (Bombay), Ellora, Kanarah and Hindostan.

More evidence may be noted in the Negroid gods of Siam and Negroid Buddhas of India. The same thing is true of the statues at Nagpoor near Benares and also in the Hindu Trinity.

So similar were the temples at Dendera, in Nubia and the Nile Valley, that Sepoys, in the British service in that area, worshipped them without any ado. Even in Japan the early gods are represented with wooly hair. It is hardly possible that these early peoples would have made their gods so unlike themselves.

The far antiquity of the African is evidenced in the fact that his primitive art and architecture, especially in South Africa, were created before Egypt was Egypt and before Mohenjo-daro, in India, was born. Living for millenia amidst the most profuse and variegated flora and under the most direct rays of the sun, the African developed a sense of beauty and a feeling for rhythm, impossible in the glacier-gripped areas or at least in the more northerly climes.

Today, for example, the art of the Eskimo gives no motif for a base to what is called "modernism" nor has it affected the tempo and rhythm in the modern song and dance. These gifts have been reserved to the African. Likewise, in antiquity, these same gifts, by successive migrations of African peoples, were carried northward into Egypt and thence southeast into India. In the latter area these gifts became infused into the Indo-European currents that pooled themselves, between 2500 B.C. and and 2,000 B. C., in Southeastern Europe.

"In the great civilizations of antiquity the inspiration of poetry and art came from the black race. The European organized his civilizations and established their laws and governments, but the source from which their art issued was foreign to the instincts of the organizing civilizers. It lay in the blood of the blacks. That universal power of imagination which we see enveloping and penetrating primordial civilizations, came entirely from the ever increasing influxion of blood from the black race into the white. The African possesses in a high degree, the faculty of emotion from the senses, without which art is impossible."

The ancient "African Volkerwanderung" was widespread. It peopled Australasia and shows its traces in the Veddahs, Todas, Tamils, and Dravidians of India and adjacent areas. Early non-white peoples were contributors also to the practical arts. For just as the Chinese created the basic mixture for powder, so the forges of the early West African were the first to bring forth iron. Tragically, however, "iron and powder," the twin-gifts of the two non-white races, have been used to bar their advancement in the present and for the near destruction of their ancient racial cultures.

Among the recognized classic types of primitive men, the "Grimaldi" are African. These "Grimaldi" peoples, covered Southeastern, Southern and Southwestern Europe. They left a primary African base for art in ancient Greece and a secondary base for color in Austria, Italy, France and Spain. The "Oldoway Man" in Northeast Africa, the "Rhodesian" or "Broken Hill Man" in South Africa, must have an unbiased re-check. Likewise a new appraisal must be made of the relics and remains of the Zymbabwe, in South Africa, in the light of very recent findings. When these things have been done new chapters in ethnology will have to be written.

The persistence of the African in the midst of western civilization is no accident. He has long been accustomed and

conditioned to radical changes. His status under such milieu
would have been greater had he earlier drawn inspiration from
his rich heritage in organization, traces of which are seen,
throughout Africa, wherever he has come into contact with
non-African races.

In our own times whites and blacks have met and mingled
in the Mississippi Valley, but only as master, slave and semi-
freeman. However, in the Indus River Valley, the Tigris-Euphrates and the Valley of the Nile, they met and mingled, in-
terchangeably, as the conquered and the conqueror; as victor
and vanquished; as equal and unequal. As nearly as 5,000 B.C.,
civilization was well under way in the Nile Valley. Co-ordinate
with other racial types in that area at that time, were distinc-
tive black men. Their traces and remains are everywhere evident. References to them may be found in far off Babylonia,
Chaldea, and Assyria. Often they are pictured as slaves and
bearers of tribute, but, in reality, they were more often actually rulers, conquerors and receivers of tribute.

Ridicule of the blacks because they lost the mastery of
Nile Valley civilization, fails of its point, due to the very hol-
lowness of its procedure. All racial and national ascendancies
have had their rise, decline, decadence and death. For example,
the culture and civilization today in western Europe will not
last forever. In spite of its recent growth, the inner soul of
European culture is already affected.

The discovery of America in 1492 blurred Europe's pris-
tine qualities through the violence which it perpetuated in the
New World and the ill-gotten wealth it secured there during
several centuries of dishonor. European art, divorced from its
basis in religion, slowly changed in form until revamped
through motifs taken from primitive African art. The Treaty
of Westphalia, 1648, is approximately the high noon of European culture. For here was a widening of the crevice made
when Protestantism collided with Catholicism, in the Thirty
Years War, a rift which is continually widening.

Later, in the middle of the Nineteenth Century, Japan
was awakened. This with the consequent stir in the Far East,

including India, were no auguries of good fortune for Western Europe. Such situations have been complicated, by rival European nationalisms, from the fall of Napoleon and the flight of Metternich, to the fighting out of old grudges by Frank and Teuton, in the Franco-Prussian War, 1870-71. Prior to this war, there was the spectacle of christian Europe lining up with the so-called "Terrible, Unspeakable, Infidel Turk," to smash christian Russia in the Crimean War, 1853-1856. More phenomenal still, was the spectacle of Nordic, christian Germany walking, arm in arm with this same Turk, in an attempt to forever blast Western Europe in the Great World War, 1914-1918.

Today super-nationalism, materialism and Caesarism are rampant in Europe. The states there, strained and bent by the very pressure of their economic weaknesses and military necessites, are rapidly turning to primitive modes of thought and action.

A revival of Islamic waves, is in the making, while a gleeful, vigorous and threatening Communism, mocks a feeble, sterile, and causeless christianity. America, which assumed the social reconstruction of the world after the Great War, is now, well nigh prostrate, under her load of crime, violence, alienism and social division. The spectre of Communism, though now only the size of a man's hand, terrifies the American church and state. The greatest of America's money changers, has sent out an S.O.S. pleading for harmony among the Protestant forces in order to gird for the battle of tomorrow, while the Catholic forces, strengthened, through ancient unity, stand their ground, now, ready to do battle with the oncoming foe. The dust of Tyre, the halls at Karnak and the stones of Babylon, all attest the wreckage of the old world, for, in them all, selfishness, the ancient traitor, hid, and thus they tottered and fell like unstable foam.

The modern nations apparently bulwarked by iron and powder, have despoiled and are still despoiling the minorities and the weaker races of the earth. Such greed was the prelude to the present war-flares in Europe which themselves may be

a preface to the decline of the west, and the rise of a newer
world destiny.

EARLY EGYPT

Few nations possess a more romantic history than Egypt.
The valley of the Nile was for many centuries the storehouse
of civilization. The most impressive thing about Egypt is its
imposing grandeur; overwhelming even in ruin and desolation.
The origin of the Egyptians has been a topic of much
speculation. Egyptologists are divided into two camps. One
side holding that the Egyptians came from Asia; the other
faction arguing that the Egyptians were of African origin. Sir
Flinders Petrie favors an Asiatic origin, for example; whereas
the late Sir Gaston Maspero advocated an African origin.
This latter view has gained much favor in recent years, and is
supported by overwhelming evidence. Even Petrie admits the
African origin of the great monument builders of the Third
and Fourth Dynasties. This culture, which Petrie calls the fifth
civilization of Egypt, "was due to an invasion from the south;
a conqueror, of Sudani features, founded the Third Dynasty,
and many entirely new ideas entered the country. This new
movement culminated in the vast schemes of Khufu, one of
history's most dominating personalities. With him the lines
of Egyptian growth were established; and the course of events
became the subject of the written record."
The Edfu Text is an important source document on the
early history of the Nile valley. This famous inscription, found
in a temple at Edfu gives an account of the origin of Egyptian
civilization. According to this account, civilization was brought
to Egypt from the south by a band of invaders under
the leadership of King Horus. This ruler, Horus, was in later
days deified, and became ultimately the Egyptian Christ. The
followers of Horus were called "the Blacksmiths," because
they had weapons of iron. Dr. Arthur G. Brodeur places the
genesis of this culture in Somaliland. In his own words:

"There are in Somaliland ruins of regular buildings of dressed stone, which show a clear resemblance to those of early Egypt. It appears probable that the ancestors of the South Egyptians came originally from this region, entering the Nile valley through Nubia, and bringing with them a civilization already fairly developed. This migration must have taken place long before 5,000 B.C."

The estimate of the French Egyptologist, Chabas, that the civilization of Egypt is at least 11,000 years old should not be considered excessive. The Great Sphinx is a statue of the sun-god Horus. It has been estimated to be at least 10,000 years old. "The origin of the Sphinx is wrapped in mystery," but according to an inscription of Khufu it is recorded "as being much older than the Great Pyramids . . . In addition to the direct evidence for its prehistoric antiquity, it is certain that if such monument had been erected by any of the historical kings, it would have been inscribed with hieroglyphics, and the fact recorded in Manetho's lists and contemporary records, whereas all tradition of its origin seems to have been lost in the night of ages." The first king of the First Dynasty is know as Aha-Mena or Menes. The authorities differ on the date of his reign. Breasted puts it at 3400 B.C., while Petrie sets it at 5510 B.C., a yawning chasm of over 2,000 years. The basis of Egyptian chronology is the lost "History of Egypt," by Manetho. Ptolemy Philadelphus, King of Egypt in the Third Century B.C. commissioned Manetho, a learned Egyptian priest of the Temple of Sebennytus to write a history from the earliest times up to his own day. Unfortunately this history has been for the most part lost; but among the surviving fragments are his list of the kings of Egypt. This list divides the rulers, of Egypt into 31 Dynasties. This scheme has been followed by the Egyptologists reluctantly, since they have not been able to devise a better one.

Sir Grafton Elliot Smith has treated the subject of ·Egyptian ethnology at length in his "Ancient Egyptians," in which we read the following:

"Not a few writers, like the traveller Volney, in the Eighteenth Century, have expressed the belief that the ancient Egyptians were Negroes, or at any rate strongly Negroid. In recent times even a writer so discriminating as Ripley usually is has given his adhesion to this view." Sir Grafton, needless to say, does not agree with Count Volney and Professor Ripley, since in his own words, there is "a profound gap that separates the Negro from the rest of mankind, including the Egyptians."

The time of the first four dynasties is known as the Old Kingdom. This period culminated in the great pyramid building reigns of Cheops, Chephren and Mycerinus (all of the Fourth Dynasty). The Great Pyramid of Gizeh is the most famous of all the pyramids of Egypt, and one of the greatest monuments of all time. This colossal structure, reared about 4,000 B.C., during the reign of the Pharaoh Cheops (also known as Khufu), embodies the amazing scientific knowledge of Egypt in its venerable stones. It contained a slab of stone (still extant) in its interior, in length, one-tenmillionth of the distance from either pole to the equator (the basis of the modern metric system of measurement). The height of the Great Pyramid is one-billionth of the distance from the earth to the sun, a measurement not accurately completed by modern scientists until 1874. The structure is so situated that the parallel of longitude which passes through it traverses the most land and the least sea of any on the globe; a fact which is equally true of the parallel of latitude which passes through it. Besides this, it is orientated within one-twelfth of one degree, a remarkable precision, difficult of attainment even in our own day. The triangular area of each of the four sloping sides equals the square of the vertical height of the Pyramid. If the length of the four sides of the base are added together they bear to the vertical height the same proportion as the circumference of a circle does to its radius. (This ratio gives us the famous mathematical constant π (pi), whose numerical value is 3.1416.) The length of each side is 365 and $\frac{1}{4}$ sacred cubits, exactly equivalent to the number of days in the year. There is a voluminous literature dealing with the Great Pyramid. Among the best works are Richard A. Proctor's "Problems of the Pyramids" and Abbé Moreux's "Mysterious Science of the Pharaohs." No one has yet "proved" that the pyramids are not the work of a Negroid folk.

THE BLACK MAN AT THE DAWN OF CULTURE

There is a definite glimpse of the wide diffusion of the African races through the discoveries made in France at the opening of the present century. In the caves at Bassenpoy, southern France, were found roughly carved quartz instruments, statuettes and bas-reliefs dating back 20,000 years ago. The caves at Grimaldi, in France, yielded similar articles but of better workmanship. To these have been added "finds" at Laussel, France and at Wilensdorf, Austria. All these early works of art are similar to types found in South Africa among the Hottentots and especially the Bushman branch of that tribe. It is of much interest still to know that there are great similarities of habit between the blacks who were in France and southern Europe 20,000 years ago and the present natives of South Africa, particularly in their wall decoration, and in the manufacture of stone and feather necklaces. In addition to art works, there were skeletal remains which were definitely native African, also found in the Grimaldi caves. Thus it can be now agreed that "The Grimaldi Man" is one of the definite, classic types which led-off in the evolution of culture.

To turn from "The Grimaldi Man" as an African "youngster" to the much disputed specimen, known as "The Oldoway Man" of East Africa, is to run into a maze of confusions, and into millenias of time.

Until now the supposition had been that modern man, homo sapiens, had not appeared until after the extinction of Neanderthal man in Europe at about the time of the last Ice Age, 40,000 years ago. Now, however, British scientists believe homo sapiens and the great apes were living side by side in Africa from early Pleistocene times, as far back as the Piltdown and Peking man skulls, between 200,000 and 500,000 years ago. These changes in point of view are due to the fact that, in 1913, in the Oldoway district of old German East Africa, Dr. Hans Reck discovered a completely fossilized man. The authenticity of this find was vouched for by Dr. L. S. B. Leakey, British anthropologist who, in 1932, made additional discoveries in the same area.

Now the celebrated Oldoway skeleton, which has been believed by some scientists to be the oldest known specimen of true man, is declared to date from a fairly recent period.

A definite announcement to this effect was made before the Congress of Prehistoric and Protohistoric Sciences at its meeting in 1932. Though the skeleton was found in 1,000,000-year-old strata at Oldoway, Tanganyika, Africa, its relative newness was said to be established by analyzing the contents of its bones—"matrixes," and then comparing the results with an analysis of the surrounding fossil beds.

The antiquity of the Oldoway man had been doubted ever since Professor Hans Reck of Berlin found the complete skeleton lying almost unharmed in a bed of shattered rocks of the Lower Pleistocene era in 1913.

Lewis S. B. Leakey examined the Oldoway fossil beds and asserted that "almost beyond question" the skeleton was the oldest complete homo sapiens ever found. But his conclusion was disputed by many scientists, including Dr. Alex Hrdlicka of the Smithsonian Institute, Washington, D. C., and Professor Elliott Smith, British Anthropologist, and even by Sir Arthur Keith, another Britisher, who had been an admirer of Dr. Leakey's work as an archaeologist.

Exactly where the Oldoway skeleton came from and how it reached the old fossil bed at Oldoway may always be a mystery.

Sir Arthur Smith Woodward, one of the foremost British geologists, said that it must have been buried there at some comparatively recent date and that in any event its antiquity was completely discredited. But how the skeleton was buried without disturbing the existing strata will continue to be a puzzle.

THE SPHINX
With Negroid Face

THOTHMES III
Greatest of the Pharaohs

THE BLACK MAN AT THE DAWN OF CULTURE 33

Tools and other objects found by the Tanganyika expedition, he said, indicated that the Oldoway Man equaled culturally the Heidelberg Man.

Although it would be impossible to date the Oldoway Man accurately he might be 100,000 or 1,000,000 years old, the skeleton is infinitely older than anything yet found, although there have been older fragments of skeletons.

In the Hall of Ancient Man of the American Museum of Natural History the chronology of the ancient fossils gives precedence to the Piltdown Man as the oldest, dating back to the Pleistocene Age, generally estimated at 1,000,000 years and over.

The late Professor Henry Fairchild Osborn, former president of the Museum, has presented evidence that the Piltdown Man lived about 1,250,000 years ago and was thus the oldest fossil of man yet found. Previous to Dr. Osborn's presentation of his new hypothesis, which has not yet been fully accepted by paleontologists, the honors of antiquity were generally bestowed upon the Java Man, known as pithecanthropos erectus, estimated to have lived about 1,000,000 years ago. The Peking Man, found in China in 1929, was supposed to have been a contemporary of the Java Man.

Next in antiquity is the Heidelberg Man, who lived in the First Interglacial Period, about 750,000 years ago.

The Neanderthal Man is the last in the series coming before modern man. His age is comparatively recent, dating no farther back than 30,000 to 40,000 years. After him came the Cro-Magnon Man, about 25,000-30,000 years, the first of the Moderns in company with the Grimaldi mentioned above.

It has been interesting to watch the flurry over this new "find" in East Africa. It need not have caused such dire misgivings. All that Dr. Leakey and his associates claimed for the Oldoway fossil was that it is the most complete skeleton of ancient man found to date. The Piltdown, Java and Peiping finds are admittedly older but their remains are fragmentary to the last degree. The skeleton of the Oldoway man is complete, was found all in one place and was fully articulated.

By 1935 Sir Arthur Keith had modified his views slightly with a fine tribute to Dr. Leakey:

"Dr. Leakey has proved that East Africa, particularly Kenya Colony and Tanganyika Territory, is a veritable museum of prehistoric man. All through the pleistocene period, which covers about one million years and corresponds to Dr. Osborn's "Age of Man," East Africa was inhabited by human beings, for Dr. Leakey has discovered their stone implements—from the crudest types imaginable to finished weapons—in all the deposits of the pleistocene period. With the tools occurred the fossil bones of many species of extinct animals. He found part of a lower jaw, certainly human, but too fragmentary to give certain information concerning the kind of man of which it had formed part. Dr. Leakey has named its owner "Kanam Man." It seems to me quite possible that Kanam Man may prove to be a near relative of "Rhodesian Man." The latter is by far the most primitive type of humanity discovered in Africa so far.

In a deposit which is later in date than that which contained the Kanam fragment, but yet much older than the deposits of Europe which contain the fossil remains of Neanderthal Man, Dr. Leakey made another remarkable discovery. He found fragmentary skulls of two men. He has named them the Kanjera skulls.

Now, touching the kind of men depicted by these skulls I have not any doubt; they represent a very early type of African Negro—by far the earliest trace of this race that has been discovered. Roughly speaking, we may give the Kanjera skulls an antiquity of half a million years. These same skulls Dr. Leakey regards as the earliest form of Homo Sapiens yet discovered. He is inclined to believe that the ancestral form of all modern races—all being embraced under the form of Homo Sapiens—was evolved in Africa, and that from that continent modern man gradually colonized the rest of the world, ousting the older and cruder forms of humanity and becoming differentiated into races as he spread.

I do not think the Negro characteristics of the Kanjera

skulls can be questioned. Also, I cannot conceive any process of evolution that 'could transform the Kanjera skulls into a Caucasian type. It is otherwise with the Rhodesian skull, that is a very primitive and generalized type which might be converted into European as well as into African forms. But the Kanjera skulls already show Negro specialization.

EVOLUTION IN AFRICA

How are we to explain this early appearance of the Negro form of mankind in East Africa? I think the most probable explanation is that the same thing happened in Africa as in Java—namely, that parallel evolution has been at work and that there has been an independent transformation of a primitive type—such as is represented by the Rhodesian skull—into a modern type, depicted for us by the black-skinned races seen in the Africa of today.

It now seems to me probable that we are making a mistake about Peking Man (Sinanthropus). Hitherto we have supposed that he, too, represents one of the early pleistocene stocks which died out and left no issue. But there are certain features in the teeth of Sinanthropus which suggest that this ancient type may not have died out but evolved in the course of the "Age of Man" into the Mongolian stock which still occupies Eastern Asia. For the time being this is a mere suggestion. Until China produces a series of intermediate stages to link Peking Man to the modern Chinese, Sinanthropus cannot claim to be the ancestor of the yellow races.

Likewise with Piltdown Man, In spite of his ape-like mandible this million-year-old Englishman may yet turn out to be an early Caucasian or "white man."

This is likely to prove true in the evolution of the modern races of mankind. We must suppose that the diverse and primitive forms of humanity, which were in existence in different parts of the earth at the beginning of the pleistocene period, are traceable to a remote common ancestor. The theory of parallel evolution compels us to suppose that in this remote common ancestor there were latent certain evolutionary tendencies. These tendencies became manifest in recent times and converted early and primitive forms of humanity into "modern" races. We have still much to learn concerning the modes in which progressive evolution works its changes in living types. Thus it does seem, as a result of discoveries made in recent years, that we shall have to change our ideas concerning the origin of the living races of mankind. Parallel evolution is to prove to be a much stronger factor in the production of new races and new species of mankind than we have suspected hitherto.

We shall have to suppose that all modern races—white, yellow, brown and black—separated from each other at a much earlier stage of their evolution and at a much earlier period of time than we have hitherto believed. Instead of searching for the common ancestor of modern races in mid-pleistocene times, we must seek for him in mid-pliocene times—which means transferring our search 2,000,000 years further back."

To come nearer the truth it should be said that too much stress is put upon geological time. Authorities differ as much as a million years on the remoteness of the lower pleistocene stratum, the same kind in which the Oldoway man was found. In comparative anatomy, type is of more significance than age. The elephant, overdue for extinction is still with us. The hairy Ainu are still in Japan and the Bushman in South Africa and Australia. To say that the Oldoway man is as old as the Dawn men, probably means very little. Even if he were not Homo Sapiens the Dawn men were still further from such an estate. It may be that the Oldoway man was an intellectual and the Dawn men merely tentative human beings.

On this very point of intellect Sir Arthur Keith jumps into the breach with the assertion that:

"No Negro was this intellectual Oldoway, but a Hamite of the stock still to be found in Northern Africa."

Such a pronouncement might well be expected from Sir Arthur Keith, for in his brochure *The Place of Prejudice in Modern Civilization,* issued in 1931, he has this to say:

"Nature has endowed her tribal teams with the spirit of antagonism for her own purposes. It has come down to us and creeps out from our modern life in many shapes, as national rivalries and jealousies and as racial hatreds. The modern mane for this spirit of antagonism is race prejudice."

This glimpse of man at the "Dawn" and at the time which might be called the cultural "Scratch" may be widened by readings listed under Anthropology in the bibliography.

When we leave the dim reaches of 20,000 years ago and more, and come into more recent times, 5,000 to 6,000 years ago, the black type and its classification are still under dispute. There is evidence that some 7,000 or 8,000 years ago a black (Negroid) race inhabited Palestine. After the scientists failed to prove them other than the descendants of people who had migrated from Africa, they immediately classified these black Palestinians as "cannibals" who devoured their enemies and burned the bones of their dead after burial.

Traces of these early men were found as the result of excavations at Shukhah, near Jerusalem in 1928, and later in caves at Mt. Carmel. Due to the fact that these Africans constituted such a puzzling find, the excavators assigned to them the name of "Natufians" and they remain to this day the greatest "riddle" in archaeology. Even Sir Arthur Keith agrees that they are clearly "Negroid," decidedly prognathous, with wide faces, flat noses and long, large heads. Sir Arthur goes on to say that these early Palestinian blacks may have been the ancestors of the Semites or Arabs of biblical times. They also show a definite resemblance to the late Stone Age men of Malta and to the remoter men of Southern Europe. Other markings found on these skeletons seem to indicate that the early black Palestinian had connections with ancient Ur of the Chaldees and also with prehistoric man in South Africa, for the latter folk burned their dead after burial instead of prior cremation. Evidence for this rite is forthcoming in the fact that Gertrude Catton-Thompson, who has long studied the ruins of the Zymbabwe in South Africa, has found burned bones there in the course of her researches. Although it may not be possible to identify the Natufians with more recent finds in Palestine, yet it is safe to say that the Natufians were living when the first city-states of Sumeria arose.

So definite is the evidence that the Natufians of Palestine were descendants of native Africans that Sir Arthur Woodward has been moved to state that after all it may be Africa and not India where the ancestral type is to be found. Again Sir Arthur Keith came to the rescue with the "assurance" that "Negroid" does not necessarily mean the actual presence of "Negro blood," but merely "Negro-like" characteristics such as are commonly seen throughout the Near East, in Southern Italy, France, Spain and even in Scandinavia. For all practical purposes, the inference from all this data is plain. That is, an African race carried Aurignacian culture into Palestine, probably after the close of the last glacial period, some 35,000 years ago. It maintained itself in that area, down to some 5,000 or 6,000 years ago. Then that culture was drafted, first into the service of Assyria, Babylonia and Chaldea and later into that of the budding cultures of the Mediterranean areas. In this latter area the Cro-Magnon ancestors of the European races, had borrowed from the black Grimaldi who preceded them and later the Cro-Magnons passed these borrowings on into what has become the Europe of today.

Few people have paid any attention to the psychic and philosophic by-products of the World War. This holocaust led to the estrangement of nearly 200,000,000 Russians from the white world with all the peril which that estrangement means to Western Europe. The backwash of that war swept the Germans into a revived and intensified Gobinism and Aryanism, which are playing havoc in Central Europe. In a word, the Germans have re-asserted their old puns that the British are beef-eaters, the French, decadent, the Italians, swine, and the Americans, mere money-grubbers. Hence the traditional pattern of Aryan-Nordic superiority, cherished by most white races, has been broken. White races have had to fight, not for superiority, but only for mere, commonplace equality within their own ranks. Superiority itself is the monopoly of the Ger-

mans and the new "Caesar" who bestrides the old Roman peninsula and the ancient land of Ethiopia.

Americans, less than a half century ago, drank deep from
the springs of the philosophy of Hegel and immersed themselves
in the educational regimen of De Garmo, Herbart and the
Prussian schoolmen. Today they refuse to go to Leipzig, Tu-
bingen, Goettingen, or even to old Heidelberg, when that venerable institution parades her Five-Hundredth Anniversary.
This is done not because there is anything more than lip-service
to the cause of the Jew in Germany, but more directly because
the Anglo-Franco-American world is distraught over the present impasse and wish to wheedle the Teutons into accord and
thus prevent Slavic-Communist tentacles from encircling Europe.

Under the pressure of emotional stress, the Germans have
gone back to their old Norse gods, the Russians have discarded
gods altogether. Under this spell, both Germany and Russia
have divulged or exposed fallacies related to the African races,
that have long cluttered the pages of history.

Just as in the ancient days, Africa, and disputes over it,
served to mend or rend the nations, so today Africa serves the
same agency. Another glimpse into the ages will probably help
to illumine the road in which the early blacks travelled.

Crete, and the other settlements in Greece and the Near
East, have yielded to the excavator, works of art which show
that there was a cultural wave in the Mediterranean area many
thousands of years before the Greeks developed. The strength
of the social and family instincts of the white races, today, is
such that they have begun to plunder the world for evidences
of a pure Nordic ancestor. But almost every time they dig they
find an African in the bone-pile.

Earlier contentions were that man's true ancestor was to be
found in China, Central Asia, India or the Tigris-Euphrates
River Valley—provided that he was non-African. There is
enough data on hand today to reject any of these regions as the
birthplace of early man and consequently early civilization. Even
if Africa is left alone there are still the Aztec, Maya, Inca and

Pueblo ruins which give no hint that they are other than non-white. Strange it is to note that even in these early American cultures, only the "swastika" hints of any connection with the cultures of the Mediterranean. And this itself leads back to Africa.

Real scientific investigators, men zealous for truth in their craft and versed in ancient and oriental history, are well aware of the fact that non-African Mediterranean cultures were long the borrowers of culture from an alien folk, namely the African. Nineveh, Babylon and Assyria all had enormous African populations. The African milieu came to full tide in mulatto Egypt, the Nile Valley and Ethiopia. The blacks who lived among the peoples in the Tigris-Euphrates area not only held full citizenship but also places of power and control, as witnessed by the art representations that have come down to us from them. There were good reasons why the ancient East made contact with the African. History will not be complete until all these reasons are thoroughly known. This can be only known by a complete, honest and unbiased archaeological study of the entire continent of Africa. Such a study is far more important than further study in mulatto Egypt, because it will illumine the ancient road and open new vistas, by the examination of the immense treasures, scattered over Africa, from the Atlantic to the Indian Ocean and from the Cape to Cairo.

Probably because of glacial action and the subsequent melting of the glaciers, flood conditions broke down the earlier cultural advancement and thus human development was set back incalculably. Accumulated knowledge and customs of thousands of years were wiped out and mankind being scattered, with the old contacts broken, sank again into barbarianism. From these flood conditions there came climatic and geographical changes which controlled new settlements, new trade routes, new forms of commerce and industry and new religious beliefs. From many points of view Africans today have the most unfavorable geographic conditions which have not only cut them off from themselves, but also from the northerly peoples, with whom, in more ancient times, they had mutual cultural contacts. In

South, and parts of Central Africa the blacks have lagged but in Egypt, the Nile Valley and Ethiopia, contacts were preserved and thus they carried on.

The areas in which the re-alignment of cultures took place after the flood conditions had passed, are much in dispute. Some seem prone to look for the new sproutings of civilization in the Nile Valley. Others lean to the area of the Aegean. If the former view is premature, the latter has data so incomplete and insufficient that it must have further and most exacting study. Even if the Aegean area becomes the post-flood proving ground, the African element will still be present, for Crete was the pivot of Aegean civilization and distributed her gifts to all the surrounding peoples. Excavations show that Crete in 3,000 B. C., had theatres, palaces and temples and doubtless was then in connection with Egypt. Indeed, Cretan frescoes show religious ceremonials done, practically in the Egyptian style, and depict priestesses at the altars, some white and others black.

Thus there appears to have been two post-flood civilizations, the one in the Nile Valley, maintained by black men, and the other in Crete, in which Africans played significant parts. Indeed the Cretans and the Colchians, were dark races with more or less Greek profiles but with full lips. No evidence exists to show that they were influenced from any source other than African. Everything so far unearthed in Crete and the Sudan apparently indicate that in the Mediterranean area, during the Stone Age, there was a common race of men. This early race, in the course of centuries, developed different physical characteristics and dispersed itself northward into Europe and Southward into Africa. Thus this ancient Aegean hegemony fell just as Rome fell quite 1,500 years ago. The latter has remained only a romance and a dream until the recent whirring of Roman wings over the Ethiopia of the present day. It is apparent now that there never was one commanding race. All have been borrowers. All have developed, in civilization, some faster, some slower, according to the nature of geographic conditions and the degree of cultural contact they had with others. But these cultural contacts, in general, have been made—westward. The strange by-product of eastward expansion, has usually been, failure. It was so with Egypt, Persia and Greece, under Alexander the Great. The Saracens stopped the Crusaders and the Turks settled an issue in 1453, at Constantinople, even though Mohammedanism had been thrown back into Asia 700 years earlier at Tours. But it was so with Napoleon, when he wrecked his armies in Egypt and with Imperial Germany, when the Hohenzollern lance was broken in an eastern thrust in the form of the Berlin-to-Bagdad Railway. Old Rome did it but died. New "Rome," under its new "Caesar," has already proclaimed itself "The Protector of Islam" and of the interests of the East. Time will mark its fate. Canny England is in the East, but she got there by going West. Ancient Ethiopia expanded Eastward and failed, because she stubbed her toes on the stones of Babylon, having been blinded by the dust of Tyre. Modern Ethiopia, metamorphosed in her ancient glory, put her trust in a League of Nations and has been blinded by Roman poison gas.

The civilization of black men, with the exception of Egypt, the Nile Valley and Ethiopia, have largely been local and geocentric. The same is true of the Mongoloid Chinese, who built a wall in order to enhance exclusiveness. However, Japan, the eldest daughter of China, is imperialistic, in the sense that she plans to bar inimical advances of the West into the East. Leagued with Japan is the "Risorgimento" in India and the might of 200,000,000 Russians, who claim themselves to be co-partners in "The Lord-ship of the East."

There was no such line-up in the era of Aegean culture, for when Aegean supremacy passed from the Cretans to the Cretanized Achaians and thence to Knossus and Mycenae, there came an abrupt halt. More than that, when Aegean supremacy reached Thessaly, it was almost ruined by the barbaric Dorians. But the seeds of culture, so lavishly spread by the Cretans were not lost. They slept through the Greek middle ages and rose again in a splendid renaissance. Thus Greek and Roman civilizations became the daughters of (Cretan) Aegean culture, which was not without its African elements. Motifs in

Greek art and nuances in Greek fables witness the African influence in Cretan culture. But Crete with more than a hundred wealthy cities was only one of the many island settlements that traded with Europe and the Nile Valley. There were also Cyprus, Sicily, Corsica, Sardinia and Malta in each of which, there are African traces.

Thus we get a glimpse of how civilizations flowered in the Mediterranean basin, thousands of years before the Christian era. Egypt, Mesopotamia and Europe are being searched today for fresh historical records which will cast light on man's early past. Only the great continent of Africa, outside of Egypt, is being neglected. There can be no full picture of the birth and childhood of civilization until Africa has been made to yield up its historical treasures. One of the most important and pressing cultural needs of today is the unbiased exploration of the antiquaries of Africa. A good history of African culture is necessary before it will be possible to work out the equation in which all men are contributing factors.

Whoever is capable and bold enough to write that history, should bear in mind that culture is the subject and man the object. That is, culture is the tutor and man the pupil. Or in terms of expansion, culture is an independent organism, in which man is not its subject but rather its object and bearer. Man does not, in reality, produce culture. Such a premise is illusory. Culture permeates man. Being bi-polar, the enhancements of culture are born of the exchanges of psychic force between two temporary opposing life streams. Such opposition may show itself in the form of the Cross against the Crescent, of Nordicism, Anti-Semitism, Communism, Imperialism or tutored and nurtured racial prejudices.

We pass now to a brief review of Bible lore in regard to the classificaton and distribution of mankind. ..

The works of Friedrich Hegel which set the norm in the philosophy of history in the early decades of the Nineteenth Century, were taken up as criteria with which to defend the system of slavery in the Americas, as part of a divine mandate pronounced through Noah.

The press, the pulpit, the platform, the legislators and the learned deans in colleges vied with each other to prove this divine mandate. No countenance, of course, could be given to any data that would show that the black race had developed any cultures, built any great empires or created organized civil life. Slavery had to be defended. Even when the slave became a christian there was great indecision as to whether he should be freed. Immediately then there had to be set up some criteria which would absolve the christian slave-holder from any guilt for his crime toward his black christian brother.

Thus it was decided that only the "soul" of man was important. That man's "true end" is to glorify God and thus save his immortal soul. Hence, the body was a mere shell, to temporarily house this immortal soul, and that whatever ills befell the body of the slave in this life, only enhanced the lustre of his crown in the hereafter. Thus proceeded the sophistry which allayed the conscience of the slave-minded groups and ostensibly proved the genuineness of the divine slave mandate against the blacks. Few of the pro-slavery class took into account the fact that slavery existed before the flood and had so existed because it has always arisen, generally, in connection with public or private war. It is written that prior to the flood, "the earth was filled with violence" and probably nothing less than a great catastrophe could have checked this violence and cleared the way for a needed reformation. But ante-deluvian slavery was a mutual thing. Then, whites were slaves to conquering blacks and conversely, blacks were slaves to victorious whites.

The mention of the "flood" here is only incidental to the story of it among various peoples widely separated. It is not held here that the "flood" was an "actuality" as recorded in the Book of Genesis. Nor is it necessary here to subscribe to it as a "myth" or "legend." Those who wish to bring themselves up-to-date on the flood, would do well to read, "The Flood, New Light on an Old Story," by Harold Peake.

When, then, in the heyday of pro-slavery agitation, Hegel laid down his propositions, there was set in motion a bigger parade of the old story of Noah—2,400 B.C.—and his three

sons, Ham, Shem and Japheth. As a matter of record the prophecy attributed to Noah says nothing at all about Ham. It appears to be directed solely and exclusively to Canaan. However,
the fulfilment of that prophecy, even as far as Canaan was concerned, was completed when the Israelites, under Joshua, conquered thee Canaanites 970 B. C. and re-asserted their ancient
rights to bury their dead in their own ancient sepulchres.

The original ethnological table preserved by Moses gives
the names and the nations recognized by him, as being the
descendants of Ham. First in the list, is "Cush" (Kush), or
Ethiopia, denoting the great and ancient kingdom south of
Egypt, which covered the Valley of the Nile to the Red Sea and
stretched even into Arabia. The land of Cush was probably
more extensive, for in the middle of the Tenth Century B.C.
it is noted that the Jewish king, Jeroboam fled, for protection
to the black Shishak, ruler of Egypt, and father-in-law of
Solomon. Shishak's army is said to have consisted of "Lubim,
Sukkim and Cushim," respectively meaning the Libyans, the
dwellers in the land of Succoth, or booths of the Wady Tumilat,
and the Sudanese. More still is the fact that the earliest Cush-
ite empire builder was the Negroid Nimrod, the Mighty Hunter and Wandering Conqueror, who set up his government in
Babylon. The Negroid Elamites came under his standard, not
for race but for conquest.

The second of the issue of Ham, was Mizraim, or Egypt,
the memorials of whose empire are the earliest known to history.

The third son was "Phut" or Libya, whose early habitat
was the site of the present Morocco. Indeed the earliest use of
the word "Africa," referred only to Libya, or the country to
the "West."

The fourth son was Canaan, upon whose sable seed there
was to be an "eternal malediction." Whatever was to have been
the punishment for Canaan's recorded offense, it was carried
out in the Israelitic conquest referred to above.

Of the children of Canaan, there were "Heth" of the Hittites, the Jebusites, Amorites, Girgasites, Hivites, and Gibeo-

nites, all tribes of the one race which was subdued by Joshua when Israel became dominant in the promised land. The vanquished Canaanites were not enslaved. Joshua had no such plan and no such intention. His mission was to drive out or exterminate. Only one of these tribes, the Gibeonites, escaped extermination and this was because its leader made a false treaty with Joshua. Even the Gibeonites were not enslaved to individual owners but were a kind of indentured servants, bound to do the common work necessary in the carrying out of the formalities of national worship.

Most distinguished of Canaan's sons was Zidon (Sidon) from whom came the Phoenicians, the earliest of commercial nations, a people who developed the arts of peace at home and plied the Mediterranean reaching the most distant parts of the then known world, even touching what is now Cornwall in England.

The land of the Phoenicians was a narrow strip on the eastern bend of the Mediterranean, less than 20 miles wide and not more than 120 miles in length. Being prevented from expanding in any other direction they took to the sea, westward, and planted colonies along the North African littoral, one of which, Carthage, was destined to later dispute, with Rome, the rght to mastery in the Mediterranean. They became teachers to the Greeks and thus helped to lay a basis for early European culture. The heights reached by the Phoenicians, children of Canaan and grand-children of Ham, disprove the "servant of servants" dictum as recorded. Furthermore the Bible supports no such dictum with the added fact that the word "Negro" appears nowhere in either the old Testament or the new. Critics may set up the proposition that the sons of Ham and Canaan were neither "Negro" nor "Negroid" and further contend that the blacks of Africa, outside the North and the Nile Valley are neither descendants of Ham nor Canaan. Such lead would only add to the wreckage of mid-Nineteenth Century sophistry and Hegelianism and at the same time obligate the critics to bring forth data more convincing than those used in the pro-slavery arguments of a century ago.

As for the Egyptian, taking sculptures and paintings as authority, he was clearly no Semite. His nostrils and lips are not so thin and his nose not so prominent. Indications are that he is a cross between certain Indo-Europeans and the black Ethiopian and Nubian. The alien races that came from the East into the Nile Valley and Egypt brought few if any women with them. Hence they readily inter-married or inter-bred with the blacks already in possession of the land. The French, for example, in North America, brought no women with them. Soon a Franco-Indian progeny began to appear. Had the French come to the New World to make homes and had they permanently remained in control, a new race would long ago have sprung up in America. The British came to the New World to found homes and in early colonial days shipments of women from England were the general rule.

It is significant that Egyptians have, even in their earliest history, freely mixed with the Nubian and the Ethiopian. They have never resented the rulership over them of a black sovereign. They followed Taharqua and Sabaco. into Syria just as quickly as they followed Sethos and Rameses. They glorified Nefertari, Ethiopian queen of Amenophis IV (Akhnaton) and paid tribute to the Great Black Pharaoh, Pianhki-meri-Amen. An example today, of what the Egyptians were in the early days can be seen in the mulatto peoples of Cuba, Puerto Rico and San Domingo, except that the Egyptian was, in general, much darker. These Spanish-speaking mulattoes are not "white" in the commonly accepted meaning of that term, nor have they much of the strain of pure Castilian. Their base is even more African than Indian. What there is of Indian in them is, for the mostpart, Carib, often a very dark type.

Again, just as Indo-Europeans entered the Nile Valley, in antiquity, mixed with the original blacks and thus produced the Egyptian, so the present contact of Italian and Ethiopian, may repeat the ancient Nile drama and create for the future a "new" race. This latter instance is significant in that it may show that black blood, which once flowed from Africa northward into southern and southeastern Europe, with the resultant creation of dark Cretans, the much darker Etruscans and probably even blondes, will, to some extent, flow back to its ancient origin. It is superfluous to mention the quadroons and octoroons in modern America, who, though "white" are classed as "black," and though "black" they "pass" as "white." Thus Cushitic Babylonia and Chaldea, Hamitic Libya, black Nubia and Ethiopia, mulatto Egypt, and her offspring, Phoenicia, have served as patrons of commerce, navigation, art, luxury, splendor and early human advancement much of which is not surpassed today even with the aid of modern science and technique. In this wise, the black, Ethiopo-Hamitic races have been servants to the Semitico-Japhetic races, in the general advancement of mankind.

Just as the old Canaanites unwittingly prepared the promised land for Israel, built in it towns and covered it with fruitful fields and vineyards, and were, in that respect, servants of Israel, so all the races of mankind have mutually served each other, by playing high and noble parts in the great drama of world renovation and cultural advancement. They have collaborated, consciously or unwittingly, in the processes of fashioning material wealth and in the slow development of religious and spiritual fibre.

Little is admitted, freely—though much is known—of the cultural contributions of the black races to civilization. However this modicum is sufficient to prevent any historian, at all mindful of the ethics of his craft, from re-asserting, that, from time immemorial, the black races have been hewers of wood and drawers of water.

We pass now to Nubia and Ethiopia as typical ancient states, sovereign in their own right and holding sway over other states.

ETHIOPIANS IN RACIAL FOG

The general status of the black race and its mulatto offshoots, from very remote times to the more or less settled life

STENIO VINCENT
President and Second Liberator of Haiti

LOUVERTURE, DESSALINES, PETION
Who with Henri Christophe, Liberated Haiti and Founded Independence

in Egypt and the Nile Valley, circa 5,000 B.C., has been set forth provisionally. This volume makes no attempt at a detailed history of the above area. It is indeed, a non-technical introductory outline in which the salient features of typical African nation-building, are interpreted.

It is hoped that racial situations in these areas, particularly, Ethiopia, long whispered about, will be brought out into the open and disposed of once for all. Ethiopia, now stripped of the pretentions of her recent rulers and even stripped of the rulers themselves, stands naked today before a puzzled world. It is difficult to find a word to adequately describe their condition. Sad, pitiful, pathetic, tragic, have in them neither the power nor the shades of meaning to fully set forth their unhappy lot. In the past forty years, Ethiopia found herself in the hands of mis-leaders who sat down, or wrangled, in the middle of the road to progress and expected a world, on the move, to march around them, only to find out, too late, that a rough-shod, modern world had walked over them.

After standing for thousands of years against the hordes of the East, against Egypt, Greece, ancient Rome and the sword of Islam, she has been blinded by Fascist poison gas and ground to dust under the wheels of the armored tanks of a new Rome. Neither pride in her ancient estate nor the marvelous example of Japan, since 1853, nor even her own victory in 1896, taught her recent leaders any effective lesson which would lead to military and diplomatic preparation for the onslaught which sooner or later, they should have known that they would have to meet.

Holding on to slavery, at this late date, and rejecting social, civil and economic modernization, her luckless leaders kept her metamorphosed in the sheen of her ancient grandeur and in the shroud of the legend of her christian primacy and, per force, expected a League of White Nations to fight for them against a white race. These leaders did not realize that white men no longer die for black men, least of all an Englishman or a Frenchman. They did not realize that white men no longer even fight for themselves, under the leadership of black commanders, as was true in the Venice of Othello, the Spain of ben Ziad, the Greece of Eurybates of whom Homer sang at Siege of Troy, the Egypt of Pianhki or the Babylonia of Nimrod. Indeed, in a world seething, more than ever, with the strife of race and color, the Ethiopian leaders remained utterly unmindful of the priceless heritage handed down to them by valorous black warriors and statesmen of long ago. In reality, the recent leaders of Ethiopia are still in the racial fog. They still believe that they are of the white race, and so believing they doubly indict themselves. For, if they be of the white race, then in the nature of the oppression which they placed upon the blacks, they should have been dispossessed long, long ago. But they have not read history aright. They did not read between the lines of the pseudo-scientific verbiage which classed them as "white." They should have seen the crass fallacy, of such verbiage. They did not have sufficient psychology, or ordinary common sense, to understand that the "white complex" drilled into them, paved the way for Europeans to get the inner-peace-time control of the country and finally, in a war, to utterly rend them and cast them aside.

They got no inference from the fact that even in ancient times, in their own country, there was a race and color flurry, when Aaron and his sister, Miriam, upbraided their brother Moses because he married Zipporah, an Ethiopian—(Midianite)—woman. If this estrangement between Moses and his relatives, was over Zipporah, then the situation is all the more interesting, for it would show that Moses had married not one black wife but two.

Indeed, some records seem to show that his marriage to Zipporah was many years before the recorded quarrel. Hence the reprimand probably came, not over Zipporah, but because he had taken a second black wife. The reference to being "black," as recorded in The Songs of Solomon, whether it refers to Solomon himself or to the Queen of Sheba, is only of indirect importance. The direct issue is that one of them was "black" and for it a sickly apology was made.

Nor have Ethiopians been able to see that their resistance

to Catholicism in the Fourth and Fifth Centuries and their later expulsions and massacres of Catholic missionaries, were situations for which they would, sooner or later, have to pay, unless negotiations, statesmanship or military preparedness calmed the religious waters that have troubled Ethiopia for 1,600 years.

Any black race in modern times which had scored a victory over a white race such as Ethiopia achieved over Italy in 1896, should have never slept, for a moment in the false security, of their ancient greatness, or of their hollow christian piety or in the flattery of being "white." Ethiopians should have known that, with Italy, there would be "un conto vecchio da soldare," i.e. an old Count to be Settled.

These are exactly the things which Menelek II saw and against which he warned. For, in 1909, he assembled the nobles, the army, the Abuna, the priests and the people into his presence and said to them:

"I have chosen Lidj Iyasu to be my heir, and I entrust him to Thee. If any man shall refuse to do his will he shall be excommunicated, and if he refuse to do thy will, he shall be excommunicated.— Cursed shall be he who shall refuse to obey him.—If, on his part, he shall betray you in any unworthy manner he himself shall be accursed."

With the above pronouncement given, he turned directly to the Abuna, the nobles, the priests and the war chiefs and said:

"Take very great care to live in unity and to watch over the safety of your country so that the enemy shall not be able to invade it."

As an earnest for the consummation of his desire, Menelek left a large sum of money, probably, $10,000,000.00, for internal improvement and for national defense. In 1913 he died. Lidj Lyasu, then in power, turned Mohammedan and tried to abolish christianity. The issue was met by Ras Tafari—(Haille Selassie) whose armies defeated Lidj Lyasu, captured him and placed him in prison. Thus by Selassie, Ethiopia was "saved" for christianity.

Selassie, then in power, 1916, immediately fell into the hands of the foreign legations which ruled the country for him. He played the role of a "white chieftain of the blacks" and squandered the patrimony of Menelek. At his coronation in 1930, with gruesome poverty throughout the land, and neither a public school system, a health service nor modernized weapons for national defense, he spent nearly a $1,000,000.00 entertaining Europeans, in a vain, fruitless attempt to win their goodwill. The irony of it is, that, during those very moments, plots were aborning among his guests whereby Ethiopia could be seized and Selassie himself dispossessed, as has been done.

In 1920 when the Hon. Marcus Garvey held sway over thousands of black men, outside of Africa and desired to turn them to the service of Ethiopia, however weak an ally they might have been, the colorphobes in control of the country refused to heed. Garvey's correspondence to them was returned unopened. Even to the coronation itself, Ethiopia invited neither the Soverign Black Government of Liberia, on the African West Coast, nor the illustrious Republic of Haiti, in the Black World of the Americas.

Ethiopians, however, are not alone in weakening themselves by worshipping the false god of an alien race. The Japanese, down to the World War, felt that they were, somehow, an appendage to the whites. At the Versailles Conference, they threatened to hold Shantung as a leverage with which to pry Woodrow Wilson into the recognition of them as such. Later, the immigration doors to America were slammed, roughly, in their faces, with laws which denied them status, either as "white" or "black." Thus they failed to gain quota privileges for entry into America. The Japanese came to himself, flouted the League of Nations, and is now well nigh on to the completion of his mastery, in the non-white Asiatic world. The racial antics of the Anglo-Indian are balking the essential and needed vigor of the program, being attempted in India by Gandhi and Nehru.

Lastly, the emancipation of the Jew in Germany in 1849, instead of energizing him to hold on to the matchless heritage of Jews, seems to have made him seek to fuse his racial ore in the deadly solution in the German crucible. In Germany, a new "Pharaoh" has arisen with a precipitant which has caused the Jewish mass, in Germany, to fall to the bottom, even into the lap of non-German Jewry which the German Jews, so recently and discreetly, affected to ignore, if not despise.

Into Ethiopia, a "New Caesar" came, with whirring wings, which made the careless Ethiopian leaders afraid. His poison gas has caused them to stumble, blindly, to their black kinsmen, however weak they may be and to the Mohammedans, to whom, earlier, Lidj Iysau tried to lead them.

In the next chapter a glimpse is given of what Ethiopia was like in the days of her glory.

ETHIOPIA AND EGYPT

There is little concern today over the impressive civilizations of the Nile Valley. But, before there was any "Glory that was Greece" or "Grandeur that was Rome," the Monarchs of Egypt were creating Empires, building pyramids, fashioning collossi, using measurements to the billionth of an inch, devising chemicals and arraying themselves in all combinations of the spectrum, surpassing, even the raiment of Solomon, in all his glory. Heeren, constant detractor of Africans, writes as follows about Ethiopia in his "Historical Researches":—

"Except the Egyptians there is no aboriginal people of Africa with so many claims upon our attention as the Ethiopians; from the remotest times to the present, one of the most celebrated and the most mysterious of nations. In the earliest traditions of nearly all the most civilized nations of antiquity the name of this distant people is found. The annals of the Egyptian priests were full of them; the nations of inner Asia, on the Euphrates and the Tigris, have interwoven the fictions of Ethiopia, with their own traditions of the conquests and wars of their heroes, and, at a period equally remote, they glimmer in Greek mythology.

When the Ethiopians scarcely knew Italy and Sicily by

name, they were themselves celebrated as the remotest nation, the most just of men, the favorites of the gods. The lofty inhabitants of Olympus journey to them, and take part in their feasts; their sacrifices are the most agreeable of all that mortals can offer. And when the faint gleam of tradition and fable give way, to the clear light of history, the lustre of the Ethiopians is not diminished. They still continue the object of curiosity and admiration, and the pen of the cautious, clearsighted historian often places them in the highest rank of knowledge and civilization."

Whether one discredits Volney or not, no one has successfully offset his conclusions. In his great work, "The Ruins of Empires" he says of Ethiopia: "Those piles of ruins which you see in that narrow valley watered by the Nile, are the ruins of opulent cities, the pride of the ancient kingdom of Ethiopia. There, a people, now forgotten, discovered, while others were yet barbarians, the elements of the arts and sciences. A race of men now rejected from society for their sable skin and frizzled hair, founded on the study of the laws of nature, those civil and religious systems which still govern the universe."

The history of the Nile Valley is an extensive panorama, stretching all the way from Ethiopia on the south to the Mediterranean, and thence eastward to Mesopotamia in the Valley of "The Two-Rivers." Contributing to the greatness of these areas were many mighty black men of whom Thothmes III is the greatest. Later came Akhnaton, 1375 B. C., of supreme individuality and personality, often called the "Heretic King," due to the fact that he was the world's first great religious reformer. Then in 947 B. C., came the black Shishak, of Libya, ruler of Egypt and father-in-law, of King Solomon of Israel and also father-in-law of Jeroboam. Jeroboam, at this time was in rebellion against Solomon and fled into Egypt under the protection of Shishak.

Then, 200 years later, the Great Pianhki, full-blooded black, arose and set himself up as "Lord of Upper and Lower Egypt." In the wake of Pianhki, came Taharqua, friend and supporter of both King Hezekiah of Judah and the prophet

Isaiah when the vindictive Assyrian tyrants bore down on the fold of the Jews.

LIBYA AND NUBIA

These two countries are treated first because their lines are much interwoven and their sovereign courses long since run. Ethiopia will be treated last and in more detail because she at least projected herself into modern times as an autonomous state.

There was comparative peace between Egypt and Nubia during the First to the Sixth Dynasties, circa 2,500 B.C. In the Sixth Dynasty, Nubians became soldiers in the Egyptian army and formed the famed "Black Battalions of Una," who was Commander-in-Chief of the armies of Pepi I, ruler of the Sixth Dynasty. From thence to the Twelfth Dynasty, Nubia went her way until the country was conquered by Usertesen III. It was under Usertesen III circa 2,000 B.C. that there arose one of the earliest flares of the race and color question, for after he had defeated the Nubian-Ethiopian forces, he set up a huge granite stele—an advertising medium similar, in a way, to modern highway advertising signs—on which, the hieroglyphics, stated the following:

> "No Black man whatsoever shall be permitted to pass this place going down stream (the Nile) no matter whether he is travelling by desert or journeying in a boat—except such Blacks as come to do business in the country or travelling on an embassy. Such, however, shall be well treated in every way whatsoever. But no boats belonging to Blacks shall, in the future be permitted to pass down this river."

Usertesen III charged his successors to keep up the fight against Nubia and Ethiopia so that the boundary would be made permanent. The stele was set up at Semnah, the modern Sennar in the Anglo-Egyptian Sudan.

All was not lost, for the Hyksos invaders began to pour into Egypt in the Thirteenth Dynasty and by the Fifteenth, Egypt was plunged into one of her darkest periods. Egypt then cried out to Nubia and Ethiopia for help. The Nubians and the Ethiopians took advantage of the disorder in Egypt and declared

themselves independent, only to find that they had a new fight
on their hands against the Hyksos. To match the Hyksos, arose
the Great Nubian, Ra-Nehesi, a full-blooded black, who organized the Nubian forces and maintained the independence of
his country.

Out of the west, from Libya, came the mulatto Ahmes I
who expelled the Hyksos, set up the Eighteenth Dynasty circa
1700 B.C., and waged two campaigns against Nubia. The country was now to have no rest, for, on the death of Ahmes I, his
immediate successors, Amenhotep I and Thothmes I, ruled
Nubia with an iron hand. Nubia, however, was pulled out of
her sorrows in a very peculiar way. When Thothmes I came to
rule, he already had two children, a son Thothmes II and a
daughter, Maken-Ra, popularly known as Hatshepsut (Hatasu)
all of whom were noticeably of mixed blood. He took to himself
an Ethiopian concubine and for him she bore a son who was to
become the Great Thothmes III. Some records indicate Thothmes
II as father of Thothmes III. At the death of Thothmes I, Egypt
and Nubia had more disorder, largely because Hatshepsut
wanted to rule ahead of her brother Thothmes II. She partly
achieved her ambition by marrying him and consequently ruled
jointly with him. At the death of Thothmes II, which his sis-
ter-wife was suspected of causing, Hatshepsut gained complete
control, utterly ignoring the rights of her Ethiopian half-
brother, Thothmes III. Hatshepsut ardently desired to be a
"man" and to simulate such, she had false beards made so that
she could wear them when she sat upon the throne.

Once in control she went through Egypt trying to destroy
all the records that related to Thothmes II but she did not raid
Nubia. These lost records are needed now to complete the picture of one of the most stirring times in which black men played
so great a part.

As for Nubia, Hatshepsut instituted a scheme of peaceful
penetration. She developed art and commerce, put ships on the
seas and sent missions to the Land of Punt. Indeed she is the
first great queen in history.

Upon her death — she committed suicide — Thothmes III,

long in the shadows, assumed the throne of Egypt. He began
with a conciliation policy toward Nubia, similar to the quasi-
liberal policy of Hatshepsut. His mildness toward Nubia caused
a rebellion against him which he speedily put down. With order
restored he led an invasion into Asia but while he was away
the Nubians regularly paid tribute, a fact which pleased Thothmes III on his return. For such fidelity he opened the trade
routes so that both Egypt and Nubia could prosper. He granted
religious toleration, respected the Nubian social customs, and
granted semi-indpendence. Thus his fame spread and his sway
stretched throughout Egypt, Nubia, the Sudan, Arabia, Syria,
Kurdestan, Armenia, even to the Tigris-Euphrates Valley. His
policy outstripped in liberality any previous Pharaoh. In religion, government, education, the fine and industrial arts,
Nubians were freely admitted. Thus from a lowly priest in the
temple of Amen at Thebes he became the Mightiest and Most
Enlightened of the Pharaohs.

Thothmes III was not the "Pharaoh of the Exodus." This
event appears to have taken place circa 1440 soon after his
death. Records seem to show that the oppressor of the Jews was
Mer-en-pthah. Recent discoveries tend to show that Hatshepsut
was the one who found Moses in the bulrushes and later it was
her favor, that brought him to power and finally her death that
made it necessary for him to flee from Egypt to Midian where
he married Jethro's daughter, Zipporah, the Midianite (Ethiopian) woman.

Thothmes III lived to the ripe age of 85 years, 53 of which
were spent as the Ruler of Egypt. In none of his conquests did
he put his vanquished foes to the sword as was so recently done
to conquered Ethiopians, on the order of the "Italian Caesar"
in Rome and the reported part-Jewish "Viceroy" in Addis
Ababa. Of the many remains commemorative of Thothmes III,
one of his obelisks stands on the Thames in London and another
in New York near the Metropolitan Museum of Fine Arts,
Central Park. Thus evidence of the magnificence of the great
Ethiopian may be seen in the centres of the cultures of two
white worlds.

Upon the death of Thothmes III, Nubia again fell into the shadows, for his ruthless successor Amenhotep II renewed the wars. Napata, the Nubian capital during the Eighteenth Dynasty and an entrepot for caravans, was seized and the trade routes blocked. In his wars against Syria, Amenhotep II slew seven of their chiefs and sent the dead body of one of them to Napata, to be exposed, in the market place as a warning to the blacks.

Thothmes IV succeeded Amenhotep II. The liberal policy of Thothmes III was revived and passed on to Amenhotep III, who reigned 1412-1380 and is popularly known as "The Black Memnon." Under Amenhotep III (Memnon)—the Nubians revolted before they knew the policy of the new king. The revolt was relentlessly crushed, yet the liberal policy was kept. To insure confidence, Amenhotep III outlawed war against Nubia, made a Nubian women, Queen Tai, his chief wife and proceeded to lay a new basis for the development of trade, the arts and religion, offering an exchange of worship between the gods of Egypt and the gods of Nubia. The fame of "Memnon" spread. He was glorified by the Greeks in song and story. Even in English literature the immortal Milton, in commenting on the wife of Moses writes:

"Black, but such as in esteem
Prince Memnon's sister might beseem."

The enlightened rule of Amenhotep III drew the Sudanese to his standard. They revered him not only as a black king who encouraged splendor, extravagance and luxury, dear to the heart of the blacks, but sensibly because he was a wise administrator who followed the pattern of Thothmes III.

Soon calm was broken by the religious wars brought on by the emissaries of the new king, Amenhotep IV, 1375 B.C., son of Amenhotep III and the Nubian woman. When Amenhotep IV broke from the established religion of Amen and set the worship of "Aten, the Solar Disk," he changed his name to "Anhk-Aten" or Ahknaton. Ahknaton is probably the "First Individual" in history. He is often referred to as the "Heretic King." Ahknaton also married an Ethiopian woman the famed

Nefertari. To them were born no sons but six daughters, one of whom married King Tut-Anhk-Amen, the splendor of whose tomb is still the amazement of the world.

The original bust of the Ethiopian Queen Nefertari or Nefertiti, is in the Berlin Museum and strangely it has won the heart of the "Lord of the Aryans" although the dark Queen is far from "Aryan." Even, Ahknaton, her part-Nubian husband should be enough to disavow her as a "traitor to the race" —the Great Race. There is hardly any need to try to make out a case that she is a "Mitannian Princess" and hence an "Aryan of the Medo-Persian" extraction. Her picture is enough. Were she dressed in modern clothes she would fit well on Harlem's Seventh Avenue, north of 110th street.

About fifty years ago excavators found 300 clay tablets at Tel-el-Armarna, since known as "The Tel-el-Armarna Letters" which have turned out to be certain official correspondence of Ahknaton with Asia. These letters are a part of the history of the black race, through the fact that the mother of Ahknaton was a Nubian-Ethiopian woman. Authorities will not admit such view. They only say that it is strange that Amenhotep III, father of Ahknaton, married "a woman" not of the royal line.

However, the attempt of "The Heretic King" to change the religion, failed. The Nubians continued to worship the gods of Amen even down to 200 B.C. when their dynasty finally collapsed. The glorious Eighteenth Dynasty ended in 1320 B.C., under Horemheb. The last 50 years of it saw the passing of Egyptian power in Nubia and the rise of the Nubians themselves to complete mastery of all Egypt.

SHISHAK, THE BLACK LIBYAN KING OF EGYPT

Seti and Rameses II of the Nineteenth Dynasty, circa 1200 B.C. claim to have destroyed Nubia but evidence shows that they scarcely penetrated the country. While rival kings were fighting at Bubastis and Thebes, Nubia regained her independence. This was possible not only due to regal strife in the delta but also because of the arrogance of the priests of Amen in Nubia and the losses which Egypt sustained in her Asiatic campaigns. The turmoil at Bubastis and Thebes, weakened the rule of the priests-kings there by 979 B.C. Such rule was finally ended in 947 B.C. by Shishak, the black Libyan, then king of Egypt. These dispossessed priests retired to Napata in Nubia, and set themselves up as priests of Amen-Ra, the god of the Nubians. They aided in the creation of a liberal regime, encouraged intermarriage with the Nubians and encouraged Nubia to expand into Egypt. The dissolution of Israel and Judah, which' had begun in 978 B.C., was completed by Shishak. Jeroboam, then in rebellion against Solomon king of Israel, fled to Shishak, his father-in-law, for protection against Solomon, and remained with the great black ruler until Solomon's death in 937 B.C. In order to off-set Jeroboam's hold on Egypt, Solomon also married a daughter of Shishak and thus Shishak became the father-in-law of two rival Jewish rulers. The plundering of Palestine and Jerusalem by Shishak, broke up the old rapprochement between the kings of Israel and the kings of Egypt. With Jeroboam on the throne of Israel he re-allied himself with Shishak in order to raid the kingdom of Judah already weakened by the secession of ten of the twelve tribes.

In this same period Zerah, the Ethiopian was defeated by Asa but not before he had over-run Egypt, assailed Judah and was ready to invade Syria. The Egyptian name of Zerah was Azerch-Amen. In later years the wars continued under Osarkon II, a scion in the line of Shishak.

These stirring times, 1000 to 900 B.C., spawned a situation, fact or legend, that has grown with interest through the years and came to white heat during the Italo-Ethiopian War. This romance of Solomon and Sheba will be treated in the section on "Ethiopia."

THE NUBIAN-ETHIOPIAN PHARAOHS OF EGYPT
750 B.C. to 200 B.C.

KASHTA, 750 B.C.

The wavering tide of black ascendancy in the Nile Valley

reached full flood in the middle of the Eighth Century B.C., The line set up by Shishak in 947 B.C. was extended by Kashta two centuries later. Kashta married a wife in the line of the great Libyan and set himself up at Napata. Here begins more glory for Nubia and Ethiopia.

PIANHKI-MERI-AMEN, 744 B.C.

The rule of Kashta was brief. However he left the throne to his son Pianhki, who blazed a trail in the Valley second only to the Great Thothmes III. Pianhki grasped the situation immediately. With his great army of black fighters under Generals Purema and Lamersekni, he, swept, from what is now Italian Somaliland on the Indian Ocean, to the shores of the Mediterranean, a stretch comparable to that from modern Spain to the Bosporus or even to the Black Sea. Thus all Egypt came under his sway. Pianhki's reign was not all one of fighting. Like Thothmes III he developed the arts of peace. He rebuilt and enlarged the great temple of Amen-Ra of "The Holy Mountain" and thus created an entente cordiale with the priests of Amen, whom Shishak drove out of Thebes during his reign. These priests were happy to carry out the will of Pianhki, especially so at Thebes.

In recent years 1927 and 1933 Arthur Brisbane, persistent detractor of the black races, commented as follows on Pianhki, The Great Ethiopian:

> "Gone is Pianhki—his court, his wives and his great temples.—He was a mighty King even if he did imitate the whiter Egyptians.—And another great Ethiopian king has left his features on the face of the Sphinx, which is a negro face.
> Who knows what the negro race might have been had it not had to fight against the destructive forces of the tropical sun? Who knows what it may become as the centuries roll by?"

SHABAKA, 715

The interminable marriage alliances and concubinage between the people of Israel and Judah and the peoples of the

East, with Nubians and Ethiopians, makes it well nigh impossible to hold to any direct line of kinship. Although Solomon, like Jeroboam, was the son-in-law of Shishak, Solomon also added to his list, a sister-in-law of Shishak, who also bore him a son. These situations were further confused when Menelik I became the issue of Solomon and the dark Sheba of Ethiopia. Quite understandable to some extent when the Delta of the Mississippi is compared with the Delta of the Nile. At all odds Shabaka was either son or brother of Pianhki.

There was a warm friendship between Shabaka and King Hosea of Israel in the beginning of the reign of the new pharaoh. But dissensions arose between them over necessary means to check the Assyrian hordes under Sargon. Shabaka however had seen service as Commander-in-Chief of the armies of Kashta, 720 B.C. which gave him an edge for Sargon. Judah, already dominated by Ethiopia, was soon to have Israel sharing her sorrows. To forestall such an event King Hosea of Israel sent a mission to Shabaka but neglected to send gifts to Sargon as he had done the year before. This slight infuriated Sargon, who immediately declared war. The Assyrians seized Samaria, Gaza and finally routed Shabaka. Shabaka knew that his defenses were well laid and could not understand the reasons for such a crushing defeat. Investigation showed him that Bakenrenef, son of Tafnecht, whom the great Pianhki had miserably humiliated, was in secret alliance with Sargon. For this plot Shabaka caught Bakenrenef and burnt him alive on the battle field. But Sargon prevailed. Shabaka fled. His troubled reign ended circa 700 B.C.

SHABATAKA, 700 B.C.

The broken threads of Nubian rule were partly mended by Shabataka, ruler of Thebes who sought peace with Palestine and Assyria. Later he sent black armies in defense of Palestine against Assyria with the result that the Assyrians overwhelmed him and thus Palestine was helpless, alone, against the aggressor. When Taharqua, then ruling at Napata, heard of the defeat of Shabakata he went by forced marches to Thebes, seized Sha-

bataka, put him to death and buried his body in Nubia. Shabataka, in his short reign of two years created a system of canals,
re-organized some of the laws and laid plans for commercial
development.

TAHARQUA, 688 B.C.

Before Taharqua could seize the reins of power, Pianhki
II the nit-wit son of a renowned forebear, threatened him for
two years until the new ruler dispossessed him. The star of
the blacks was again in the ascendancy. He made peace with
Palestine and set his plans for administrative reforms. In this
he had the co-operation of the priests-kings at Thebes in whose
line he was a descendant. He had a double coronation, one at
Tanis-Zoan and the other at Thebes. He brought his mother
from Napata to rejoice with him at the beginning of his new
royal estate. No sooner was he safely in power than the Assyrians bore down once more upon Palestine and Egypt. King
Hezekiah, though warned against trusting Taharqua, finally
cast his fortune with the black king. Sennacherib was no friend
of Taharqua yet he did not invade Egypt. Later, however, Essarhaddon, son of Sennacherib, launched the attack. The first Assyrian army, against Taharqua, was wiped out and buried by a
sandstorm but the second defeated him. Taharqua fled to Mem-
phis. Assyria was now in control through twenty princes set up
by Essarhaddon. When Essarhaddon died in 608 B.C., Taharqua re-entered the delta, probably at the invitation of these
princes, either in good faith or in a plot to seize him. However
that may be, he raided the delta and dispossessed them. Fired
by this new insurgency, Ashurbanipal, son of Essarhaddon,
rushed to Egypt and halted the Nubian revolt. While Taharqua
was making ready for further resistance, secret communications
between him and King Hezekiah were intercepted by the Assyrians which enabled them to make a surprise attack and utterly
rout Taharqua's armies. Assyrian records of this rout do not
indicate whether the informers were friends of the deposed
Pianhki or from the sources in Israel which had earlier warned

Hezekiah against Taharqua. The records only state that the Assyrian armies sent Taharqua "to his dark doom." During the 25 years of his reign he pushed forward administrative reforms, kept the peace with Palestine, promoted commerce with the Sudanese, built temples, especially the great monolithic sanctuary at Gebel Barkal and lesser temples at Tanis-Zoan and Thebes.

ROT-AMEN AND AMEN-MERI-NUT

Rot-Amen, the son-in-law and successor of Taharqua, allied himself with Phoenicia and warred on Persia and Assyria. Though he was defeated he made Egypt well-nigh untenable for Assyria. He died without heirs and a weaker ruler, Amen-meri-Nut succeeded him. The latter tried a reunion of Ethiopia and Egypt by conquering the twelve reigning Egyptian chiefs. They soon rallied and drove him out. The leader of these chiefs was Psammtek, a Libyan.

TANUT-AMEN, 661 B.C.

This feeble monarch, nephew of Taharqua, was no match for the times. Under him Nubia defeated herself, by unnecessary interference in Syria and Palestine. His miserable failures kept Nubia on the wane until the appearance of another strong man, Nastasen. Because of Tanut-Amen's constant blunders, the Nubian leaders created a "High Priestess" of Amen, a master stroke, which could have kept Nubia supreme in Egypt but for the wavering policy of the king. A policy which soon brought down upon his head the wrath of Assyria. For about a century the Persians over-ran Egypt and about 525 B.C. Cambyses attempted to invade Nubia and Ethiopia. Before launching his adventure Cambyses sent a mission to the king of Ethiopia with gifts and the following message:

"'Cambyses, anxious to become thy ally and sworn friend, has sent us to hold converse with thee and to bear thee the gifts thou seest, which are the things wherein he himself delights the most.' Hereon the Ethiopian made answer: 'The king of

QUEEN TAI
Mother of Akhnaton

Typical Official of Ancient Nubia

the Persians sent you not with gifts because he much desired to become my sworn friend . . . nor is the account which ye give of yourselves true, for ye are come to search out my kingdom. Also your king is not a just man, for were he so, he had not coveted a land which is not his own, nor brought slavery to a people who never did any wrong. Bear him this bow and say . . . The king of Ethiopia thus advises the king of the Persians, when the Persian can pull a bow of this strength thus easily, then let him come with an army of superior strength against the long-lived Ethiopians. Until then let him thank the gods that they have not put it into the hearts of the sons of the Ethiops to covet countries that do not belong to them.' "

Enraged at such a taunt from the king of Ethiopia, Cambyses set out overland with an army of 50,000 to even the score with his dark challenger. Not a fifth of the journey was completed before food was exhausted and lots cast in order to determine who should be killed and eaten. These spectacles sickened Cambyses who made his way back to Egypt. The remainder of his men were buried in a huge sandstorm such as had happened to the first army sent out by Essarhaddon in 681 B.C. against Taharqua.

This incident, highly debatable, as of 525 B.C. is still unsettled for, although records show that such a tragedy did happen, other sources tend to show that Nastasen reigned at a later date, probably, 328 B.C. It appears that Nastasen did confront a certain "Kambastian" but in all probability, not Cambyses.

It is recorded that the defeat of Cambyses drove him insane. On his return to Egypt he found much merrymaking going on, in honor of the Sacred Bull-Apis. He mistook this as rejoicing over his defeat. Angered, he personally stabbed the Apis to death, murdered many Persian nobles and commoners, the priests and officials responsible for the festival, including his own brother. He sent an arrow through the heart of the little son of his trustworthy bodyguard and had the body ripped open to see how perfect a shot he had made. He wound up by killing his sister because she would not marry him. A year later, revolt broke out in Persia. On mounting his steed to begin his journey, he accidentally cut himself with his sword and died in squalor in a Syrian village.

ARNQ-AMEN OR "ERGAMENES."

A final fleeting glimpse of old Nubia before the theatre of empire is moved to Meroe, is afforded by Arnq-Amen known to the Greeks as "Ergamenes," one of the last Nubian kings. The Ptolemies refrained from warring on Nubia. They sought to conquer her by pacific means. Accordingly they brought Arnq-Amen to Alexandria and trained him in all the wisdom and culture of Egypt and Greece, so that he might be "used" for the stealthy subjugation of Nubia. With his training over he ascended the throne. Before he had reigned very long, the priests of Amen ordered him to commit suicide as was their habit when they wished to get rid of an unwanted ruler. Arnq-Amen, irked by this command, laughed ironically and strode into the temple, with his guards, slew all the priests and ended once for all, the suicide mandate. Thereupon he made offerings to all the gods although he was worshipper of none of them.

The Ptolemies had gained their point, but not by violence. Nubia passed into the shadows.

ANCIENT ETHIOPIA

One tradition holds that shortly after the flood Cush, the son of Ham, founded the city of Axum. He named his son Aethiops and called his country Aethiopia. Another tradition holds that either Homer or Herodotus invented the name Aethiops, which in Greek means "black or burnt faced," and thus the country got its name. There is great doubt that either of them did any such thing. However, the latter view appears more tenable. Upon the exact people known as Ethiopians and the exact location of the various Ethiopias, authorities fail to agree.

The bane of all discussions, on Ethiopians and other native Africans, is the persistent search for a "true Negro," a human being so low in intelligence and so wanting in initiative, and so shorn of achievement, that he would be the proper specimen to represent the black races in all past history and all that which is to come. As it was, then in the courts of Axum and Greece, so it is today in the courts of Virginia and New York, namely neither "Negro" nor "true Negro" can be defined. It is best that the word be discarded, abandoned, and forgotten.

With the word "Abyssinia", there is no great difficulty. It is evidently derived from the "Habashat" Arabian tribe which early entered East Africa. Even though contention be made that the Ethiopians came from the stock of the "Himyarite Arabs," would scarcely alter the Africian equation, because, in the Arabian peninsula, there has always been a large infiltration of African blood. Whether "science" will admit it or not, is of no great importance. It is well known that, early Nineteenth Dynasty inscriptions speak of the blacks from the "Land of Pun," meaning the area known today as Hedjaz and Yemen on the Arabian shore of the Red Sea, and Ethiopia, French and British Somaliland, on the African shore of the Red Sea.

Indeed, as early as the Seventh to the Ninth Egyptian Dynasties, large numbers of Nubians, Ethiopians and Sudanese had crossed the Red Sea into Hedjaz and freely mixed with the Arabs and the already "Arabianized" blacks who were there earlier. The Bischarin folk in East Africa, are probably the nearest residue of that ancient fusion. If the Egyptian monuments of the Eighteenth and Nineteenth Dynasties tell anything at all, they can only tell that, at that time, Ethiopia was predominantly the land of African blacks. The word Habashat has been softened into "Habsh," to "Habshine," and finally, to Abyssinia. Such, for example, as Penn's Woods became Pennsylvania, and Lothairingia became Loringia and finally Lorraine. The word Axum, by some authorities, is attributed to a certain Malaka Axum, grandson of Aethiops, the son of Cush, the son of Ham, the son of Noah. Malaka Axum had five brothers and the six of them are considered the founders of Axum. Ex-emperor Haile Selassie, considered a twig from this ancient black tree, by way of Solomon, Sheba and Menelek I, has detached him-

self from its trunk. He has had the Ethiopian version of the
Bible changed so that his ancestral stem would proceed from
the sons of Shem, rather than from the sons of Ham. This was
no great legerdemain, for Lidj Iyasu, whom Selassie
deposed, threw over, not only Ham and the Axums, but also
Solomon, Sheba, Menelek I and Menelek II, in order that his
ancestral stem would be from the Mohammedan tree. Thus, he
tried to appear as a son of Islam.

At any rate, Axum is noted as the home of the Dragon Wai-
naba, which lived in the Tembien mountains. According to tradition, he occasionally raided Axum. A certain Angabo, said
to be the father of Sheba, killed the Dragon. For this exploit
he was made king of Axum. Through him, therefore, Sheba
received the right to rule. Later came the Solomon-Sheba situation and finally, their son Menelek I. He is reputed to have
brought to Axum an Ark of Covenant, either bogus or genuine.
Thus Axum became the Holy City.

Sheba is said to have reigned there for 50 years, 1005-
955 B.C., and Menelek I, 24 years, 954-930 B.C. Some records
seem to show that Axum was not founded until the First Century
A. D., contemporary with the fall of Napata under the blows
of the Roman general, Petronius. The true origin, then of
Axum appears to be as much in the mist as the true meaning of
the word "Black" in the Songs of Solomon, as whether it
was applied to Solomon, himself, or to Sheba.

The Falashas, the so-called "Black Jews" in Ethiopia appear
to have entered Ethiopia as early as 300 B.C., of them more
will be said in succeeding chapters.

MEROE 325 B.C.

After nearly four centuries of Nubian rule at Napata, the
line set up by Kashta in 750 B.C. ended. The deputies which
had ruled in the name of Piankhi at Meroe declared themselves
kings. The Meroitic line began about 328 B.C. and lasted nearly
six centuries. During the reign of the Ptolemies, Nubia pros-
pered. It looked as if the good old days of Thothmes III had

returned. Not the least among the Ptolemies whose liberal policy gave peace to Nubia, was the dark Cleopatra, who conquered the heart of Marc Antony on the return of Roman legions to Egypt from an attempted conquest of Ethiopia. After her death, Roman power took over the Nile Valley. About 30 B.C. the Nubians revolted against the Roman regime, as an act of resentment to the claims made by Rome to sovereignty in Nubia. A hurried conference was held by Cornelius Gallus, Roman Governor of Egypt, under Emperor Augustus. In this conference Nubia was granted independence on condition that Rome be considered paramount in Nubia. Just, for example, as the British Government wanted to grant a certain limited independence to the American colonies but retain the right to tax. Gallus granted independence to Nubia, for which he was deposed. Thus disgraced, he committed suicide, 26 B.C.

The new Roman governor, Petronius, immediately waged war, beginning first in Arabia. The Nubians knew the plans of Petronius and without delay they struck in self-defense, and attacked the Roman garrisons in the Valley, over-threw the statues of Caesar; subjugated the populace and extracted heavy indemnity. When the word of the rebellion reached Rome, Augustus ordered Petronius to quell the revolt. He, instead of waging war immediately, sent for the Nubian leaders and inquired of them the reasons for their uprising. He suggested that they give back the booty which they had taken and warned them that they were not the lords of their country, now that Egypt had come under Roman rule. The Nubian chiefs asked for three days in which to consider the demands of Petronius. Receiving no reply from them, he opened war and utterly defeated them. Among the captured chiefs were some of the generals of Candace, queen of Meroe.

Petronius then set out to capture Candace. She fled, but left with her son a plea for peace which promised agreement to his demands. Petronius disregarded the plea and raided the country. When the Roman army withdrew, Candace emerged from hiding, raised an army and renewed the attack. When the Nubian army was in sight of the advancing Romans, Candace sent envoys ahead to treat with Petronius. They were told to refer their case to Caesar.

Hostilities were stopped while the Nubian envoys, under Roman guard, journeyed to confer with Caesar. The great oratory of the Nubian envoys, before Caesar, softened his heart. He granted all their petitions and cancelled the tribute which was overdue him from Nubia.

Two kings ruled in Nubia after Candace, but nothing definite is known about them. Later on Meroe came under the power of the kings of Axum, and thus a more definite history of Ethiopia began. Of the various Candaces, five are known. The Candace who warred against Alexander the Great, the Candace who warred on Petronius, the Candace of Acts VIII: 27, and the Candace that warred on Nero, and another, of whom there appears to be no dependable record. The word "Candace," no doubt, is equivalent to the word "Kantiba," the Ethiopian word for governor. Meroe, ancient and celebrated made laudable progress in social, civil and intellectual cultivation. It had a fixed constitution, a government, laws and religion. It sent out colonies one of which was Thebes, celebrated in Egyptian history.

Meroe was the center of the great caravan trade between Ethiopia, Egypt, Arabia, Northern Africa and India.

ETHIOPIA SINCE 330 A.D.

For the next four centuries Nubia and Ethiopia went their way. This was made possible because the Roman Empire was crumbling. The death rattle, in its throat, began to click in 180 A.D., and resounded more and more until the final crash of Imperial Rome, 476 A.D. Prior to 330 A. D., a Syrian merchant, Frumentius, made a chance landing on the coast of Ethiopia. He was captured and presented to the king and queen. On the death of this Ethiopian king, the queen asked Frumentius to help her to rule. When the queen's son became of age and began to assist his mother, Frumentius returned to Egypt and asked Athanasius to send a Bishop to Ethiopia. Athanasius, pleased with the work of Frumentius, returned him there as Bishop, about 330 A.D. He succeeded in converting Ezana (Abreha) to Christianity. This aroused the jealousy of Emperor Constantine of the Greek Orthodox Church, who wrote to Ezana and asked him to expel Frumentius and put in an Arian Bishop, contending that Athanasius had no right to approve him. Thus Ethiopia was drawn into a religious war, which has continued to the recent Italo-Ethiopian war, through which the Roman Church has finally come into control of the religious life of the country.

From 330 A.D. until the middle of the Tenth Century, Ethiopia passed through many religious conflicts. She regarded the Canon law, both of the Greek and Roman churches, including the Apocrypha, but not the Book of Maccabees. The Ethiopian church apparently accepted certain findings of the Council of Nicaea 325 A.D., but the Council of Chalcedon, 451 A. D., condemned the Ethiopian church for its contentions on the single nature of Christ, which makes its religion a "Monophysite" form of Christianity.

By 525 A. D. Axum was at the height of its power and apparently, the title Negus Negusti, King of Kings, was used for the first time. To what extent the writings of the early church Fathers, especially Origen and St. Augustine, aided Ethiopia, is not known. It is conceivable, however, that Ethiopia was not wholly neglected by them.

With the rise of Islam in the Seventh Century the fortunes of Ethiopia declined. Something like an entente cordiale grew up between Ethiopia and Islam, first because Axum protected Mohammedans, who had fled from persecution at Mecca, and also because Bilal, an Ethiopian, was one of the chief advisors and collaborators with the Prophet of Allah. Though Ethiopia became surrounded by Mohammedan states, Mohammed, himself, never invaded it, and is said to have left a decree that his followers, in the future, should come to the aid of Ethiopia whenever she was in distress.

In the middle of the Tenth Century the Falashas or "Black Jews," under their mulatto queen, Judith, drove Emperor Del-Naad from the throne and reigned for 40 years, from about 940 to 980 A. D. Del-Naad fled to Shoa where his descendants reigned until near the middle of the Thirteenth Century. The Falasha power in Ethiopia was broken at the turn of the Eleventh Century by Takla Haimanot, who became the first and only native Ethiopian to rule as Abuna. Haimanot achieved mastery in Ethiopia in a very romantic fashion. He was counsellor to Del-Naad. Del-Naad suspected his own daughter of plotting against him, and to preserve his power, ordered her killed. Haimanot not only obstructed the will of Del-Naad, but asked for the hand of his daughter in marriage. Infuriated at this request, Del-Naad ordered the guards to slay Haimanot. When they refused so to do, he engaged Haimanot in personal combat. Haimanot killed him, married his daughter, and assumed authority in Ethiopia.

The dynasty which he set up became known as the House of Zagwe, and with the exception of Shoa, it controlled the country until 1275 A.D. The last ruler of the Zagwe line abdicated in favor of Yekuno Amlak of the line of Solomon, but a branch of the Zagwes continued to rule until the middle of the Eighteenth Century. The rule of the Yekunno, real Negus Negusti ended about 1285 A.D., and for the next two centuries Ethiopia was again in religious conflicts. At the opening of the Fourteenth Century a mission of Ethiopians, the records seem to show, went to Avignon in southern France where a Papacy had been set up in opposition to the ancient Papacy at Rome. They conferred with Pope Clement V, the results of which are not known. Whatever they could have been would have been voided anyway after the Roman schism had passed.

Again, about 1450, two Ethiopian priests were sent to Jerusalem to confer on a merger of the Greek and Roman churches. This matter was later taken up by Rome and Portugal, which led John II of Portugal to send an emissary, in 1490, to Ethiopia. These connections enabled Ethiopian rulers to secure help against the forces of Islam, which was finally accepted by the middle of the Sixteenth Century.

But Ethiopia was not yet free of religious struggles. The coming of the Jesuits created new conflicts which resulted in their massacre by king Fasiladas between 1632 and 1665. The country was then closed to Europeans. Under Iyasu I, 1680-1705, communications with Europe were re-opened. In this period, 1701, Louis XIV sent a mission to Ethiopia, which met the same fate that Fasiladas had meted out in 1636 to the Jesuits. Ethiopia then lay in the shadows until the reign of Batafa, 1720-1730, the last of the early rulers, who displayed new energy.

Citations of outstanding movements of the earlier Ethiopian rulers are interesting. Theodore I, 1411-1414, annulled the agreements made by Yekuno Amlak and Takla Haimanot, that one third of the land be given to the priests. The other agreements made by Yekuno Amlak and Takla Haimanot were, that the rulership in Ethiopia was to remain in the line of Solomon, that no Ethiopian, after Haimanot, should become Abuna, and that the Abuna be forever sent down from Alexandria. Thus Ethiopians, unlike the great Nubians of old, denied themselves the spiritual guidance of their own country. The baneful effects of such a policy were made clear in the recent Italo-Ethiopian war.

This action kept the country in turmoil until the appearance of the great Zara Yakob, 1434-1468. In statesmanship, Yakob may be compared to the great Count Cavour who helped to bring order in Italy in the middle of the Nineteenth Century. He created a great literature, did much building, sent monks to the Council of Florence, 1431-1445, under the patronage of Pope Eugene IV. However, he brought down the wrath of his people on his head when he signed a decree which would join the Ethiopian church with the church of Rome. The presence of Ethiopians in Rome at that time resulted in the establishment of an Ethiopian monastery there, which today is being used in training Ethiopians for service in their country as Roman Catholic priests. It is conceivable that Ethiopia's failure to take part in the Crusades may have prevented her from getting certain types of help from Europe. It is known that the rulers, during the Crusades, were approached on this subject, but nothing is definite as to what was done. It may be that the Ethiopians refrained from such an adventure because of the old agreement, in the Seventh Century, with the Prophet of Allah.

Baeda Maryam, the son of Yakob, succeeded him and ruled until 1478. His first act was a mis-step, which upset his entire rule. He had a picture painted of Christ and the Virgin Mary, which was offensive to a people, who detested such things, especially so, to the Gallas. The picture was preserved until 1700 when the Gallas, in their reign, destroyed not only the picture, but the bones of Maryam as well.

Then towards the end of the Fifteenth Century, came a series of weak rulers whose feebleness and duplicity kept the country in turmoil until the appearance of Claudius in 1540. From 1478 to 1494 Emperor Eskender was in control. He, it was, that leagued with John II of Portugal in 1492. Displeasure over this alliance resulted in his assassination. His death was kept secret for three years to prevent usurpation, but when his seven-year old son finally came to the throne he was killed after reigning only six months.

One Naod, brother of Eskender had an insipid rule, 1494-1507. Naod leagued himself against De Covilham, and thus, increased the religious schism. The legend of Prester John need only be mentioned here. It constitutes a story which will be given separate treatment.

Following Naod came Lebna Dengel, 1508-1540. His easy victories turned his head. He did not realize the threat to Ethiopia of Turkish encroachments. He soon had to face the Sultan of Egypt in 1516 and also the king of Portugal. The great Queen Helena died in 1525, which left Dengel without a needed advisor. The Turks, now ruling Egypt, poured into Ethiopia in 1527 under the leadership of Ahmad Gran. Gran immediately asked for the hand of Dengel's daughter in marriage. When refused, he raided the country from end to end. An ironic corollary is the fact that during the pounding of the armies of Gran, the Ethiopians weakened their forces by quarrels among themselves over the proper day on which to observe Easter. Dengel, in a last stand, begged help from Portugal and promised to accept the supremacy of the Pope. Help came too late.

The Arabs had wrecked the country, razed the temples and buildings in the principal cities, and murdered the adult christians. The remaining christians accepted Islam. Famine filled the land. Dengel, insane, roamed the forests, and died alone. To turn from this sordid picture and look towards the north in Southern Italy, a bright light is shone through the birth of St. Benedict the Moor, 1524, at a small place just outside Palermo. He was patronized by a rich and practical Catholic, Vincent Manasseri and later became an intercessor, through whom many miracles were wrought. He died in 1597, and is honored today by the church. At about the same time a South African had been created Bishop in Portugal.

Persistent rumors have it that the Roman Church has had three black Popes in its line of Pontiffs. St. Vicor I, the fifteenth Pope, St. Melchiades, the thirty-third, and St. Galatius, the fiftyfirst. Some controversy has raged, too, as to whether Origen and Augustine were black or white. Such inference extends also to St. Luke, Simon the Cyrenian, Simon Niger, prophet and teacher at Antioch, Julius Africanus, St. Cyprian, Tertullian, Lactantius and Terence. The controversy in regard to St. Augustine was apparently settled when, in 1921, an American priest appeared to have raised the question. The up-shot of this discussion was a statement from the American priest which read: "I simply remark that his color was black; by this I, by no means, intend to insinuate that St. Augustine was a Negro, but that as a native of Africa, he represented one of the four great divisions into which the human family is divided, so far as color is concerned, namely, white (Europe), black (Africa), yellow (China), red (American Indian). I have not been able to understand what possible difference the mere accident of color can make in a man's right to salvation."

To counteract the wreckage in Ethiopia through the clash between Gran and Dengel, there arose (1508-1540) Emperor Claudius. He summoned his warriors, and in the spirit of the great Piankhi, the Nubian king who in 744 B.C., told his men that, "with the help of Amen one man could lead captive a thousand." Thus steeled, Claudius led the fight for restoration.

He whipped together a motley army of Ethiopians, Arabian deserters and Portuguese adventurers, and stood off Gran sufficiently well to allow the people to return to their homes and fields. Finally, 1543, Gran was killed by a Portuguese soldier, and the Arabs routed. Claudius, then proceeded to subdue the Gallas and restore peace. With the king of Portugal he made an agreement in 1555 for the establishment of a new Jesuit mission. He finally made a confession of faith acceptable to the Roman church, which he disavowed in 1557. In 1559, he was murdered.

He developed the arts of peace, in spite of the continuous call to arms. After his death, Emperor Minas, violently anti-Catholic came to the throne. His brief reign (1559-1563) was hampered by the revolt of Yeshak, who is reputed to have secretly sent out letters to the enemies of the king. The new emperor, Sarsa Dengel, 1563-1597, was indifferent to Rome. Although he was engaged in wars for nearly 30 years, he also developed the arts of peace. Yeshak, formerly estranged from Sarsa Dengel, finally made peace with him, only to betray him to the Turks. Upon the death of Yeshak, which was ordered by Dengel, it left the latter free, enabling him to secure victory over the Turks and the Jews. In later years Dengel was attacked as a proselyte to the Roman faith because he had asked Portugal for missionaries. As a matter of fact, he also asked for gun powder, for muskets and for makers of cannon. The rumor persisted, and one, Za Selasse used it to force himself into position as the power behind the throne, which he held for three successive administrations. Confusion reigned until 1603, when Za Dengel was recalled. Immediately on his assumption of power, he became a Catholic and made contact with Pope Clement VIII and King Philip III of Spain.

For the next 50 years, 1553-1603, Ethiopians were left alone. As a matter of fact, Europe, herself, was engaged in the blood-letting Thirty Years War, 1618-1648, which was to determine the supremacy of Protestantism or Catholicism in that area. Hence the European nations had no time to interfere, effectively, in the affairs of Ethiopia. The flare of light thrown up by the great

St. Benedict, the Moor, 1524-1597, had its counterpart in
1649 through a distinguished Ethiopian, known as Abba Gregorius, to whom the world is indebted for authentic information
on the history of Ethiopia. Gregorius was a highly educated
man. It appears that he had displeased the king of Ethiopia by
going to India without permission and therefore, was exiled by
royal order. In 1649 Gregorius, then in Rome, met Hiob
Ludolf a great German scholar. He instructed Ludolf in the
language and lore of Ethiopia, and through this, Ludolf came
to be known as the founder of Ethiopian Studies. Whatever
became of Gregorius after 1649 is not known, but he maintains
a high place, not only in the history of the black race, but also
in the cultural history of the world. In the next century 1799
was born, Pushkin, Russo-Ethiopian, renowned in Russian and
world lierature. Emperor Susenyos came to the throne 1607-
1632, amidst petty strife and later civil war. He courted the
Jesuits and finally became a convert to Catholicism. Thereupon
Father Mendez, of the Jesuit Order, in 1626, disestablished the
Ethiopian church and instituted Roman ritual. This brought
on a religious revolt led by Takla Giorgis in 1628.

Fasiladas opposed his father's act and by 1632 caused
him to abdicate. In power himself, 1632-1667, Fasiladas embraced the Roman faith for which act he had so recently upbraided his father. This, apparently, was tactical, for the Jesuits
met their worst treatment at his hands. Aside, however, from
his rift with Father Mendez, and his later expulsion of the
Jesuits, Fasiladas gave a worthy rule as such fragrants of this
era can reveal.

In 1667-1682, John I (Yohannes) assumed control. He
immediately set up the cry, "Ethiopia for the Ethiopians," and
warred on Catholics, Mohammedans and Jews.

The next reign, 1682-1706, under the great Iyasu I, saw
Ethiopia at the Religious Council of 1686 in regard to the
nature of Christ. Thence, they proceeded to re-examine and
classify the Fetha-Nagast, or Book of the Four Gospels. Iyasu
had to face a Catholic mission sent out in 1701 by Louis XIV,
but the mission came to grief, as did the earlier Jesuits in 1636.

Aiding Iyasu in expelling the Louis XIV Mission was Takla Haimanot I, 1706-1708. In this period, 1708, Ethiopia re-examined the findings of the Council of Nicaea, of 325 A. D. For the next 50 years, there was petty strife in the country under the Emperors Justus, David III, Asma Giorgis and Iyasu II, 1730-1755. In this latter reign Ethiopia made war on the Fungs, a Sudani-Nubian folk—and brought to a halt attempts of Europeans to change the Ethiopian religion. From 1755 to 1800 there was a rapid succession of rulers. The country was filled with intrigue. John II, 1769, who bade fair to give a good administration, was poisoned. From 1769 to 1788 there was a continuous feud between Takla Haimanot II and Ras Michael. The most significant thing in this period, 1755-1777, was the rise of the Gallas, one of the most interesting peoples in Ethiopia. They had been gaining ground since the Fifteenth Century. Ras Kassa, now in England with Ex-emperor Haile Selassie, is in the line of the Gallas, and was one of the most distinguished generals during Ethiopia's late war with Italy. Confusion and disorder, at the turn of the Nineteenth Century paved the way for dissensions, divisions and for submissions, so evident among Ethiopian leaders, during the war of 1933-1936, with Italy.

These divisions around 1800 came about as follows: Ras Sahla Selasse, of Shoa, was a vassal of Ras Hailou; Ras Hailou, himself, was in control of Amhara and Gogam. The continual bickering, between Ras Hailou and Ras Ube, kept the nation in turmoil. With the accession of John III in 1840, wilder disorder reigned. Ten years later Sahla Dengel came into power for four years. Still the anarchy did not abate. Finally, Lidj Kassa, torn with the strife that had been created by Ras Hailou and Ras Ube, took matters into his own hands, waged war, and placed himself (1855-1868) in control of the country. Lidj Kassa, chose as his throne name, Theodore II in honor of the Great Theodore four centuries ealier. He proceeded, immediately, to limit the aristocrats and to try to force the Gallas and Mohammedans out of the country, unless they became christians.

By holding two Englishmen, Bell and Plowden, as hostages he incurred the wrath of the British. Records seem to show that Theodore was lured into writing amorous letters to queen Victoria, which asked her hand in marriage. He felt, doubtless, that the white queen of the British would not disdain to accept an Ethiopian of such distinguished lineage. It is doubtful whether the great queen ever saw the letters. Although Theodore received gifts of various sorts from England, yet he persisted in holding Bell and Plowden in custody. Whether his obstinacy was based on his failure to get a favorable reply on the question of marriage, has not been so clearly shown. However his failure to release the Englishmen after repeated warnings from England did cause that country to send an expedition into Ethiopia which warred against him, routed his forces and caused him to commit suicide rather than fall into the hands of the British.

But Theodore's undoing was not all due to his defiance of England. While he was making war against the English forces, a certain Negusi, anxious to gain control in a part of Ethiopia, turned Catholic and made an alliance with Napoleon III of France in exchange for French help to attain his ends. The deal brought no aid to Negusi, but it did result in gaining Somaliland for France, which she still holds. Theodore discovered the treason of Negusi, but too late to stop its effects.

The fall of Magdala in 1868 marked the end of the first great Ethiopian leader in modern times. There was now, no peace in the country. John IV, 1868-1889, not only courted the favor of Napier, leader of the British expedition against Theodore, but he was also truculent to the Italian forces which had begun to get a foot-hold in Ethiopia in 1838 through the missionary work of Father Massaia. In 1868 there were two kings in Ethiopia, Menelek, king of Shoa and John IV, king of Tigré. Against both of them, the Gallas made war. To add to these disturbances, there appeared in Ethiopia, Dr. Sapeto, reputed to have been an Italian Secret Agent. He sought to gain a footing on the Bay of Assab, by direct negotiation. In this he failed. Soon he organized a dummy steamship company and bought the desired land through its name, and turned it over to the Italian Government.

Ethiopia was now faced by penetrations on the part of both Egypt and Italy. Menelek II, displeased with the turn of things, warred on John, but was defeated. John, later leading a war against the Dervishes of the Sudan, was struck by a stray bullet which caused his death in 1889. Thus, the way was opened for Menelek II. In the intervening years, 1868-1889, Ethiopia had been triumphant in many wars against Italy. Some of them were carried on by John, and others by Menelek II. With Menelek now in full control, 1889, the Italians sought to bind him by a treaty. Accordingly, they drew up the infamous Treaty of Uccialli, in which they sought, by trickery, to force Menelek to agree, that Ethiopia's foreign affairs be directed from Rome. In this treaty was the disputed Article XVII, signed by Menelek through which the Italians claimed that Menelek agreed to be "obliged" to turn Ethiopian affairs over to the Italian foreign office. One word in the Article, "Icciaullacciaul," appears to have been misinterpreted. The Italians claimed that the word meant "must" and Menelek claimed that the word meant "may or might;" hence, Menelek, not only disregarded the terms of the treaty, as he had a right to do, but also communicated with other sovereigns in Europe.

Out of this welter of dispute, the tottering Crispi ministry, in Italy, ordered the Italian soldiers to strike. The world knows the outcome of the war of 1896, and the great battle of Adowa, so fateful to Italy in men and so damaging to her prestige in diplomacy. Menelek emerged as the greatest black leader, soldier and statesman in modern times. He represented a flare, not only of the struggle against the French, in Haiti by Touissant Louverture, 1799-1804, but also of the great warriors in the glorious days of old Nubia, and Thothmes III in Egypt. A final treaty was made in which the Italians recognized the sovereignty and independence of the reborn black empire.

Ten years later, 1906, France, England and Italy drew up a treaty in which they virtually partitioned the country. Ras Mangasha, who did yeoman service for his country prior to

HAILLE SELASSIE
(*Self-Exiled Ruler*)

RAS DESTA DEMTOU
Noblest Ethiopian Since Menelek

1896, two years later rose in revolt against Menelek II, and his chief advisor, Ras Makonnen. Both of these leaders would have been used to strengthen the empire, but the services of both were cut short by their deaths in 1906. Menelek, now shorn of his great advisor, Ras Makonnen, managed the ship of state until 1909, when his mind became affected, and partly so on to 1913, when he is reported to have died.

A certain Ras Gugsa, who had begun opposition to Ras Makonnen as early as 1902, brought on a schism similar to the three-way quarrel among Sahla Selasse, Ras Hailu and Ras Ubi, a century earlier. Menelek, while yet in the strength of his mental powers in 1909, warned the Abuna and all the leaders, against dissension and division which might cause them to lose their country. At the same time, he ordered that his grand-son Lidj Iyasu succeed him, which was done. No sooner was Lidj-Iyasu on the throne, than he turned Moham-medan, and opposed the christian religion. For this apostasy, has was deposed by Ras Tafari-(Haile Selassie).

In 1923, Ras Tafari was successful in getting Ethiopia into the League of Nations. This move oddly enough, was sponsored by Italy and supported by France but upon it, the British frowned.

Later on, 1928, Italy made an additional Treaty of Friend-ship with Ethiopia and in 1930, Ras Tafari was crowned Haile Selassie I, King of Kings and Conquering Lion of the Tribe of Judah. To some extent, he carried on the reforms instituted by the great Menelek, but apparently was not as zealous for the real interest of the country as was that incomparable states-man.

In 1933, Italy renewed her old war cry: "Un Conto Vec-chio da Soldare," i.e., "An old count to be settled." The Fas-cist forces began plotting war. In 1934 at Wal Wal, a boun-dary dispute brought on the needed excuse which Italy desired in order to launch the actual attack. Wal Wal, however, was at least 60 miles on the Ethiopian side from the stated boundary line between Ethiopia and Italian Somaliland. Disputes, ac-cusations, and recriminations continued until October of 1935, when the Fascist air forces and armored tanks launched one of the most unaccountably indefensible wars in history. The League of Nations wavered and did nothing, except a temporary blockade by the way of imposing sanctions. The Ethiopians, practically unarmed, and their leaders torn with strife and dissension, fought bravely, until Fascist poison gas blinded them and ended the war.

As a last resort, ex-Emporer Haile Seelassie gathered around him selected chiefs and nobles and fled in the night to a waiting train and on to the safety of a British warship thence to the calm of the British countryside. The war, after his flight, dragged on without the aid of the great Ras Nasibu, mighty holder of the southern line against Marshal Graziani. He fled with the emperor, but went to Switzerland where, tended by his Russian brother-in-law, he died.

Bravely fighting alone within the country, was Ras Imru, who finally was subdued, captured and borne to the island of Ponza in the Tyrrhenian Sea, where he now languishes in exile. Of the great Rases who might have given a better account of themselves were: Gugsa, Seyoum, Ghetacchio and Chebdebbe, all of whom submitted. General Takla Hawariate made valiant pleas for his country before the League. He inadvertently referred to his countrymen as members of the black race, which partly accounted for his recall as Minister to France to the Ethiopian Delegate to the League. Though trained in the Russian Military School, he failed to get a command, although he returned to the country before the war was over.

Wolde Maryam, who succeeded Hawariate as Ethiopian Minister to France, submitted to Italy while still in office, and Afwerk Jesus, Ethiopian Minister to Italy submitted and returned to his country in the Italian service. Ras Desta Demtou, though he fled from the country with his father-in-law, Emperor Haile Selassie, returned to the war for a last stroke at the Fascist invader, just as the mighty Taharqua returned to the wars in 688 B.C., in an effort to stem the tide of Assyrian power led by Essarhaddon. Ras Desta was betrayed into

the hands of the Italians by a petty chieftain, who had long
borne a grievance against him.

In the meantime, an attempt had been made on the life
of Marshal Graziani, the Italian viceroy at Addis Ababa. The
Fascist forces took swift vengeance, which included the murder
of Ethiopian civilians, the approximate number of which is
undetermined. Ras Desta, assumed to have been connected
with the attack on Graziani, was captured and made to face
a firing squad of twelve men. He was the only great chief that
died on the land and under his own flag.

ETHIOPIA AND THE LEAGUE OF NATIONS

It is interesting now to review the blandishments of Count
Bonin-Longare of Italy which lured Ethiopia into the League
and thus aided Italy to become one of the "satisfied" nations.

The Count, on September 19, 1923, before The Sixth
Committee, of the Fourth Assembly of the League of Nations,
said, that:

> "Abyssinia's request constituted a tribute to the League
> of Nations. This tribute was of great value as coming from
> a distant nation which had hitherto remained outside the great
> international movements, but which by the remarkable tenacity
> with which it had been able to preserve its religious faith and
> and national character, throughout the ages, had acquired
> titles of nobility to which due justice must be paid here.—
> The request for admission should be welcomed and considered
> in a friendly spirit, in order to pave the way for favorable
> developments.—The Sub-Committee had therefore been grateful
> to the Abyssinian Government for having authorized the high
> officials, whom it had instructed to submit its request for ad-
> mission, to furninsh information and explanations; these had
> been of great value, and several of them had thrown a favor-
> able light upon the situation."

Count Bonin-Longare was supported in these high sentiments by M. de Jouvenel, of France and M. Freire d'Andrade,
of Portugal. Though the Portuguese delegate had a faint remi-
niscence of the medieval feuds between Ethiopia and Portugal,
yet he leaned towards the "right," which Ethiopia should have
had, to import arms. To this view the Italian delegate was
heartily opposed, and expressed himself as follows:

"—the fewer arms there were in Abyssinia the less scope there would be for slave traffic, for the importation of arms enabled traffickers to conquer the sturdy tribes of Central Africa. If, however, there were free traffic in arms, a vast quantity of rifles would pass across Abyssinia into Central Africa, and the sanguinary warfare of previous centuries would be again resumed between those tribes. It was the task of the Third Committee to disarm Europe; the Sixth Committee would not submit the error of arming Central Africa."

The Count concluded with an appeal that the Committee adopt his conclusions and the report submitted with them. He closed by stating that he:

"—was sure that the Abyssinian Government would accept the engagements required of it and that it would accept them frankly and with that loyalty which consisted, in the first instance, of gauging how far it would be capable of keeping any engagements it undertook. The Abyssinian Government would no doubt appreciate the assistance which the League of Nations could give it in its fight against slavery, and thus prepare itself to become an ever more active and effectual pioneer of civilization in Central Africa."

These sentiments of the Count prevailed and Ethiopia entered the League a shorn lamb ready for slaughter in the House of Peace—in the House of her "friends" who had supported her entrance with their fingers crossed and their tongues in their cheeks.

Ethiopia at the Crossroads

T HE Italo-Ethiopian War quickened interest not only in that ancient land but in all Africa. Of special interest is the fact that the Ethiopians have finally been listed with the black races. This action, so long delayed by biased writers, opens an unquestioned vista into the cultural past of the Nile Valley and the part which Ethiopians and allied black races have played in the civilizations of the ancient East.

In all the flare of the sadistic war in East Africa, not one scientist, not one anthropologist, not one ethnologist came boldly forth to declaim that ruthless Fascism was destroying a "white race." Of all the writers who, in the past have classified the Ethiopians as "Caucasian" not one during the war has successfully defended his thesis. The few who did essay a clarification of the racial skein in Ethiopia and East Africa, in general, sought only to show that at least the "Amharas" were "Hymarite Arabs" utterly different from the so-called "true African."

This was saying very little in view of the fact that the "Hymarite" Arabs came chiefly from the Adites, Joktanite and Johramite tribes in the old land of Saba and were themselves heavily "Africanized." Not even the Jews, who have long had a sort of drowsy interest in the assertions that the Ethiopians were a "Semitic" race and that the "Falashas" were actually "Black Jews," came forth boldly to the defense of Ethiopians either as Semitics, of a sort, or actually, Jews. What little contact the Jews did make with Ethiopia during the war was not that of co-racialists or co-religionists, but merely on the general horror of war. These Falashas seem to know nothing of the Babylonish captivity. They do not know the Talmud nor do they speak Hebrew. What little interest the outer world has had in them has been fostered, chiefly, by Dr. Jacques Faitlovitch, long a champion of their cause and claims. They are religiously called "Beta Israel."

In order to be able to check with a degree of accuracy on the question of racial classification in Ethiopia, the author visited the chief Ethiopian Legations in Europe in the summer of 1935 just prior to the outbreak of the war. The expressions received regarding the question of race may be summed up as follows:

"The Emperor is very conscious of the fact that he is today the only Black Sovereign in the world, and he considers himself as the natural leader of the (black) Negro race. He is fond of repeating the phrase that 'Ethiopia is the trustee for the future of the black races,.'"

His Majesty, Emperor Haille Selassie I, regards himself as the Guardian of the interests of black men everywhere and the symbol of their hopes throughout Africa, which interests and hopes will be dashed to pieces if Ethiopia is vanquished in this struggle.

On August 9, 1935, while appealing to the Mohammedans in Ogaden, Southeastern Ethiopia, for help, the Emperor is reported to have said: "I am the chief of all the blacks. I am Emperor of all Negroes, even those under foreign domination."

Much was made of this in the Italian press, from which the story probably originated. It is certain that, whatever his private opinion on race may be he has never made any such statement. Haille Selassie is too cautious, wily and wary, to make any such acknowledgment. There are, however certain things in politics, so evident that there is no need to formulate them in public speeches. And there are certain consequences that inevitably result from certain events even though these events be far from the intention or even the consciousness of those responsible for the shaping of the events.

As a belated gesture to racial brotherhood, after the war had been lost, ex-Emperor Haille Selassie has sent his personal physician to America as his personal representative to the blacks. But even in his trans-Atlantic broadcast to America endorsing the authority which he had given to his representative, the former Emperor failed to make any definite commitments on racial brotherhood. Among the Ethiopians in authority who

were definitely race-conscious were, Ras Nassibu, great leader
of the Ethiopian forces in Ogaden—now dead; Wolde Giorgis, former private secretary to the Emperor, General Tecla
Hawariate, former Ethiopian Minister to France and Delegate
to the League of Nations, Ras Kassa, the Galla chieftain now
with the ex-Emperor, in England, and Dr. W. C. Martin, Ethiopian Minister to Great Britain, now in charge of Ethiopian
Legation in London.

Back in August 1919 an Ethiopian Delegation of three
Imperial Dignitaries came to the United States on a business
and diplomatic mission. They were, Dedjazmatch Nadou, later,
1923, one of the signatories for Ethiopia when she was admitted to the League of Nations, Kantiba Gabrou, then governor
of Gondar and Belanghetta Herouy, then Mayor of Addis Ababa and later Minister of Foreign Affairs. While in New York
they received, in the old Waldorf-Astoria Hotel, the following
committee of Harlem citizens: Rev. W. P. Hayes, then pastor
of Mt. Olivet Baptist Church; Rev. W. W. Brown, then pastor
of the Metropolitan Baptist Church; Elder J. E. Humphrey,
of the Seventh Day Adventists Church; Mr. Chas. T. Magill,
publicist; Mr. J. A. Davis, realtor and the author.

From the Waldorf the Delegation went to the Metropolitan Baptist Church in Harlem where Rev. W. W. Brown welcomed them, not only in the name of Harlem but in the name
of black folk throughout America. Mayor Herouy responded
to the welcome address through Mr. Topokyan, an attaché of
the Persian Legation in New York.

At the end of the service the audience was assembled in
front of the church where a picture was made with the Ethiopian Delegation in the centre. This was done, not merely in
the course of ordinary courtesy but especially to show good-will
and racial recognition for the blacks in America. To the author
the Delegation gave the following message:

> "On the part of the Ethiopian Empire we desire to ex-
> press the satisfaction we have felt on hearing of the wonderful
> progress the Africans have made in this country. It gives us
> great confidence in the Government of the United States to
> know that through the independence given you by America, you

have increased in numbers and developed in education and prosperity. We want you to remember us after we have returned to our native country. In order to help you do this we suggest that you turn to your Bible and in our memory, read to yourselves, from time to time, the first Chapter of the first Epistle of John. This is the first thing read by our children after they have learned the alphabet, and is called the Alphabet of the Apostles. Please also tell this to such of your friends whom we did not have the opportunity to meet and kindly convey to them our farewell."

In 1927 Dr. Azaz Wahrnek Martin, now Ethiopian Envoy Extraordinary and Minister Plenipotentiary to the Court of St. James, London, England, came to America on a special mission in connection with diplomatic relations between Ethiopia and the United States and also the matter of getting American aid in the development of the Lake Tsana water project.

While in New York, a committee headed by Mr. Arthur Schomburg, Curator of the African History Section of the 135th Street Library, Harlem, called on him in the Astor Hotel, 45th Street and Broadway. Dr. Martin, at that time, invited American blacks to come to Ethiopia as mechanics, professional men, farmers and settlers. There seems to be no record of any public appearances made by him while here.

In 1933, the late Prince Desta Demtou, loyal son-in-law of ex-Emperor Haile Selassie, came to these shores accompanied by Ato Manamano, then Ethiopian Consul to Jerusalem. Their special mission was to pay official visit to the United States Government in return for the visit of Hon. H. Murray Jacoby who was America's official representative at the coronation of the Emperor in 1930. Incidentally they pushed forward the work of the missions of 1919 and 1927.

While in New York a committee headed by Capt. Arthur P. Hayes and the author called on Prince Demtou and Ato Manamano in their suite in the Hotel St. Moritz. During a two hour interview the Prince inquired of every phase of the life of black folk in the United States. To such inquiries the author made brief but inclusive reply. He also asked that the statement given by the 1919 Mission be re-published as his sentiment. At the end of the interview Prince Demtou placed a golden ring on the author's finger as a mystic circle of friendship and bade him to keep interest in Ethiopia alive in the hearts of the American blacks. The Prince also discussed at length the question of the Nation's new program of school building and educational administration in Ethiopia. Dr. Malaku Bayen, a native Ethiopian, then (1933) a medical student at Howard University and later, during the war, was personal physician to the Emperor, was present, as interpreter, throughout the interview. When the Prince sailed on the Ile de France, he gave a final greeting to a group from the Universal Ethiopian Students Association which had come with a huge Ethiopian flag and a bon voyage basket of flowers. He reiterated his hope that American blacks trained in engineering, general mechanics, teachers, nurses and physicians would come, for service, and make their homes in Ethiopia.

RAS DESTA DEMTOU

The Most Defiant of Ethiopian Chieftains Fell Before an Italian Firing Squad February 24, 1937

As a result of the author's contacts with Minister Martin in London and Minister Hawariate in Paris he brought back with him the following messages:

MESSAGE FROM DR. MARTIN
Ethiopian Minister to Great Britain
IMPERAL ETHIOPIAN LEGATION
LONDON

August 7th, 1935

To the Friends of Ethiopia in the United States of America
Greetings:—

I have this day received Dr. Willis N. Huggins in official interview and listened carefully to his statement of aims and plans initiated in America for the benefit of Ethiopia.

While we do not necessarily seek sporadic collections indiscriminately made, yet we do most ardently desire a public loan which should be arranged by responsible business men and managed through a reputable banking house.

We welcome medical supplies, nurses, doctors, veterinarians, industrial and technical men to come to us. However we desire that those who will come will also become a part of us in building the Ethiopia of the future. It is also desirable that an independent Red Cross of colored people act with other groups for us.

Dr. Huggins has my full approval to proceed in the organization of such activities in connection with committees which may be arranged.

Your efforts will be recognized officially from our London office.

Yours for Service,
(Signed) W. MARTIN,
*Ethiopian Minister to The Court of St. James
London, England.*

MESSAGE OF GENERAL TECLE HAWARIATE

*Ethiopian Minister to France and Delegate to the
League of Nations, Geneva*

Imperial Ethiopian Legation, Paris

August 9th, 1935

To the Friends of Ethiopia in the United States of America: Greetings:

Dr. Willis N. Huggins was officially received by me today with letters of introduction from my distinguished colleague and fellow countryman, Dr. Martin, Ethiopian Minister to Great Britain.

I have carefully read Minister Martin's instructions to Dr. Huggins and heartily concur in them. I would add however that the black race in America forms a salient angle of Ethiopia which cannot be ignored in its relation to the one independent, indigenous black government remaining in the world.

Speaking unofficially, I can say that His Majesty, Emperor

Haile Selassie regards himself as the Guardian of the interests of black men everywhere and the Symbol of their hopes throughout Africa, which interests and hopes would be dashed to pieces if Ethiopia is vanquished in this struggle. Coming out of this struggle victorious and sovereign, as with the help of God we will, 'Ethiopia will be stronger than ever. It will afford a profitable field for investments and commercial enterprise. A part of the surplus capital in America could then be safely put into Ethiopian gold bonds and would bring a sure return, higher, perhaps, than elsewhere.

As soon as conditions permit, representatives from Ethiopia will come to place these matters before the great American public. Meanwhile, through the best way possible, help Ethiopia in this hour.

(Signed) TECLE-HAWARIATE,
Ethiopian Minister to France and
Delegate to the League of Nations, Geneva

AN APPEAL FOR ETHIOPIA
TO THE LEAGUE OF NATIONS

Memorandum presented by the International Council of Friends
of Ethiopia to the Council of the League of Nations,
Geneva, Switzerland.

Transmitted August 15th, 1935, to the Honorable Joseph C. Avenol, Secretary to the League of Nations, by Dr. Willis N. Huggins, Executive Secretary of the International Council of Friends of Ethiopia.

Africans and persons of African descent throughout the world, have always looked with pride at the Empire of Ethiopia, which alone of all the ancient empires of black men in Africa, still maintains its independence.

The nefarious will of Italy to conquer Ethiopia is expressed at present, by the concentration of men and munitions on the Ethiopian frontiers. This is viewed with righteous indignation by the blacks in the western world who are bound by racial kinship to the ancient and illustrious Ethiopian people.

The planned destruction of Ethiopia, if actually executed, will not only be a catastrophe for all black men, but such a heinous crime will:

(1) put the peace of the world in peril,

(2) provide stronger arguments for the spread of sub- versive political theories,

(3) increase the hollow mockery of the professions of Christianity thus bringing more and deeper disgrace to Christian principles,

(4) increase the guilt of modern Christian nations who, yesterday raped Africa and carried away millions of her children to be enslaved in the Americas.

Today these same Christian nations actually aid or tacitly stand by, while plans are made to slaughter the people in the most ancient Christian land in the world.

The idea that the League of Nations would tolerate a war, so fraught with peril, so pregnant with dire consequences for the world and one, so utterly based upon such evident pretexts, is altogether repellent to the common judgment of mankind.

Ethiopia is a member of the League of Nations. Article X of the Covenant guarantees the territorial integrity and political independence of its members. Her membership was sponsored by France and welcomed by Italy both of whom considered Ethiopia's membership a credit to the League.

Great Britain, France and Italy have agreed (a) in the Tri-Partite Treaty of 1906, to co-operate in maintaining the political and territorial status-quo in Ethiopia and (b) in the Treaty of 1930, to assist the Emperor of Ethiopia to obtain arms and munitions necessary for the defense of his territory from external aggression.

The Italian and British governments have unequivocally recognized the exclusive rights of Ethiopia to grant or refuse any request in connection with economic questions which either of these governments may make—the Italian Government in its note to His Highness Tafari Makonnen of June 9th, 1926, and the British Government in its letter of August 3rd, 1926, to the Secretary General of the League of Nations.

The International Council of Friends of Ethiopia ardently hopes that the League of Nations will;—

(1) take measures to restrain Italy from this gross infringement of international law and agreements often ratified;

(2) assure the Emperor and the people of Ethiopia that it whole-heartedly supports them in their efforts to preserve and maintain their rights;

(3) protest to the Italian government against its immoral and unwarranted attitude toward Ethiopia;

(4) send a neutral commission to Ethiopia to observe and report before September 4th on boundary disputes;

(5) conform to its Covenant as stated in Articles X and XVI respecting territorial integrity, national independence and the sanctions for the violation of these Articles.

This memorandum faithfully translates the sentiments of millions of blacks in the Americas who plead that Ethiopia be safeguarded as a question of sacred honor and of human duty. They are convinced that the peace machinery of the world will do all in its power to give to the Italo-Ethiopian Dispute a solution in peace and mutual honor.

You will find in this Memorandum, honorable Members of the Council, the expression of our high consideration.

For the International Council of Friends of Ethiopia.

(Signed) WILLIS N. HUGGINS,

Executive Secretary.

The French text of the above plea was published, in its entirety, in "Journal des Nations" in Geneva, August 16th, 1935.

While in Switzerland the author made a special trip to Villeneuve on the Lake where he spent a half day with the renowned Romain Rolland. M. Rolland was sought because his great personal influence might be used to help sway Premier Litvinoff, as president of the Council, to come to the aid of Ethiopia.

Other men whose voices were raised on behalf of Ethiopia in the ominous days of mid-August, were Hon. Gratien Candace, Member of the French Chamber of Deputies from Guaduloupe, Hon. Galando Diouf, Member of the French Chamber of Deputies from Senegal, General Nemours, Haitian Delegate to the League of Nations and Hon. Constantin Mayard, Haitian Minister to France.

Before leaving Europe the author sent a telegram of thanks on behalf of the International Council of Friends of Ethiopia to President Eamon de Valera, of the Irish Free State, for his expressed intention to use his influence for Ethiopia.

A LETTER OF APPRECIATION

HIS MAJESTY, HAILLE SELASSIE

to

Dr. WILLIS N. HUGGINS

for his efforts in Europe and his activities in America on behalf of Ethiopia.

IMPERIAL PALACE

Addis-Ababa, le 24 Septembre 1935

M. le Dr. W. N. Huggins,
1890 Seventh Avenue,
New York.

Monsieur,

Nous avons l'honneur de vous informer que votre lettre du 16 Aout 1935, addressé á Sa Majesté l'Empereur, Notre Auguste Souverain, est parvenue á Sa Majesté.

Sa Majesté a été tres touché de votre activite au nom du Conseil International des Amis de l'Ethiope, en notre faveur,

et de la sympathie et des bons voeux que vous lui exprimez.
Sur l'ordre de Sa Majesté nous avons l'honneur de vous
en remercier.

Veuillez, agreer Monsieur, l'expression de notre consideration.

Signed: (for the Emperor)

TRANSLATION

Dear sir:

We have the honor to inform you that your letter of August 16th, 1935, addressed to His Majesty, the Emperor, Our
August Sovereign has come to His Majesty.

His Majesty has been very much touched by your activity
in the name of The International Council of Friends of Ethiopia, in our favor and of the sympathy and the good wishes
that you have expressed for Him.

We beg you to accept, Sir, the expression of our consideration.

THE HOARE-LAVAL PLAN

OFFICIAL publication of the Hoare-Laval peace plan on December 13, 1935 only served to increase world indignation at the manner in which Britain and France, claiming to act as the League's representatives, had intended to dismember a League state to satisfy the territorial ambitions of a declared aggressor. The plan provided for an "exchange of territories" under which Ethiopia was to cede outright 60,000 square miles in return for a corridor of 3,000 square miles through Italian Eritrea, including the port of Assab. In addition, Britain and France were "to use their influence at Addis Ababa and Geneva" to secure the formation in Southern Ethiopia of an Italian zone of economic expansion and settlement totaling 160,000 square miles, for which Ethiopia was to receive no territorial *quid pro quo*. In this zone Italy was to enjoy "exclusive economic rights," to be exercised by a "privileged company" which would acquire all unoccupied lands and a monopoly of exploiting mines, forests and other natural resources. This company would be "obliged" to contribute to the economic "equipment" of the country and to expend a portion of its revenue for the benefit of the natives. The Italian zone was to remain an "integral part of Ethiopia" but to be controlled by League "services" in which Italy was to play "a preponderant but not exclusive role." Questions regarding administration of the zone were to be handled by one of the principal League advisors, "who might be of Italian nationality," and who would act as assistant to the chief League adviser at Addis Ababa. The League services throughout Ethiopia "would regard it as one of their essential duties to insure the safety of Italian subjects and the free development of their enterprises."

An immediate outcry was raised against the Hoare-Laval proposals by Ethiopia, the British press and Parliament, the

AKHNATON
First Religious Reformer

NEFERTARI
Wife of Akhnaton

French Radical Socialists, and the small League powers in Europe and Latin America. Captain Anthony Eden, British Minister for League Affairs, figuratively washed Britain's hands of the whole scheme on December 12, when he told the League sanctions committee that the peace proposals were "neither definitive nor sacrosanct," and that Britain would "cordially welcome any suggestions for their improvement." At his request the sanctions committee, convoked for the specific purpose of considering an oil embargo against Italy, postponed action until after the League Council—summoned for December 18—had passed on the peace plan.

Various considerations have been mentioned in justification or extenuation of British action: Japan's renewed drive into China; unrest in Egypt; Italy's threat to Lake Tsana, the confusion of France's internal situation; the reluctance of British financial and industrial interests to support an oil embargo; Tory sympathies for Mussolini; fear that the British fleet, immobilized in the Mediterranean since September, would not prove a match for that of Italy. All these considerations, however, were present in actual or potential form at the outbreak of the Italo-Ethiopian war and must have entered into the calculations of a government with the least pretensions to foresight. The key to Britain's action must be sought elsewhere— in the attitude of France. The Baldwin government had repeatedly declared that it would support the collective system only on condition that all League powers, great and small, pulled their full weight; should the collective system prove ineffective, it intimated that Britain might have to loosen its ties with the continent and look to its own defenses by unilateral action. Again and again during the Ethiopian crisis Britain had sought to obtain a definite pledge of French naval assistance in case of Italian attack on the British fleet, only to receive ambiguous assurance from M. Laval.

END OF THE ITALO-ETHIOPIAN WAR

As 1935 closed, Marshal Pietro Badoglio succeeded the aged General Emilio de Bono as commander-in-chief of the

Italian forces, while General Graziani remained in command of the southern army operating from Italian Somaliland. In the north, de Bono had advanced no further than the Makale-Seket line, having been forced eastward, from the Angli-Egyption Sudan frontier, almost to Adowa. Badoglio planned three offensives, while Graziani was to offer a distraction by advancing on Wardara, 175 miles south of Addis Ababa. He defeated Ras Desta, occupied Wardara January 26, and halted. Badoglio had as immediate objectives the regions of Tembien, where de Bono had been defeated; Enderta and Scire. In the last, Ras Imru was preparing an offensive with 40,000 or 50,000 men. Badoglio neutralized this offensive, reached his other objectives and then defeated the Negus's reorganized army at Lake Ashangi—the turning point in the war.

The rapidity with which the Ethiopian defense crumbled constitutes one of the most disgraceful episodes in history.

But the Italian victory was no miracle. Untrained tribesmen armed with antique weapons, save in some instances where modern equipment was used, were no match for one of the most powerfully mechanized fighting forces in the world today. The crumbling of the black empire began on January 22, 1936 with the loss of Neghelli. This was followed by the defeats of Ras Mulghetta and Rases Seyoum and Kassa on February 16 and February 28, respectively.

March brought the defeat of Ras Imru and a second defeat for Ras Kassa and the bombing of Harar.

Early in April the Emperor's personal army was broken, and Gondar, the ancient capital of Ethiopia taken. Towards the middle of April the Lake Tsana region was invested while Ras Desta and Ras Nasibu failed in the south. The last week in April disaster came. Addis Ababa was bombed, April 14 by 22 planes and simultaneously attacked, north and south, by Italian armies. On April 30, the defense of Addis Ababa was abandoned. doned.Two days later the Empeor and his selected personnel fled, leaving the capital to flames and riot. The Ethiopian masses, now leaderless, and blinded by Yperite, the most deadly poison gas, struck out aimlessly at everything "white" until the Italian forces invested the capital on May 5 under Marshall Badoglio. Thus was halted the continued independence of a black sovereign state whose roots go back beyond the great sovereignties in the Nile Valley and the Ancient East. Desultory fighting continued until December 17, 1936 when Ras Imru was defeated and later in January of 1937 carried into exile on the lonely island of Ponza in the Tyrrhenian Sea.

Meanwhile Ras Desta Demtou, who fled the country with his father-in-law, Emperor Haille Selassie, had returned to the wars, and had successfully eluded capture. However, the attempted assassination of the viceroy at Addis Ababa, early in February, quickened the Fascists forces to hunt down this wily Chieftain. Desta, now in the hands of the Fascists, was shot down by a 12-man firing squad, February 24, 1937.

It is difficult to assign actual blame in a situation so complicated. A venturesome opinion would indicate that the Emperor, at least, after the Hoare-Laval abortion, might have salvaged the core of his empire by negotiation after the "powers" had practically deserted him. To be sure such would have been a bitter draught but certainly it would have been better than his pell-mell flight, and the populace left leaderless.

Now—May 1937—he toys in England with the fatuous verbiage of the League Covenant scheming how to be represented at the coronation of a king of the British, the very British who lured him into an unequal fight with a mighty power and left him adrift. Indeed the British who originally opposed his entry into the League. The Emperor hopes for another assault upon the League in plenary session assembled, probably in September, but the machinations of Italy and France, have apparently led the Swiss into recognizing, as de jure, the present Italian occupation. Hence the plan is to halt Ethiopian delegates at the Swiss border on the score that, not having a sovereign government, they therefore have no valid passports. Thus the "powers," ashamed to face the issue directly, have elected to hide in the shadow of Helvetius.

Haille Selassie, the Emperor of Ethiopia, who trusted his empire to the word of the League of Nations and lost it, stated early in April, 1937, in an exclusive interview to the French newspaper *L'Intransiegeant*, that he would have sought an agreement with Mussolini but for his confidence in the League. The Emperor said, "My people would have been able to defend themselves very differently from the way they did. But we were not prepared. It is my fault. I did not think that war would come. We were always uneasy when we saw foreigners in our land, so it was an immense joy to us when we were admitted to the League of Nations in 1923. We were saved. To us the word 'League' had a sacred meaning.

"My people imagined the chiefs of 52 white nations seated with me and a cup passing from hand to hand. The foreign chieftains have drunk from the cup. Therefore they are bound to aid us.

"When I received the dispatches announcing that English battleships had arrived at Gibraltar, I thought to myself, 'I was right to maintain my trust.' But . . .

The Negus went on, "If I had known, I would have sought an agreement with Mussolini. I would have spared my people. "I was misled.

"Now who will put an end to the sufferings of my people?"

Arab-Moorish Civilization and Culture

THE story of the great Arab-Moorish civilization begins with the birth of Mohammed. This celebrated personage was born about the year 571 C. E. (Christian Era). It is claimed by his followers that his birth was heralded by a spectacular display of miracles. Mohammed himself, however, seems to have never suspected that there was anything unusual about either his birth or his career until he was about thirty years of age, when he began to hear strange voices. While in a cave on Mount Hara, his mind sank in religious meditation, the angel Gabriel appeared before him, proclaiming him as Mohammed, the prophet of God. Gabriel brought Mohammed the Koran, or Mohammedan Bible, page by page, as they met clandestinely in the desert. In Mecca, Mohammed was so unpopular that he was forced to flee to Medina. Here he was received with open arms, in the year 622 C. E., known as the Hejira (Flight), which is the beginning of the Mohammedan Era.

The doctrine of the Arabian prophet spread like wild-fire. Its success was based on environment and the sagacity of Mohammed. A period of drought had desolated the Arabian peninsula shortly before the advent of Mohammed and the tribes were restless. They were ready to listen to a new prophet. The cardinal doctrine of Mohammedanism is very simple:— "There is no god but God. (Allah), and Mohammed is the Prophet of God." This very simplicity appealed to many. Then large numbers of Christians and Jews were converted, because Mohammed also recognized Jesus and Moses as prophets of God. Islam, as the Mohammedan religion is called, appealed to all classes of people. The Doctrine of Equality and Brotherhood appealed to the oppressed. The Doctrine of Conquest appealed to the desert tribes. City-dwellers were pleased by Mohammed's

102 AN INTRODUCTION TO AFRICAN CIVILIZATIONS

encouragement of commerce, and the superstitious were flattered by Ceremony and Ritualism.

After becoming the prophet of Allah, Mohammed decided that it was more expedient to spread his doctrine by means of revolution rather than by the slower method of evolution. He challenged all opponents to mortal combat, saying boldly: "I, the last of the prophets am sent with the sword. Let those who promulgate my faith enter into no argument or discussion, but slay all who refuse obedience to the law. Whoever fights for the true faith, whether he fall or conquer, will assuredly receive a glorious reward."

"The sword is the key of heaven and hell; all who draw it in the cause of faith will be rewarded with temporal advantages; every drop shed of their blood, every hardship and peril endured by them, will be registered on high as more meritorious than even fasting and prayer."

One achievement of Mohammed stands out above all his other works; i.e. his teaching not only by word but by example, of the Brotherhood of Man. One of Mohammed's earliest and most zealous followers, was Bilal, a full blooded Ethiopian. The prophet so cherished the friendship and loyalty of this Ethiopian that he granted him an honored station in paradise. Mohammed became the benefactor of the slave when he ruled that any slave accepting Islam should be immediately emancipated. And though we say today that Mohammedan countries are backward, we must admit that they are happily free from that reprehensible race prejudice which so disgraces Christendom. No Mohammedan in Europe, Asia or America dares look down on his brother in Africa, for when he dies every true Moslem expects to have his soul weighed in the balance of works and judged by two black angels. Unless the soul of the true believer is absolved by these angels, he cannot pass over the infernal pit on a bridge as narrow as a hair and as sharp as a sword; which he must do in order to reach the celestial regions.

The head of the Mohammedan religion bears the title of Khalif, a word meaning "Successor" or "Representative" of Mohammed. On the death of the Prophet of Islam, his father-in-law, Abu Beker, was elected Khalif. This however, caused a split among the faithful. There were many who thought that the office should have gone to Mohammed's son-in-law Ali. The partisans of Abu Beker justified their stand by claiming that the office should be filled by election, whereas the advocates of Ali claimed that the succession was, by rights, hereditary. The first group is known as the Sunnites, and is dominant in Turkey, Turkestan, Africa and Arabia. The second sect is known as the Shiites, now dominant in Persia and India.

Despite their differences, the successors of Mohammed vigorously pushed their campaign of conquest. Six years after the death of the Prophet Asia Minor and the Tigris-Euphrates Valley had been captured. Soon afterwards Persia and India were conquered. A century later the Moslem dominions stretched from Spain through North Africa across Asia to China. The Arabs have been accused of destroying the Alexandrian Library in their conquest of Egypt, but reputable historians regard the charge as untrue. One of our leading authorities on medieval history, Professor James Westfall Thompson, remarks that: "The hoary tale that the Arabs destroyed the great library at Alexandria is false. There was no library to destroy. One great library at Alexandria was burned in 48 B. C. The second great library was destroyed in 389 A.D. by fanatical Christian monks, and never rebuilt." There was much inexcusable plundering in the early days of the conquest, but fortunately the conquerors were finally subdued and refined by the conquered. At the capture of the Persian city of Madayn, the Moslems destroyed a magnificent palace, the ceiling of which represented the sky, with stars and planets in motion. But let it be remembered that they created a greater culture than the ones they destroyed.

The first great line of Khalifs in the East were known as the Ommayads, being members of the aristocratic and powerful Ommayad family. They were followed by a line of rulers known as the Abbasids, descendants of Abbas, Mohammed's uncle. In Egypt, the Fatimite Khalifate was established. The Fatimites traced their descent from Mohammed's daughter Fatima. After being ousted in the Near East, the Ommayads gained control of

Spain and North Africa. This internecine strife greatly weakened the Islamic states.

The Bagdad Khalifate, founded in 750 A.D. reached its zenith during the reign of the Khalif Ha-run-al-Rashid (786-809), remembered by all who have read those delightful stories, "The Arabian Nights." At its height, the Bagdad Khalifate stretched from the Oxus River to Tripoli and from the Arabian Desert to the Caucasus Mountains. A fine description of this great empire is given by Sir Richard Burton in his celebrated translation of the "Arabian Nights," from which the following extract is taken:

"A well regulated routine of tribute and taxation personally inspected by the Khalif, a network of waterways, irrigation canals, a noble system of highways provided with viaducts, bridges and caravanserai, and a postal system of mounted couriers enabled it to collect, as in a reservoir, the wealth of the outer world . . . Under iron administration, agriculture and commerce, the twin pillars of national prosperity, necessarily flourished. A scientific canalization, with irrigation works inherited from the ancients . . . rendered cultivation a certainty of profit, not a mere speculation, as it must ever be to those who, perforce, rely upon the fickle rains of heaven. The remains of extensive mines prove that the source of public wealth was not neglected; navigation laws encouraged transit and traffic, and ordinances for the fisheries aimed at developing a branch of industry new to the Arabs. Most substantial encouragement was given to trade and commerce; to manufactures and handicrafts, by the flood of gold which poured in from all parts of the earth; by the presence of a splendid and luxurious court, and by the call for new arts and industries, which such a civilization would necessitate."

The Saracenic commerce with Europe was much more extensive than is generally thought. There was a brisk trade between the Moslems and the Russians at Astrakhan, Kiev, Sari and the Black Sea ports. The Russians sold them slaves, furs, hemp, cordage, lumber, and bought in return, fruits, spices, perfumes and other luxuries. A Mohammedan traveller visited

Germany during the reign of Otto the Great (936-973), and found spices and silks from the Orient on sale in the city of Mainz, and saw money from Samarkand. The great volume and extent of this trade is graphically illustrated by the numerous Arabic coins which have been found widely scattered in Eastern, Northern and Central Europe. "Great quantities of coins that bear the stamp of Arabic sovereigns," states Professor Thompson, "have been found on the higher and middle courses of the Volga, the territories on the upper courses of the Dnieper, the upper shores of the Baltic Sea and the Gulf of Finland. On the islands between Finland and Sweden, on the south shores of Norway, on the islands of Denmark, in Jutland and Schleswig, many coins of Arabic rulers from the 7th to the 11th centuries have been found . . . The wide extent of Arab commerce is interestingly attested by these numismatic specimens, in all more than 13,000. Some Arabic coins have been found even in Mecklenburg, Pomerania and western Prussia."

THE BRILLIANCE OF MOORISH SPAIN

The Moors, natives of Morocco, in North Africa, were converted to Islam during the Mohammedan Conquest in the 7th century. In the year 711 C.E., under the leadership of the Emir Musa and Tarik-bin-Ziad, veteran Arab generals, the Moors swarmed across the Strait of Gibraltar into Spain. After completely over-running the Iberian Peninsula, the invaders pushed on through to France. Here they were repulsed with heavy losses by the Franks, under the leadership of Charles Martel. After this defeat they retired into Spain, and there laid the foundation of a new civilization. The country was incalculably enriched by their labors. In the field of agriculture they were highly skilled, and introduced sugar-cane, dates, rice, cotton, ginger, strawberries, lemons into Spain. Their enlightened policy, in respect to agriculture, is expressed in the following Moorish Proverb:—"He who plants or sows, and who causes the earth to produce food for man or beast, does a service the account of which will be kept for him in the sky."

Ibn-al-Awam and Abu Zacaria, of Seville, wrote learned

works on agriculture and husbandry. A translation of a treatise on agriculture, by Ibn-al-Awam (12th century), was published in Spain as late as 1802, for the instruction of Spanish farmers. Ibn Khaldun, another Moorish expert on agriculture, wrote a valuable treatise on farming, and worked out a theory of prices and the nature of capital.

Besides being scientific agriculturists, the Moors were engineers of great ability. The Khalif Abd-er-Rahman III had an aqueduct constructed, which conveyed water from the mountains to Cordova through lead pipes. Modern Spain retains only a fragment of the fine irrigation system built by Moorish engineers, who also erected large underground silos for the storage of grain, in case of emergency. Nor did they neglect to mine gold, silver, copper, quicksilver, tin, lead, iron, alum. Up to the 12th century the maritime commerce of the Saracens on the Mediterranean was greater than that of the Christians. Hundreds of ships were engaged in it. This widespread commerce naturally stimulated manufacturing. The sword blades of Toledo were the most excellent and beautiful in Europe; and a shield factory near Cordova had an output of 12,000 shields per year. Murcia became famous for the manufacture of all kinds of brass and iron instruments; the tanneries of Cordova and Morocco were the best in the world; Almeria produced sashes famed the world over for their bright colors and fine texture; carpets were made in Teulala and bright hued woolens in Baza and Granada. The Moors also produced glass and pottery vases, mosaics and jewelry. They introduced the silk industry into Spain. On this matter of conquering Spain, J. A. Rogers, research student in European archives, states, from his correspondence with Mme. Halideh Edib, noted Turkish writer that—

"The two greatest Negro figures in the history of Islam are Bilal of Ethiopia . . . and Tarik-bin-Ziad, who was the CONQUERER of SPAIN as commander of the Moorish army which invaded Spain . . . Gibraltar is named after him. The great Turkish classic, 'Tarik-bin-Ziad', is also named after him." That was 711 A.D., while Negro slavery in Spain began in 1442.

(2) in 1086 the Almoravide Africans from Upper Sengal came to the aid of their brothers in Spain against the Chris-

tians. Their leader was Yusuf, who with only 25,000 men de-feated a white army of 70,000, and also the Cid, the great white champion of Christendom. Now even the Encyclopedia Brittanica admits that the Negro had a hand in this. It says, "The Almoravides, who were Berbers, and were largely mingled with pure Negroes." (Vol. 21, p. 128, 14th edition.)
  (3) In 1280 the Sultan," Abu Hassan Ali, known in Moroccan history as "The Black Sultan," because he was an unmixed Negro, ruled Southern Spain. The fleets of this great African monarch dominated the Mediterranean, including the shores now ruled by the mighty Mussolini. Ali's fleet defeated that of the white Christians under Godfrey Tenorio. (Consult any history of Morocco and the works of V. C. Scott O'Connor.)

The Moors built magnificent cities. Cordova in the 10th century was much like a modern city. The streets were paved and there were raised sidewalks for pedestrians. At night "one could travel for 10 miles by the light of lamps along an uninterrupted extent of buildings." This was several hundred years before there was a paved street in Paris or a street-lamp in London. The population of the city was over one-million. There were 200,000 homes, 800 public schools, many colleges and universities, 10,000 palaces of the wealthy besides many royal palaces, surrounded by beautiful gardens. The palace of the Khalif was like a dreamland castle brought to earth. Surrounded by magnificent gardens, the palace had 15,000 doors, a central hall supported by columns of marble and rock crystal, decorated with precious stones and covered with a roof of gold and silver. The palace was ventilated with perfumed air and had 300 ornate baths, with hot and cold running water. Fountains, some even of quicksilver, spouted skyward in the gardens, among bright colored flowers, luxuriant shrubs and chirping song-birds. This one palace employed a retinue of nearly 25,000 servants. The great size of the palace gardens can well be imagined if we note that the gold-fish in the fountains, streams and pools of the palace grounds consumed 12,000 loaves of bread per day. (This sounds incredible, but S. P. Scott, whose monumental three volume work "History of the Moorish Empire in Europe," is the most authoritative history of Moorish Spain in the English language, does not regard it as untrue. The loaves of bread were perhaps very small in size.) The Great Mosque of Cordova, another grand structure, happily still extant, had a scarlet and gold roof, with 1,000 columns of porphyry and marble; was lighted by over 200 silver chandeliers, containing over 1,000 silver lamps burning perfumed oil. This mosque was built at the huge cost of $300,000,000. There were 5,000 mills in Cordova at a time when there was not even one in all the rest of Europe, and there were 90 public baths, besides many more private ones, when the rest of Europe considered bathing as extremely wicked, and to be avoided as much as possible. Cordova was also graced by a great system of over 4,000 public markets. Granada, Seville and Toledo were rivals of Cordova in respect to magnificence. Education was universal in Moslem Spain, being given even to the most humble, while in Christian Europe 99% of the people were illiterate, and even kings were unable to read or write. The Moorish rulers lived in sumptuous palaces while the monarchs of Germany, France and England dwelt in big barns, with no windows and no chimneys and with only a hole in the roof for the exit of smoke. And lest we forget, the Moors introduced changeable and washable underclothing into Europe.

The first light that burst in upon the long night of Europe's Dark Ages and heralded the dawn of a new day was from Moorish Spain, and from their Saracenic comrades who had settled in Sicily and Italy. In the words of Harold Peake, the English scientific writer: "Light first dawned on Europe from Spain, by means of the foundation by the Moors in the 9th century of a Medical School at Salerno in South Italy. This developed into a university about A.D. 1150 and received a new constitution from the Emperor Frederick II in 1231. Thence the new civilization spread up Italy to France and soon penetrated all parts of Europe except the north-eastern section."

All over the Arab-Moorish Empire a brisk intellectual life flourished. The Khalifs of both the East and the West were, for the most part, enlightened patrons of learning. They maintained immense libraries and offered fortunes for new manuscripts. Khalif Harun-al-Rashid founded the great University of Bagdad, at which the most celebrated professor was Joshua ben Nun, a Jew. Here, Greek classics were translated into

Arabic. Emperor Michael III, of the Byzantine Empire, was forced by treaty to send Greek books to Bagdad. Harun was a patron of the Medical College of Djondesabour; and graduates in medicine had to pass an examination given by the faculty of that school or by that of the University of Bagdad before practicing. In other fields of science the Arabs and Moors were equally brilliant. Djafar or Geber, in the 8th century, was an outstanding chemist. He has been called the founder of scientific chemistry. It was he who discovered nitric acid and aqua regia. Then we have Rhazes (9th century), who discovered methods for producing sulphuric acid and absolute alcohol. Achild Bechl, another noted chemist, obtained phosphorous by distillation. The names of some other savants and their fields of study will show us the extent of Arab-Moorish erudition. There were: Assamh, a topographer and statistician; Avicenna, physician and philosopher; Averroes, philosopher and scientist; Abu Othman, Zoologist; Alberuni, mineralogist; Rhazes, Al Abbas and Al Beithan, botanists; Avenzoar, pharmacist; Albucasis or Abulcasis of Cordova, surgeon; Al-Razi of Bagdad, physician and surgeon; and Omar Khayyam, mathematician, astronomer and poet. Also, let us bear in mind, the Arabs and Moors adopted the system of numerals which we now use from the Hindus, and introduced them into Europe. Al Kharizmi (9th century), improved this number system by introducing zero (0), as a mathematical quantity. The Moslem mathematicians added algebra and plane and spherical trigonometry to the Euclidean geometry. The mathematician, Mohammed Ben Musa, substituted sines for chords in trigonometry, and in algebra, devised a method for solving quadratic equations. There were many experts in the physical sciences. Al Maimon (9th century), determined the obliquity of the Ecliptic and calculated the size of the earth by measuring a degree on the shore of the Red Sea. In the 10th and 11th centuries there flourished the two great physicists, Al Hazen, a famous optician and Ali Ibn-Isa, a noted oculist. Most of our school histories teach us that it was the prevailing belief, before Magellan circumnavigated the globe in 1519, that the world was flat. This popular view is not buttressed by evidence, for the Moors taught geography from globes in their schools long before Magellan was born. They also built the first astronomical observatories in Europe. The unusual industry and ability of the medieval Moslem scholars may be well illustrated by considering the achievements of Avicenna of Bokhara (980-1037), who was a philosopher, physician and geologist. Avicenna was the author of many treatises on various scientific and philosophical subjects. Among his works were the following: (1) Utility and Advantage of Science, (2) Health and Remedies, (3) Canons of Physic, (4) Astronomical Observations, (5) Mathematical Theorems, (6) the Arabic Language, (7) Origin of the Soul and the Resurrection of the Body, (8) an Abridgment of Euclid, (9) Physics and Metaphysics, and (10) an Encyclopedia of Human Knowledge, in 20 volumes. Avicenna's knowledge of geology is aptly illustrated by the following passage from his works:

"Mountains may be due to two different causes. Either they are effects of upheavals of the crust of the earth, such as might occur during a mighty earthquake, or they are the effect of water, which cutting for itself a new route, has denuded the valleys, the strata being of different kinds, some soft, some hard. The winds and waters disintegrate the one but leave the other intact. Most of the eminences of the earth have had this latter origin. It would require a long period of time for all such changes to be accomplished, during which the mountains themselves might be somewhat diminished in size. But that water has been the main cause of these effects is proved by the existence of fossil remains of aquatic and other animals on many mountains."

The outstanding characteristic of the Arab-Moorish rulers was tolerance. Their relations with the most distant nations were most cordial. The Moslem traveller journeyed with utmost freedom in such widely separated lands as China and the Sudan. About the year 1000, of our era, Mohammedan merchants reached the Sudan and established commercial relations with the flourishing kingdoms of that region. "When Mohammedan merchants came to the Sudan, about 1000 A.D." writes Lady Lugard, the distinguished British explorer, "they already found a well arranged system of commerce . . . When the Arabs first visited Negroland by the western route in the 8th and 9th centuries of our era they found the black kings of Ghana in the height of their prosperity." Besides Ghana, the other great Sudanese states of the medieval period were Songhay, Melle and Ethiopia. The Songhay Empire rose to its greatest height in the 16th century, and at that time it was greater than any contemporary European state. This empire stretched from the Atlantic almost to the Indian Ocean, and covered a vast territory almost equal in size to the entire continent of Europe. Felix Dubois, the great French authority on Africa, describes this African culture in his "Timbuctoo the Mysterious," saying:

"This accomplishment brings the greatest honor to the black race, and merits from this point of view all our attention. In the 16th century, the Songhay land awoke. A marvelous growth of civilization mounted there in the heart of the Black Continent.

"And this civilization was not imposed by circumstances, nor by an invader as is often the case even in our own day. It was desired, called forth, introduced and propagated by a man of the black race." This celebrated African was Mohammed Askia, Emperor of Songhay. American writers have as a rule been blissfully ignorant of Africa, considering it as a land of savagery unworthy of study. There are however some exceptions, Mr. V. F. Calverton, Editor of *The Modern Monthly,* being one. "In the Songhay Empire, for example," writes Mr. Calverton, in *Current History,* for September 1929, "education was advanced to such a point that people came from all over the Islamic world to teach in its schools, and the savants of the Songhay were active as well in the Mohammedan countries to the north and east. In fact, throughout the Sudan, university life was fairly extensive. Ahmed Baba, one of the strongly arresting figures of his period, stands out as a brilliant example of the sweep of Sudanese erudition. An author of more than forty books upon such diverse themes as theology, astronomy, ethnography and biography, Baba was a scholar of great depth and inspiration. With his expatriation from Timbuctoo— he was in the city at the time that it was invaded by the Moroccans in 1592, and protested against their occupation of it — he lost in his collection of 1,600 books, one of the richest libraries of his day; and Ahmed Baba, although the most conspicuous, was only one scholar among the many.

"All through West Africa the natives had established many centers of learning. In their schools and universities courses were given in rhetoric, logic, eloquence, diction, the principles of arithmetic, hygiene, medicine, prosody, philosophy, ethnography, music and astronomy. The Negro scholars in many instances surpassed the Arabian. In Ethiopia their contributions to culture streamed far beyond the borders of their own nation in influence and power, as every new exploration and excavation of African materials reveals. We see rising before us, in obscure manuscripts, relics of apparel and architectural remains, the lives of peoples and the movements of civilizations, once buried in the sands of a dead world."

Our knowledge of the past, as the preceding section on medieval Africa shows, has been greatly enriched by the industry of Moslem travellers, historians and scholars, since this knowledge, had it not been preserved in manuscripts written in Arabic, would most certainly have been lost to the world. How many of us who have seen the beautiful natural color photographs of the magnificent ruined temples of Cambodia, know that the Arab historian, El Masudi, described this region in the 10th century, when it was the center of a flourishing culture. The people of this lost empire were known as the Khmers, and were Dravidian in origin. The Dravidians were the aboriginal inhabitants of India; they are referred to by Herodotus as "Ethiopians of the sun-rising" on account of their Eastern habitat and the blackness of their skins. El Masudi, in a work on history and geography, entitled "Meadows of Gold and Mines of Gems" states that: "India is a vast country, having many seas and mountains, and borders upon the empire of ez-Zanij, which is the kingdom of the Maharajah, the king of the islands, whose

QUEEN TEGA MANEN
of Ethiopia

MENELEK II
Greatest Modern Ethiopian

ALEXANDRE PUSHKIN
Russo-Ethiopian

dominions form the frontier between India and China, and are considered as part of India." He also informs us that these people were of black complexion, that their culture was one of "splendor and high civilization;" that "the Maharajah is lord of the sixth sea" (Indian Ocean), "king of the islands from which drugs and spices are exported," that "the population and the number of troops of his kingdom cannot be counted; and the islands under his sceptre are so numerous that the fastest sailing vessel is not able to go round them in two years."

Angkor, the capital of the vanished Khmer Empire, contains some of the most beautiful as well as the best preserved ruins of any of the deserted cities of the past. The interested reader may verify this by obtaining *The National Geographic Magazine*, September 1928, which contains Gervais Courtellemont's wonderful natural color photographs of the ruins of Angkor, the mysterious city of the Cambodian jungles.

Edrisi (12th century), was another great Saracen scholar. He travelled widely, studied for many years, then settled at the court of Roger II at Palermo, Sicily, and composed a valuable geography of the Arab-Moorish world. Then, there was Ibn Batuta (14th century), a native of Morocco, and the world's greatest globe-trotter. He travelled continuously for thirty years, visiting Russia, Egypt, Palestine, Syria, Asia Minor, Constantinople, China, India, the Malay Peninsula, Sumatra, Borneo, Java, the Sudan and Arabia. He journeyed far enough north in Russia to see the "Midnight Sun"; made four pilgrimages to Mecca; crossed Africa from the Atlantic Ocean to the Red Sea twice; travelled through the perilous passes of the Hindu Kush Mountains. Finally he wrote the most fascinating of all books of travel.

After several centuries of brilliance the lucky star of the Saracens began to wane. The Arabs never recovered from the conquests of the Seljuk Turks in the 11th century and the Mongols in the 13th century. The Mongols under Hulagu Khan captured and destroyed Bagdad in 1258. The great irrigation system of Mesopotamia dating from ancient times, was also destroyed. The Khalifate of Cordova had begun to break up in 1031, since the internal troubles of the Moslems made it impossible for them to preserve an adequate defense against their Christian enemies. By 1492 the Moors had lost all of Spain except the Kingdom of Granada. The Christians, although they had their internal disputes also, were finally united by the marriage of Ferdinand and Isabella, which joined in peace the formerly hostile royal houses of Aragon and Castile. The united Christian forces surrounded the city of Granada and blockaded it for eight months. The Moorish ruler, Abu Abdallah, finally surrendered.

The Moors lingered in Spain for a little more than a century. By 1610 through expulsion and migration, a million — among them many Jews—had returned to North and West Africa.

In the Seventeenth Century the inept Don Sebastian king of Portugal, led his army and the flower of his nobility into Morocco—and to speedy death. Those of his troops which escaped the sword were enslaved except the converts to Islam. These were adopted into the nation.

Probably recalling the Almoravides Movement in the Eleventh Century, the inhabitants of Morocco and the desert spread, after their defeat of Sebastian, to Guinea, re-mingling their blood with the peoples of the West Coast.

Black Mohammedans in the latter area and in the Sudan today represent the projection into the present of the Islamic influence initiated by the Almoravides. Among the Moors of today are to be found all shades of color, from white to black. Today the Moors are back in Spain, as mercenary soldiers, in the Spanish civil war. Great alarm is felt over their presence there by the christian forces in Spain who deplore the fact that "black infidel forces have been brought into Spain by those who, in their madness, have taken the religion of Christ as a war banner and have flouted Western Civilization by bringing back the Moors as their allies to kill other Spaniards." Such pronouncements are interesting in view of the fact that Spain has, practically, been in cultural doldrums since the expulsion of the Moors and the Jews.

South Africa

I NSCRIPTIONS on the Egyptian monuments show that Egypt
had connections with South Africa in the days of Queen Hatshepsut, and her Ethiopian half-brother, Thothmes III, 1700
B.C. Motifs in the primitive art of South Africa were carried
into the art of Egypt. What is still more interesting is the fact
that there are resemblances between the language of Egypt and
that of the Hottentots and Bushmen. These peoples were flourishing when Solomon and Hiram of Tyre joined in an adventure in 900 B.C. to find the gold of Ophir. Legends of the
great flood seem to be unknown in South Africa; except among
the Basutos, who probably got it from modern missionaries.

But South Africa has enough unfavorable environment
without an additional set back by what was called the "ancient
flood." Her vast deserts and her rivers, broken by yawning
cataracts and chasms, and her mighty inland seas, have always
barred her from having regular contact with the peoples of
the north. Even in this, South Africa has followed the strange
geographical pattern of having a "North" more advanced than
the South. For example, Northern Europe as compared with
Southern Europe; Northern Germany and Southern Germany;
Northern Italy and Southern Italy; Northern Ireland and
Southern Ireland. When it is considered that the whole of
North America is more progressive than the whole of South
America, it may still be interesting to note that New England
is more advanced than the cotton States; and even Northern
Alabama boasts a superiority over her Gulf Coast. Probably,
the only exception to what seems to be the rule, is China, in
which Southern China takes the lead over Northern China.

The author, one day, asked a pupil in an ancient history
class, why, in his opinion, the Chinese varied from the apparent
geographical norm. In a flash, and in true American style, the

youngster replied, "The Chinese are naturally cock-eyed, anyhow, and they see things upside down." The author learned a lesson from that boy. It may be that investigators and "standard" historians have been seeing the civilization of the black races upside down.

With all of South Africa's deterrents, she still holds a high place in human culture. Out of her deserts may have come an early man even more important than the Rhodesian or Broken Hill man. No scientist has yet successfully denied the possibility that the earliest migrations of human beings came from South Africa and spread westward, northward and eastward. Nor is it settled yet that there was not at one time a continent which joined Africa with India.

Whether the theory of "floating continents" be accepted or not, it is still an interesting observation to note that the concave west coast of Africa and the convex east coast of South America would snugly fit, where they pulled together. It is significant, too, that in South America black gods with African features are venerated and worshipped.

To turn to cultural evidences in South Africa, there are the indisputable ruins of the Zymbabwe rivaling, to some extent, the ruins in Egypt and the Nile Valley. The unsettled question is, by whom were they built? On the Mapungubwe Hill in Mashonaland, there are many, many skeletons. Are these skeletons the remains of the "Red Men" in many native legends, or, are they all that remains of an indigenous culture and civilization? Do they represent peoples who drifted south with the culture of Egypt? Or, are they natives who once conquered and then fell? If they are not of the Bantu races, nor Hottentots, or Bushmen, then who are they? It is an interesting problem from every point of view. After all, what is the Zymbabwe? First it is a Bantu word which means "stone building" or residence of a great chief. They are fragments of walls built with chipped granite blocks, 6 x 12 inches in size and larger. These blocks have been put together without mortar or any form of cement; they are laid in herring bone fashion so neatly set together, and the walls so thick that they make a compact, cohesive mass. Such walls are scattered all over Southern Mashonaland and Matabeleland. Often the walls rise in seven terraces and vary from six to forty feet high, and from five to six feet wide. In a way they are comparable to the walls of China. Recently on the Mpungubwe Hill skeletons have been examined that had been buried with gold ornaments, apparently of extreme age. In the Sixteenth Century, the Portuguese mentioned Monomatapa, the supreme African king, who long ago presided at Zymbabwe and used gold ornaments similar to the ones recently found. There were also green and blue beads similar to those found in West Africa and in Egypt. It is hoped that re-examination will keep the scientists from reaching conclusions that are upside down. Evidence shows that these early peoples were not Islamic, and that their work could not have been the work of Portuguese, for the latter did not go that far inland. The Semitic cast in the faces of certain Kaffirs are too weak to conclude that the Zymbabwe builders were either Jews or Arabians.

Concerning leadership among South African peoples in modern times, the traces become warmer and far more stirring than the cold stones of the Zymbabwe. Dingiswayo, a mighty Zulu, at the turn of the Nineteenth Century, took notes from the British soldiery stationed in Zululand. He passed these new military tactics on to Chaka, his chief commanding officer. Chaka was an apt pupil. He whipped together an army and organized them in phalanx on the old Spartan model, and soon he became lord and master of valley and plain in South Africa. The Zulu's rise was a phenomenon such as the world had not seen before. Through three lines, the Zulu Federation developed: Chaka to Dingaan, his brother, in 1828, then to Panda, a younger brother, and finally to Cetywayo, son of Panda, by 1879, when Zulu ascendancy was blocked by the British.

Between 1879 and 1893, Lobengula harried the British until his defeat in the latter year. Though Dingaan burned a trail which the Boers fear and even honor today, yet of all the South African leaders, Chaka was the greatest. Just as

Napoleon Bonaparte changed the map of Europe, so did Chaka change the map of South Africa with, of course, allowances for area, and the magnitude of the people and their administrative problems. Chaka was violence personified, yet he spared the Swazis, a kindred Zulu tribe. They were later spared again by the British because of the heroic effort they made against them. The British linked all the Swazis with the Basutos, than whom, there is no finer race in the world. They were made so by their great leader, Moshesh I. Indeed, South Africa can boast of three leaders comparable to great men found anywhere. Chaka, the warrior extraordinary, whose ambition, perfected military drill, army discipline and swiftness of military movement, made him the terror of Europeans. Second, Khama, king of the Bechuanas, a great social reformer, administrator, peacemaker and protector of his people from the effects of the baneful side of white civilization, and lastly, Moshesh, the great Basuto diplomat and enlightened ruler, comparable to the enlightened rulers in Eighteenth Century Europe.

About 1880, there appeared a new and different type of South African leader. Hendrick Witbooi, in many respects as remarkable as the triumvirate just mentioned. He was race conscious and probably the first nationalist in South Africa. He ordered every black man to fight for the possession of Africa, the chiefs who refused to cooperate were driven out or killed, and their tribes annexed to the insurgents. Joining military power with religious zeal, he widened his national mission. When the Germans came to South Africa in 1884, he was found issuing proclamations calling all black men to arms. The Germans engaged him in battle and with superior arms, over-awed his troops and forced temporary treaties. This, however, failed to stop Witbooi. Though harried by the Germans, he escaped with his warriors. It was not until 1894 that he was subdued. He made a treaty of friendship and protection with the German Kaiser, but in that very year, Witbooi again resorted to arms and called his followers to save their race from German bondage. Witbooi ordered the murder of all Germans, and in the insurrection that followed, he fell, mortally wounded. But the uprising was not put down until 1907. In 1933, the world was astonished to read of Chief Tshekedi, chief of a tribe of Bechuanas and grandson of the great Khama. Tshekedi, in 1933, flogged an Englishman because of his debaucheries with native women. He was called before a British court at that time, and relieved of his power. Upon the plea of his mother, the Dowager Queen, to Queen Mary of England, Tshekedi was restored to his throne. During his trial in the open air, fifteen thousand natives looked on. But the machine guns of the British maintained order. Today, 1937, Tshekedi is in trouble again. A recent court decision has shorn him of much of his restored power. In order to off-set him, the British have raised a subject chief of Tshekedi's to coordinate rank with him, thus, with a rival, the British hope to off-set his insurgency in the future. At present, he is the outstanding ruler in South Africa. Bechuanaland, his province, is quite the size of France and Italy combined. It is surrounded, except, on the west by white communities anxious for invasion. Basutoland, known popularly as the "Switzerland of South Africa" is about the size of Belgium, and is wholly surrounded by whites. Its fertile valleys and mountain ranges have given the enterprising Basutos superior advantages to the other South African peoples. Their cattle, their ponies and mules, and above all, their great output of wool and mohair, placed Basutoland, for more than a half century, in an excellent economic position. The budget surplus permitted the highest expenditure for education and social development. They have even made loans to other native governments. Their country is covered with telephones and telegraphs owned by the government. During the world war, the Basutos sent $250,-000 to the various war funds in England, and $200,000 more, with which to buy twenty airplanes.

Thanks to the foresight of Moshesh, who in 1879 trained them to pay-as-they-go, the Basuto Government was never in debt to anyone until 1921, when its exports began to fall off. Before the war, its wool and mohair exports combined, were nine million pounds, worth, in the Basuto market, $2,000,000.

By 1923 it had dropped to five hundred thousand pounds, and by 1936, to less than one hundred thousand pounds. This was due largely to the "freeze out" policy of the British and the fact that the Germans, who took the entire Basuto wool export, were no longer able to buy in that market. Basutos are forced today to call on special hidden reserves in addition to being compelled to go outside of their country and sell their labor in the open market.

The people of Swaziland, a country about the size of Wales, are in just about as bad an economic condition. Agricultural possibilities there are great, hence, the Swazis have been treated more disgraceful by the white races than any other South African people. By every species of fraud and misrepresentation, concession hunters of all nations, have worked in conjunction, in every illegal way, to obtain contracts. Today, all the land of the Swazis is in the possession outsiders, whose contracts call for the expropriation of all values above and below the land. One concessionaire, who arrived too late to get such a contract, finally sought to get a blanket contract for a concession for anything of value not contained in any other concession. The land area of the Union of South Africa, originally belonging to the natives, totals 300,000,000 acres. Today, 2,000,000 white men hold 86 per cent of the land in South Africa and 6,000,000 natives hold the remainder.

Dr. Max Yergan, formerly a Y.M.C.A. leader in South Africa, recently withdrew from that organization. For a quarter of a century he worked among the peoples there, all the way up to Kenya and Uganda. Today, he has joined a new organization, known as the International Committee on African Affairs. The plan of this new body is to take carefully chosen Africans and train them for intelligent leadership, in cooperation with those movements in Africa and Europe, that are for the best interest of the people. This new work of Dr. Yergan is more than timely because the anti-African forces have sounded, what they consider, the death knell to native advancement.

Recently the Native Representation Bill was passed by

the two houses of Parliament, 169 to 11. This bill, temporarily, ends the experiment of giving the black man the vote on terms of equality or at least in proportion to his taxation. This right, apparently lost, has been treasured by the natives for 90 years. In an earlier day, the right of the native to vote was spared even by Cecil Rhodes, the arch despoiler of the South African people. Jan Hofmeyer advised, 25 years ago, that a European population of less than 2,000,000 in the southern end of the continent, populated by 200,000,000, could best serve itself and its security, by retaining the good will of the 5,000,000 blacks, among whom they immediately lived. History has yet to record whether the black man in South Africa will be the rear guard of a white civilization or the advance guard for a new civilization of the blacks.

West Africa

D RAW a line through Africa along the southern edge of the
Sahara. To the land north of that line, add Ethiopia and
the Sudan and Africa will have been practically divided into two
equal parts. Glance down the West Coast as far as Angola
and areas will be noted, which are climatically unsuited for the
permanent settlement of white men. The West Coast then is
a part of Africa which belongs and probably always will belong
to black men, in spite of the European power to which they may
owe allegiance. Any interests which whites may have there,
will probably never go beyond trade connections which the
whites may build up in competition with each other. Thus at
least, for modern times, nature has fought for the blacks in
West Africa as she fought for them in Haiti, as an "ally" of
Touissant Louverture, against the French. But black men must
not idly trust their fortunes to nature. Ethiopia, largely did that
and lost. Sandstorms did defeat the first thrust of Assyria against
Taharqua in 667 B. C. and again buried the armies of Cambyses
in the ancient campaign, 525 B.C., of frightful memory, but
the "rainy season" added naught to black fortune recently in
East Africa.

The road to empire in West Africa has been a circuitous
one. Only the great work of Maurice Delafosse has made a
closely knit pattern of its threads. Similarly history is indebted
to Ibn Batuta who was in West Africa in 1352. It appears that
as early as 1600 B. C., certain Hebrews—the Beni-Israel—
scattered westward on the Mediterannean shore of Africa, and
southward into Nubia and Ethiopia, thence west again, in the
Eleventh Century A.D. through Central Africa to the Atlantic.
To the indigenous cultures, already established in these areas,
they added a Semitic element, represented today by the Falashas
or "Black Jews" of Ethiopia and various types of Hebrew isms in

West Africa. For example, the Moors, the Fulani, the Ashanti and the Fanti.

Some light was cast on West Africa in 750 B.C., by Hanno, the Carthaginian, but only a flash. Later, in 450 B.C. a Persian rebel, who had offended Xerxes, was penalized by that great warrior by "dooming" him to circumnavigate Africa. The exile failed in his attempt but brought back to the great king data, though incomplete, which hinted that a dark race lived beyond the desert sands.

Definite states became discernible in West Africa in the Fourth Century A.D. with the appearance of Ghana, an Afro-Semitic community. These reached their maximum in the middle of the Sixteenth Century but, by the close of the Nineteenth Century they had languished.

If the Semitic kings of Ghana be granted before the Seventh Century A. D., it is still tenable that, after that era, black kings were in control. Thus, from the middle of the Seventh Century to the end of the Eleventh, Ghana, though beset by Islamic waves, nevertheless set a standard for empire building by black men in West Africa.

The empire of the Songhay, 690-1335, outshone the lustre of Ghana. The victory of Gongo Mussa, Mandingo chieftain in 1325, signalled the power of Songhay. Ten years later Berber control was halted. A century later the Touaregs ousted the Mandingoes from Timbuctoo only to lose it in 1468 to Sonni Ali who set up Songhay against Melle. In surge of triumph Sonni Ali was opposed, in 1374, by Mansa Mussa. To such heights did the Mandingoes reach that, in 1481, John II of Portugal, made a treaty with their Emperor, practically at the same time in which he was making contacts with the emperors of Ethiopia.

Sonni Ali was a wise administrator. He warred against the Moslems though a Moslem himself. His intrepid, reckless campaigning brought him in conflict with the Mossi, in a war with whom he was drowned in 1492 fording a stream.

The next year the Sonni dynasty was overthrown by

Mohammed Askia, full blooded black, who ruled until 1529. He instituted a rather liberal regime. He systematized the farms, and re-organized commerce, the trades, the arts and crafts, and initiated a new religious development. He was a patron of scholarship and literature as evidenced in the great intellectual centers at Jenne and Timbuctoo. These arts of peace were coming to their height, in the Sixteenth and Seventeenth Centuries, according to the record as shown in the Tarikh-el-fettach and the Tarikh-es-Sudan, Arabic documents of the type in which much of the history of West and Central Africa may be found.

There arose also in the Seventh Century the Mandingo or Mellestine Empire, one of the greatest of the middle ages. Except for a period of 15 years following 1285, it had 1300 years of unbroken power.

For four centuries the Mandingoes went their way but by the middle of the Eleventh Century Mohammedanism captured West Africa. The Mansa embraced Islam and went to Mecca. New international and intellectual relations were then opened to West Africa. These ties were continued, for, in 1213, Mansa Mussa made three trips there.

The Mansa had a brief set-back in 1224, when his forces were defeated by the king of Soso and annexed. Sundeasa, the grandson of the Mansa, rallied an army and defeated Soso. Five years later he annexed Ghana and then settled down to the development of the arts of peace.

About 1285 there arose a certain Sakura, a serf, whose prowess enabled him to keep up the Keita (Mandingo) tradition. He enlarged Melle and created newer international relations. On his return from Mecca, by way of Ethiopia, in 1300, he was assassinated by Danakils, Ethiopian tribesmen, who grudged him his gold. His body was dried and brought to his home for a royal Keita burial. The Keitas were restored with the great Gongo Mussa in control, 1307-1332. In 1324 he went to Mecca in magnificent style. His retinue numbered more than 60,000 and the expense of the trip ran well beyond $5,000,000. The Mansa met the distinguished men of Egypt, Mecca and the East and on his return, a new architectural pattern was created for West Africa, in addition to a revival of learning and the arts. Troubled by wars, especially with the Mossi, Melle waned. The rod of empire was taken up by Songhay, and carried to a height never before attained in West Africa. Reference has already been made to Sonni Ali and Mohammed Abou Bekr, "The Askia." The latter made an intellectual trip to Mecca in 1324. His trip enabled him to make detailed inquiry on education, economics, trade, commerce and the amenities of life in the East. In Egypt discussions were held on the matter of a Calif for the Sudan.

Disorder followed the death of Sonni Ali in 1492, but "The Askia" was still in the ascendant. Melle had weakened. The Askia spread his power into the Haussa states. He took Katsena in 1513 and two years later he took Agades. The king of the Haussas, though an ally of the Askia, turned on him and defeated him. Thus Haussa independence was restored, though Agades did not recover until the end of the century.

Blindness in 1529 barred further assaults by the Askia, in consequence of which his son deposed him.

Five years later Melle subsidized the Fulani and aided them in attacks on Songhay but both were defeated. Melle, then, 1534, appealed in vain to John III of Portugal for military aid against Songhay.

The anarchy which followed the dethronement of the Askia, was resisted by Daoud, who ruled from 1550 to 1585. Daoud was a liberal but before he could get his policies in action, he was beset by the Sultans of Morocco who were determined to get salt from the mines at Tegazza. When Daoud refused to be bribed with gold, the Sultan dispatched a force of 20,000 to take Tegazza. All died of thirst. In 1590 another expedition of 3,000 was sent against Songhay, composed chiefly of Spanish renegades. In a year they had been reduced to less than 1,000. Though the new Askia, Ishak II, had a strong army of infantry and cavalry, the Sultan's forces were armed with muskets, implements unknown in West Africa. Ishak II, placed cows between his forces and those of the enemy but, frightened by rifle fire, they turned on Ishak's men and created greater disaster. Songhay's power broken, she languished until 1660. In the next 120 years, 128 "pashas" ruled at Timbuctoo and revelled in every form of Spanish debauchery. After 1780, pasha rule disappeared but Timbuctoo had no peace or rest until 1894, when Major Joffre, of World War Fame, came to West Africa. Though Songhay had become feeble a new bid for power on the West Coast was shown by El-Hadj Omar.

In 1776 the Moslem Tukulors conquered the Fulani and set up a state that lasted until 1881, when it was annexed to Senegal.

In the center of this period, Omar did his best work. By 1820 he had sufficiently entrenched himself so that he might go, with authority, to Mecca, and thereby courted the title of Caliph of the Sudan. By 1848 his army was powerful enough to over-run and subjugate Mande, a struggle which lasted until 1854. Three years later, Omar had to face the combined forces af Paul Holle, a mulatto warrior fighting under the French, and also Gen. Faidherbe, the French strategist, himself. He emerged victor in 1861 and the next year he put to death the rival king in that area. Omar over-reached himself by his attacks on Timbuctoo. So weakened by these forays, he was no match for the Fulani, before whom he fell in battle, 1864. The anarchy which followed his death was not ended until Lieutenant-Colonel Archinard took over the area, 1890-1893.

In the meantime a new leader had appeared in the person of Samory—Samori Touré—a Mandingo warrior, who harried the French for 18 years, 1880-1898. He fell into the hands of the French through the strategy of Gen. Alfred Dodds, a mulatto officer, in the French service.

The Haussa peoples centered largely in the areas of Tessava, Kano, Katsena, Sokoto and Kebbi. Under a female ruler, all of them were merged into a loose federation. By 1,500 the king of the Kebbi deposed the female line and assumed the rulership. Soon Bornu fell under the control of the Kebbi. To defeat the Kebbi, the sultan of Bornu allied himself with the Askia, 1513, and captured Katsena and Agades. Quarrels developed between the sultan of Bornu and the Askia which resulted in the defeat in 1517 of the Askia and the consequent freedom of the Haussas from the power of the Kebbi.

During the closing quarter of the Sixteenth Century, 1571-1603, Bornu was at its height. During a part of that time she was in temporary alliance with Ethiopia. For two centuries Bornu and Haussaland showed no great high lights. However, Sheik Ousman, 1801-1815, came to power in Haussaland and the old wars were resumed with Bornu. Disorder in Bornu continued, intermittently, throughout the century. In 1900 the old kingdom fell into the hands of the British.

Meanwhile, Ousman in 1815, had passed his rule in Haussaland, over to his son, Mohammed Bello, who kept the state intact until 1837. From his death in 1837 disorder continued until, in 1904, the British captured Sokoto and spread their authority over the entire area.

In order to vitalize the panorama of the West Coast, teachers should stress certain definite facts in regard to Sonni Ali and his great Prime Minister, Mohammed Abu Bekr, who became, "Mohammed Askia" and the first of the Askias; Mansa Musa, Mohammed Bello, Tutu Kwamina of the Ashanti and Fanti folk; Behanzin, Samory, Yussef ben Tachfine and his work under the Almoravides; Bishop Crowther, Dr. Blyden and Dr. Aggrey. Into this skein, also, should be drawn such characters as Massanissa, Syphax and Jugurtha, kings of old Numidia, for often, as in the case of the kingdom of Ghana, the West Coast was drawn into the theatre of the civilizations of the north African littoral, and thence into Spain.

Students should see clearly that there were definite native rule in old Songhay 700 to 1528; Ghana, from the Fourth Century to mid-Thirteenth; Bornu, from the Tenth Century to 1900; the Bambara, from 1660 to 1861; Bagirmi, from the Fifteenth Century to 1912, and that Kano, Katsena and Zaria were military powers and commercial entrepots of a very high order. In general special detail work may well be done in the study of the Mellestine and Songhay Empires at their greatest extent. For this the works of Woodson, George W. Ellis, A. B.

Ellis, H. H. Johnston, Melville Herskovits, W. E. B. DuBois and Maurice Delafosse, will be especially needed. Further south in the bend of the Niger there were the Bini folk of the old kingdom of Benin. Portuguese navigators discovered this area in the Fifteenth Century. It was then a great metropolis and significant for its religious and political sway over extended territory. So disciplined was old Benin that, when the Great Oba sent generals out to battle, few returned, that is, if they were vanquished they dared not return and if they were victorious, they preferred to set themselves up as chiefs in the newly acquired territory and pay tribute to the Oba, rather than return to his service. Such military methods are similar to those used by the Convention in Revolutionary France, when a Representative on Mission, accompanied generals to the wars, in order to capture or slay them if they failed.

It is thought that the Bini are an offshoot of the Yoruba nation. Though their language differs somewhat from the Yoruba, their customs, traditions, religious practices, and beliefs definitely link them together ethnologically.

According to the accounts of early European navigators, the King of Benin, although a mighty ruler of a great kingdom, received his investiture from another powerful monarch who lived "toward the east" and who sent each new king of Benin a staff, a cross, and a cap of shining brass. Heads of bronze were also sent as gifts to these new kings. It is believed that this mysterious potentate was the Awni of Ife, the spiritual ruler of the great Yoruba nation.

Ife, the sacred city, boasts a long and glorious past. The Yorubas have a tradition that their ancestors came from Egypt and settled there, and their nation increased and spread until it now numbers more than three million people and covers a huge area in southern Nigeria.

Native tradition tells that through the centuries there always have been a war-king and a priest-king ruling equally. The first king was Oduduwa, a mythical personage, a great leader who brought his people safely through the northern desert to Nigeria. He died at Ife and later was deified and identified with the Earth Goddess. His grandson, Awranyan, who succeeded him on the throne, is regarded as the father of all the Yorubas existing today.

Catholic missionary work was attempted in Benin as early as 1485 but the indifference of the people to christianity and the additional factor of climate, made it impracticable, at that time, for the missions to flourish and soon they were abandoned. The Oba, however, kept up trade with Europe throughout the Sixteenth and Seventeenth Centuries when mission work was again resumed with a fairer measure of success, down to the present day.

The exquisite "Bronzes of Benin" compel the admiration of the world. Attempts to prove them other than native craftsmanship have all failed. Arguments which tend to label them as Portuguese have not stood the test. These arguments were generally set at naught in 1910 after a visit to that area by Leo Frobenius, the world's greatest authority on African art.

There is nothing like the bronze castings in Benin in any other part of the world. They were produced by the "cire perdue" process, with an accuracy and a fidelity to detail, unmatched anywhere. It is interesting to note that the complicated method used by the people of Benin, is identical with the same processes used in Italy during the Renaissance, of which movement, in Europe, the Benin folk knew nothing. As was the splendor of Benin art so was the splendor of the court of the kings and the discipline of the armed forces of the kingdom, especially so with the "Amazons", who feats of daring in Dahomey, dismayed Europeans who attacked them.

After nearly five centuries of unbroken native rule the splendor of this mighty sovereignty had waned by 1825. Europeans entered in that year and by 1892 the reigning Oba forbade all trade with the Continent. In 1896 British troops invaded Benin. After a year's fighting the city was captured. The Oba was exiled to Calabar and his domain passed into the shadow of the British flag.

Thus in the Nineteenth Century, black sovereignties in West Africa were finally snuffed out, save Liberia which eked out its existence by grace of its step-childhood to the United States of America. With an inauspicious beginning in 1820-1821, Liberia managed by 1837 to achieve a central government and in 1847 it became a Republic on the American model.

Its territory has been repeatedly encroached upon by the French and the British. Frightened at the growl of the "wardogs" in Europe, Liberia entered the World War on the side of the Allies and received one shock from the impact of battle when a German Gunboat shelled its coast. Since the war, Liberia has been able to secure financial help from America and also has permitted the Firestone Rubber Company to secure a large concession of land for the production of that product.

As Liberia stands today she is ripe for international complications. Germany is still an "unsatisfied, land-hungry" nation, whom the League of Nations would not hesitate to "satisfy" by casting Liberia into the maw of the Aryan Moloch. Fortunately the Liberians sense their plight which the leading Monrovian newspaper sums up as follows:

As stated in Monrovia's *Weekly Mirror*: "It is evident that Liberia is destined to be the next objective of European imperialism and unless Liberians refuse to be a nation of orators and cease from idealizing, and look to machine guns and bullets and gases and explosives as the god of the ark of the covenant and not the covenant of the League of Nations, they are doomed because the republic is unarmed and is incapable of any resistance from without."

Normally the blacks in America and the West Indies should serve as a bulwark for the safety of the country, and for its further territorial expansion. Unfortunately, however, not only Liberians, but most West Africans, remember the needless and terrific treatment meted out to West Coast natives by West Indian soldiery and civilian administrators, who were employed in the British service.

Hence the Garvey Movement, foresighted as it was, fell on deaf ears in the Republic. Today, neither "foreign" blacks from the United States or the West Indies receive hearty welcome despite the good work done for the country by the late

Minister, The Hon. Chas. E. Mitchell and the present Minister, The Hon. Lester H. Walton, both American blacks. Or the fact that President Barclay, who has re-made the country, is himself part West Indian.

The Nineteenth Century closed with the final defeat of old Kordofan in East Africa. It is needless to relate how the Sudan was conquered. It will be sufficient to state that Egypt seized Kordofan in 1800-1840. This was the completion of the fall of the Fung dynasty which flourished from 1515 to 1789. The Fungs reached their height in 1643 under King Badi, one of the greatest intellectuals and administrators that East Africa has produced. By 1778, under King Adlan II, the kingdom waned and crashed in 1789 when it was taken over by Kordofan.

From 1878 to 1900 a certain Rabah, petty officer in the army of Suleiman, broke with his chief, seized a part of the regular army of Suleiman, and ravaged the Sudan in an unorganized effort to stay the hand of Egypt and Europe. In 1881, Mohammed Ahmed came into control and four years later he had four-fifths of the Sudan under his control. His death in 1885 cut short his venture. He was followed by Abdullah, who sought to restore a semblance of sovereignty for Kordofan. In his attempts so to do he encountered Ethiopia, took Gondar and in a subsequent war with John II, of Ethiopia, killed the Ethiopian ruler and incidentally, opened the way for the Great Menelik II. But Kordofan lost her chance to regain or to create, sovereignty.

Menelek II saved Ethiopia and brought it safetly through the perilous Nineteenth Century, with the aid of Ras Mangasha and Ras Makonnen. Menelek died in 1913. After a brief reign of Lidj Iyasu and a Regency, directed by Ras Tafari, 1916-1930, Ras Tafari was crowned, 1930, Haille Selassie I, King of Kings, Elect of God and Conquering Lion of the Tribe of Judah.

With Italian and French aid he manoeuvered Ethiopia into the League of Nations 1923. In October 1935, Italian legions poured into Ethiopia and in May 1936, Emperor Selassie fled from his country.

Recent Tendencies

ALTHOUGH this section deals with recent tendencies and attitudes on this subject, we find no better way to open the discussion than by referring to the opinion of Dr. Blyden, uttered back in 1881. We quote from his address on the occasion of his inauguration as president of the Liberia College:—

> The people generally are not yet prepared to understand their own interests in the great work to be done for themselves and their children. We shall be obliged to work for some time to come not only without the popular sympathy we ought to have, but with utterly inadequate resources.
>
> In all English-speaking countries the mind of the intelligent Negro child revolts against the descriptions of the Negro given in elementary books—geographies, travels, histories. . . .
>
> Having embraced or at least assented to these falsehoods about himself, he concludes that his only hope of rising in the scale of respectable manhood is to strive for whatever is most unlike himself and most alien to his peculiar tastes. And whatever his literary attainments or acquired ability, he fancies that he must grind at the mill which is provided for him, putting in material furnished to his hands, bringing no contribution from his own field; and of course nothing comes out but what is put in.

A year after the above pronouncement by Dr. Blyden, the Honorable George W. Williams published his *History of the Negro Race in America,* in two volumes. The first volume covers the period from 1619 to 1800. It contains 464 pages of text, 125 of which are devoted to the African background.

The second volume, 584 pages, takes the story from 1800 to 1880.

In 1891, Honorable E. A. Johnson, then of Raleigh, North Carolina, now resident of New York City, published his "School History of the Negro Race in America and History of the Negro Soldiers in the Spanish American War." This is one of the first attempts to bring the subject within the range of elementary school children. Since 1890, under the leadership of Dr. DuBois, Dr. Moorland, Dr. Woodson, and Mr. Schomburg, the field has been widened. Emotion, passionate dogma and mere assumption have been ruled out and a critical, scientific basis has been laid.

Father John LaFarge, editor of the Catholic Weekly, *America,* in an article in his magazine, July 21, 1928, under the title, "The Unknown Field of Negro History," sums up briefly:

> Negro history is a wonderful tale. You must go back to the ancient world to get the effect of the Egyptian Queen, Nefertari, of ivory thrones, leopard skins, processions of slaves, or the Negro poet Nosseyeb of Damascus. The grandeur was left over in Africa and so was the remote but vivid past. Yet there is a special story to be told of the Negro in our latter times and especially in our own country. Instead of thrones and kings, it will tell of the great cloud of humble folk, and the few that with infinite toil and pains managed to rise above their surroundings.
>
> All kinds of adventures are there, each in its own way, with its own atmosphere and meaning. The sole reason why it should not be told after all, is that we are shy of reality. . . .
>
> Negro history may be a good tale, but has it any real significance? To get at its significance, one must realize that the expression "Negro History" is a little misleading. . . .
>
> I believe it (the Catholic Church) has, and that moreover Catholics both at home and abroad can do a great deal towards shedding light on this little-known phase of the world's history. . . .
>
> From the standpoint of policy, the adaptation of the Church to racial tradition and cultures is the major missionary problem of the present day. Our Holy Father's own utterances and acts, the discussions and plans of leaders in the field of mission studies, all bear this out.

Miss Odette Keun is one of the bitterest critics and opponents of this subject, that has come forth in recent years. Browsing among the books of the Clarendon Press in the city of Oxford, England in 1931, the writer picked up an innocent looking pamphlet entitled *A Foreigner Looks at the Sudan.*

Excerpts from the pamphlet will illustrate Miss Keun's point of view:

The little museum at Omdurman, on the White Nile, plunges the visitor straightway, into one of the blackest, most cruel and lawless chapters of African history—and no human record will ever set down all that African history has really been. It was Africa that made Winwood Reade call his great world-history the "Martyrdom of Man."—In 1821, Mohammed Ali the Great, subjugated the peoples he called the Sudan, the "Country of the Blacks."

Still further back in the savage past, one catches elusive glimpses of native empires and emirates, barbaric and uncontrolled. . . .

. . . And here I am going to hold forth on a subject that is a source of indescribable irritation to any sociologically disposed traveller. Let us get it into our heads once for all, we Europeans, that the Sudan never had a civilization—for I take my solemn oath that in thirty years or so from today the "Jeunes-Soudanais," who are inevitably beginning to come into existence, will assert that once upon a time it had a glorious past. This is a depressing prophecy, but it will come true. Every subject race, as soon as it becomes conscious of its subjection, seeks compensation in the spontaneously created legend of a glorious past.

The Poles have bored us to death with this legend; so have the Irish, the Hebrews, the Arabs; India has made herself an intolerable nuisance with the same sort of nonsense. All alien-governed people develop this obsession, and so too will the Sudanese invent in the near future, the romantic and fantastic annals of a gorgeous national history. They will prove that they have anticipated everything that the West has accomplished.

They will find fragments that they will patch together to testify that the fountain of all wisdom, virtue and science was in their ancestors. Those of Arab speech and Moslem faith will claim that their blood links them to the makers of Saracen civilization, the greatness of which . . . has been immensely exaggerated into the legend of a golden age. And the others—to whom even the strain of Arab blood is denied—Nubians, Hamites and Nilotic negroes, will learn (from their English teachers) of Taharka and Candace, of the temple of Ammon at Napata, of Meroe and its table of the sun, and they will seek in the world of those forgotten shadows the glories of "nationhood" and "culture" which their recent past and their present withhold. They will discover that they too possessed an Alexander, a Caesar, a Napoleon, or, to come to modern histrionic antics, a Mussolini. . . .

. . . Too far back for any clearness of record, there was,

—for as much as I can make out in the intricate tale,—a medley of aboriginal potentates, all barbaric; on the primary Hamitic stock, were grafted later, numberless foreign shoots, originat ing from East and Central Africa; Egyptian penetration took place as early as the Old Empire, and the archaeological vestiges of grandeur are faint materialized echoes of Egyptian civilization. In the early centuries after Christ some Christian kingdoms arose, notably those of Dongola and Aloa; with the Arab invasions beginning in the seventh century, Moslem religion and influence prevailed in the north—Nubia, Sennar, Kordofan—while in the south the pagan negroes held unassail ably to their beliefs and customs.

Of course I realize that what I have given is the most rudimentary historical glimpse conceivable, but it is hardly worthwhile breaking one's head over such futile and irrelevant jig-saw puzzles of rule and conquest, when there are so many vitally important problems to grapple with in contemporary science, politics, ethics, industry, commerce. To be aware of one's past is a symptom of a disease.

Miss Keun has made a study of the Sudan. She probably has an "Aryan" complex. In her attempt to pay tribute to the British for what they have done since the occupation of Khartoum, she, incoherently, has sought to damn the natives. It is quite likely that her diatribes are, after all, unreal. It may be that her real bitterness is not towards the natives, but towards other Europeans, the Germans, for instance, who failed to hold their own in Africa. Complexes have a peculiar way of registering themselves.

Indeed the finest gem in recent opinion dealing with this subject is an article which appeared in the *Crisis Magazine,* July 1933, from the pen of Mr. Alfred Edgar Smith, under the title, "An Outline of the World History of the Negro, in a Thousand Words."

It comes as an antidote to the vitriolic attacks of Miss Keun. Mr. Smith's article is accompanied by two charts. One shows the relation of Negro History with the History of Man in general. The other shows the relation of Negro History in America to this World History. This article and these charts are invaluable to the proper study of this subject.

In the past quarter of a century, many white men who can speak with authority and conviction, have expressed themselves definitely and objectively on the subject of African culture. John W. Vandercook, in his book, *Tom-Tom*, 1926, expresses amazement at the indifference of the black man, in the western world, to the glory of his ancient heritage and rebukes him unsparingly: (pp. xiii-xvi).

Yet, with so few exceptions that the rule is merely strengthened, negroes have tacitly accepted and, deep in themselves, actually believe that they are somehow lower in the scale of things than those of us who have glory in white complexions.

In Western theology God is white, Christ is white, the Church is white. Yet the "free" black has swallowed this bait, hook, line, and sinker. I cannot see how any one with respect for what is called "the human soul" can view without distaste and a secret sense that something is amiss in a race of men admitting in their every act and thought their own inferiority.

And now each Africa-bound ship carries American negro missionaries of the white church who are off to risk their lives in the pitiful task of telling their "heathen" brethren in the homeland that the old gods are wrong, the ancient pride is false and the wonderful tales of the forest children are merely antique lies.

Yet in the jungles to which these modern slaves are going there exists a marvelous world that they have forgotten and the white conquerors have never known or tried to know. . . . Yet since morning broke above the world they have sheltered a people who have survived, who in the warmth and wonderment of the sun have reared up dreams that comfort, states that last, and imaged gods who are supremely kind and wise. It is a black world, a foreign world. But it is their own.

To my mind there is no hope for the modern negro in the way that he is vainly going. Slavery lasted too long and ended too suddenly for the whites ever to forget and forgive enough to allow the black people into our sancta. Our state, our civilization is our own, for we made it. It is fair, as things in this partial world can be fair, that we should keep it, use it for ourselves, and shut the outcasts that we made away from it.

A race is like a man. Until it uses its own talents, takes pride in its own history, and loves its own memories it can never fulfill itself completely. The civilized negro must lose his contempt for his "heathen" brethren in Africa and in the jungles of Melanesia and Suriname. He must learn that the fathers of the race had and still possess blessed secrets, wonderful lores, and great philosophies, that rank the jungle negro's civilization as the equal, and in many respects the superior of any way of life that is to be found anywhere in the world, whether among white or yellow, black or red.

In an Encyclical Letter issued March 5, 1924 by Pope Pius, XI, the following declaration appears:—

> The belief that the dark-skinned races are inferior to the white is a mistaken one . . . long experience proves that these peoples, erroneously termed inferior, can compete with the white races in mental acumen.
> If in the heart of barbarous lands, there are found men slow to learn, this is explainable by the conditions of their life, of which the restricted needs do not allow them to make large use of their intelligence.

Dr. Albert Einstein, has an article in the *Crisis, Magazine* for February, 1932, as follows:

> "It seems to be a universal fact that minorities, especially when their individuals are recognized because of physical differences, are treated by the majorities among whom they live as an inferior class. The tragic part of such a fate, however, lies not only in the automatically realized disadvantages suffered by these minorities in economic and social relations, but also in the fact that those who meet such treatment themselves for the most part acquiesce in this prejudiced estimate because of the suggestive influence of the majority and come to regard people like themselves as inferior. This second and more important aspect of evil can be met through closer union and conscious educational enlightenment among the minority, and so an emancipation of the soul of the minority can be attained. The determined effort of the American Negroes in this direction deserves every recognition and assistance."

On August 8, 1933, Arthur Brisbane, in an unguarded moment, while reproving the sponsors of *Negro Day* at the *Century of Progress Exposition, in Chicago*, had this to say in the *New York American* of that date:

> "Next Saturday is set apart as 'Negro Day' at the 'Century of Progress Exposition' in Chicago, with athletic sports, including colored Olympic champions and a pageant at Soldier's Field called 'The Epic of a Race.' 3,000 Negro voices singing 'spirituals.'
> "The committee in charge might have reproduced on Soldier's Field the great Sphinx that stands on the Egyptian desert. That Sphinx has an Ethiopian face, proving that the Negro race was important far back in the night of time. Many colored men and women would be more proud of the fact that one of their race once ruled over Egypt than in any modern 'spirituals,' 'Green Pastures' or athletic records."

The writer immediately sent a letter to Mr. Brisbane asking him for citations to authorities which inspired him to offer such a suggestion and pay such a glowing tribute. The return registry card was of course received, but nothing further from Mr. Brisbane.

The teacher must ever be on the alert to the slightest suggestions in periodical literature, checking and running down clues when possible.

Book-burning in Germany and the silencing of German-Jewish writers is a serious blow to the world. It is particularly so to African history because of the wealth of dependable information which proceeded from that source. Something has been salvaged out of the holocaust, after all, and placed in other centers in Europe and in New York. Happily the books of Frobenius, are still available which means that threads of the truth in this field, are not utterly broken. On the credit side, the "extreme racialism" in Germany has had a tendency to loosen tongues, in many quarters, which hitherto have been mute on phases of African history, and sources to it, by which the subject can profit.

For example, certain intellectuals in the present set-up in Germany, in order to irk the French, refer to them as "negroid" and similarly have these intellectuals referred to the Jews. These two classes so "shamefully abused" have retorted in ways which have thrown light on a few facts which black folk have wanted to see brought out into the open.

Apropos the banter of white races with the word "negroid" or "negrophile," the following has come to light. St. Maurice, pictured on the imposing coat of arms of the city of Coburg, Germany, is now an "Aryan worry" since Coburg has become a Nazi stronghold. St. Maurice is a fast-black, changeless-skinned Ethiopian. Though honored and adored for, lo these many years, he must now be de-hallowed in order that a new patron, of Nordic persuasion, may soothe troubled souls and lure the unwary German into paths of truth and light.

On the other hand a distinguished white American, travelling in Europe in 1933, was reported to have reminded the

French that the Nazi press was referring to them as "negroid."
The writer opened communication with him in regard to the
reported incident.

His representatives replied, in part, as follows:

> Dr. — asked me to reply at once to your letter of in-
> quiry and to say that he cannot at this moment,—place his
> hand on any one reference to the French race as negroid or
> semi-negroid—but again and again the Nazi press refers con-
> temptuously to the "negroid French race." And again;
> I am unable to find a reference in the Nazi press at my
> disposal wherein the French are called a "negroid race," but
> I know there is ample substantiation for that charge.
> I should like to bring to your attention that in 1932 the
> Nazi Governor of Thuringia, Sauckel, declared in a speech—
> that the French are a negroid race with whom the Germans
> should be too proud to deal.—The savage tendencies of the
> French are an inheritance from their negroid strain.—
> (The Book) "Mein Kampf"—compares the negroes with
> black poodles which can be trained to learn the tricks of their
> white superiors—etc., etc.

Since Dr. ——— is a "friend" to the blacks in America, and
never fails to speak for and to counsel them, it is difficult to
see what service he could perform for the French by his reported statement.

During the period of this correspondence a chain letter
came to the hands of the writer from the "Aryan Book Store"
said to be in Los Angeles, California. After its anti-Semitic
spleen had run its slimy course, it ended with the statement,
that:

> The Jews are not of the white race, they are Semites.

It would seem that only the Germans are excited;
neither the Hebrews nor the French are perturbed. Meanwhile,
black folk, humorously, watch the intra-white propagandist
parade.

Brief Statement of Courses in Schools Today

IN THE SUMMER of 1911, during the sessions of the Chautauqua held that year in Bay-View, Mich., Dr. Erwin H. Richards, Missionary to the Inhambane, East Africa, under the Methodist Episcopal Church, was one of the principal speakers. In the course of his address he so distorted the folk-ways of that area and claimed so positively that the ruins of Mashonaland were not of native origin, that he was immediately challenged by members of the Chautauqua. His reply was:

> I beg you to point out any standard author who holds that the black man built any of the ancient ruins in Africa, anywhere, save as a slave. I am after the truth as much as any one. I have distinctly called attention to the positive fact, undenied by the vast majority that it is not the black man alone, but the fellow of any color and often of another language that provokes instant dislike to some extent. I shall be glad to hunt for the truth with any one and exchange views so long as they are mutually helpful.

The views of Dr. Richards were submitted to Dr. Franz Boas, then in Mexico City. A letter received from Dr. Boas at that point reads:

> "I want to thank you for calling this incident to my attention. The question seems to my mind a simple one of fair-play, while it is difficult to others on account of inherited prejudices. I shall always count it my duty to help to dispel these so far as it is in my power. With serious work on the part of your people, we shall succeed ultimately.

In 1916 letters were sent to representative men and catalogs were secured from various institutions in an endeavor to get expressions on the desirability of African history as a school subject. A cross section of opinion, at that time may be seen through the following replies:

The only way I can think of for studying Negro history is
to learn more about Negroes. This for me is aim and value
enough.

W. E. B. DuBOIS
Editor of CRISIS MAGAZINE, N. Y.
Author of "THE NEGRO," *etc.*

I have not given this particular matter sufficient thought
to' come to any definite conclusion in regard to it. Naturally
one of the first questions that comes to me is as to where such
a course could be put into the curriculum without crowding
something else out. A second question is as to what suitable
textbooks could be secured. The third question which I at
once raise is what particular advantage is to be derived by the
students in taking the proposed special course. Unless a course
has a well defined, constructive and useful aim, it would seem
to me unwise to take the student's time for it when there are
so many things which he obviously needs to know if he is to
be well prepared to take up his own work in the world.

GILBERT W. BRINK,
Superintendent, Educational Work,
American Baptist Home Mission
Society, New York.

I have considerable sympathy with the general ideas which
your questionnaire expresses as to the desirability of teaching
Negro history in Negro schools, but I find it difficult to make
any statement of my position except in terms of some particular proposition. Thus, I doubt whether Negro history as a
formal subject has any place in the elementary school.

Its place in the secondary school would be in close conjunction with civics and economics along the lines of the
revolutionary new conceptions of secondary history which are
being formulated by a committee of the National Education
Association. This committee has made a preliminary report.
Its chairman is Dr. Thomas Jesse Jones, United States Bureau
of Education, Washington D. C. According to the conception
of that committee, not only Negro history but all histories
would be taught much less as a story of separate groups of
people, and much more as a fundamental inquiry into human
society and its processes with special reference to present
duty. In the standard courses and especially the research work
of the college, Negro History might have a large place and
be carried out into minute specialization.

H. PAUL DOUGLASS,
Corresponding Secretary,
American Missionary Association,
New York.

The aim of Negro History should be to acquaint Negro youth and the country at large with the outstanding characters that the race has produced and to impress students with the important achievements of the race, singly and by co-operative enterprises, whether in war or civil life. This as with other groups of people will bring self-respect to the group in question and a proper appreciation of them as a factor in the body politic by others than themselves. The object is a worthy one, and should be carried out in a broad, scientific way—not with a narrow self-centered purpose or mere bit of bragging; but let the values be true.

They are bound to have a good influence.

J. E. MOORLAND,
International Committee of Young
Men's Christian Asssociations,
New York.

The course should acquaint the young student with the basic facts in Negro history giving the relation of it to the larger field of American history and thus some idea of his own citizenship. I note that you are using my book on the Negro. May I ask you to correct two typographical errors more glaring than some others? On page 108 read 1895 for 1893 and at the bottom of 229 read 1806 instead of 1906.

BENJAMIN BRAWLEY, Dean
Morehouse College,
Atlanta, Ga.

The subject of Negro history, more generally taught in our schools is something we have long since needed. For centuries the Negro has been taught that he has no honorable past and the teaching has been so effective that even some of our leaders have accepted the doctrine as true. It seems to me that it should be our purpose to acquaint the student with our noble past; to create in him that pride, self-respect, and confidence which will enable him to reassert the man that is in him by enlarging his racial vision.

M. W. BULLOCK, Dean,
A. and M. College,
Huntsville, Alabama.

In the Foreword to my "Negro in American History", the necessity for the work is briefly stated.

I stand ready to render whatever additional services correspondence and further research here in Washington, where there is good available material, should bring forth. When this cannot meet your needs, call on the Society for Negro Research for assistance.

JOHN W. CROMWELL, Corresponding Sec'y,
American Negro Academy,
Author, "NEGRO IN AMERICAN HISTORY"

I do not see how I can answer your question with regard to the value of Negro history to the Negro student except by answering the question: What is history anyway and why do we study it. This I shall not attempt to do. I refer you to the German philosopher, Hegel, whose conception of the meaning and significance of history I accept.

To state the matter briefly, however, it amounts to this: Every race that is going to succeed must have its own heroes. The Negro is an American, and so far as he is an American, he admires and pays homage to American ideals as represented in her best men. Within this larger group, however, the Negro has been set apart, rightly or wrongly, by his color, traditions, and above all by his struggle for fair-play for his own people. The men who have taken part in that struggle are necessarily closer to him and more particularly his heroes than they are those of the rest of America. That does not mean that Frederick Douglass and Booker T. Washington are not accepted as great Americans but they are Great Negroes or if you please Afro-Americans. Their lives are an inspiration to all of us but it seems to me that they should be a special inspiration to the people of the Negro race. That is about the way I look at it. I am sending you enclosed an outline of the general course of my lectures.

ROBERT E. PARKS,
University of Chicago.

. . . unless our schools utilize for educational purposes the careers and personalities of colored men and women as well as of white our children will be overwhelmed by the perstige of the white man and their own initiative impaired . . . Our children should be trained to a knowledge and a due appreciation of all the makers and sustainers of civilization. It is true that for my boy there is something of inspiration, something I would not have him lose in the life of St. Francis of Assisi. But there are some modern saints who bear a more intimate relation to his experience; I certainly would not have his life untouched by the spirit of Alexander Crummel. Our schools must have shut their eyes to the very educational material best fitted to develop in our children race pride, self-confidence, a spirit of brave and noble emulation.

ROSCOE C. BRUCE,
Assistant Superintendent,
Washington, D. C. (1914-15)

I would suggest the biographical approach, using, for example, such men as: Frederick Douglass, Alexander Crummel, Martin R. Delaney, W. H. Council, Paul Dunbar, Peter H. Clark, H. H. Garnet, Benjamin Banneker, Bishop D. E. Payne, Booker T. Washington.

These rounded out with organized material on our contribution to the economic progress of the nation and our status in industrial and higher education, the value and benefit of which is so obvious that there seems to be no need for long discussion here.

JOHN E. BRUCE, *"Grit"*
Contributing Editor,
Colored American Review,
New York.

Excerpts from the catalogs of twelve institutions which were attempting to give courses prior to 1916, will furnish some idea of the scope of the work at that time:

ATLANTA UNIVERSITY, Atlanta, Ga.

"United States History and the History of the Negro in America; Modern European History and the History of Africa; General Economics and the Economic History of the Negro American; General Sociology and the Social Conditions of the Negro American."

FISK UNIVERSITY, Nashville, Tennessee.

A course in Negro history which "aims to give historical perspective for the understanding of present conditions, and an appreciation of honored names of Negroes of the past and an estimate of the genuine contributions the Negro has made to the labor force, military strength, musical culture and general trend of American civilization."

The courses were given, apparently, without an African background.

WILBERFORCE UNIVERSITY, Wilberforce, Ohio.

A "Review of certain aspects of the Negro Problem with a history of the African Peoples in the Western World."

HOWARD UNIVERSITY, Washington, D. C.

A course in "The History of the Reconstruction Period" which "aims to give a clear conception of the new birth of the nation and to ascertain the re-adjustment rights, liberties, immunities, obligations and duties of the emancipated and enfranchised race and the contribution of the Negro to American civilization."

MOREHOUSE COLLEGE, Atlanta, Georgia.

A "half-course" in the essentials of Negro American History with a wide and rapid reading in such writers and authorities as Du-Bois, Brawley, Williams, Blake, Merriam and

Cromwell. Special emphasis is placed upon the economic history of the Negro in American life."

SELMA UNIVERSITY, Selma, Alabama.

Under the heading "Sociology and Economics" was given a course on "The Life of the American Negro which is a careful study of the health conditions, skilled and unskilled Negro laborers, home life, schools, and the Religion of the Negro and his Moral Status as revealed in his churches and in his daily life." Another course was given in "African History" which is "intended to carefully study the Colonization of Africa by European Nations, Tribal Migrations, and the Causes of the Present Political Situation in Africa, special attention given to the Republic of Liberia." A third course was given on "The Negro in America which is a careful study of the facts and forces which have affected the Negro in American Society, with special attention to the institution of slavery and state legislation."

PAINE UNIVERSITY, Selma, Alabama.

A course in "The Ancient History of the Negro in Africa". This was followed by a course in the "history of the Negro in America from 1619 to Emancipation and a history of the race from Emancipation with his progress and institutions."

HAMPTON INSTITUTE, Hampton Virginia.

The course here "aims to study and understand the relative efficiency of the Negro and Indian as laborers as compared with other races; the importance of the Negro and Indian Races as factors in agriculture." The last half of this course "aims to show the Negro and Indian the place of the individual, the home and the community in the social whole."

VIRGINIA UNION UNIVERSITY, Richmond, Virginia.

The course here was "intended to acquaint the student with the most modern and scientific methods of social research as applied to the study of community problems, especially related to Negro life both in the country and city." This was followed by "a survey of the anthropological and ethnological traits of the African Negro; a historical review of his transference to America; social and economic conditions under slavery; status in Reconstruction Days and progress since then; present conditions among various classes of Negroes in various parts of the country with emphasis upon Negro health, economics, crime, education and general betterment."

SPELMAN SEMINARY, Atlanta, Georgia.

A course was offered here in "The Essentials of Negro History with a general outline and a special study of the social condition of the Negro race in America."

TUSKEGEE INSTITUTE, Tuskegee, Alabama.

Two courses were given here; one on "The Negro in Africa" and the other on the "Negro in American History." The first makes "a study of Africa, the continent and its resources and political conditions." Special attention was given to "the natives, their habits of life and their past and present history. They were reviewed from the standpoint of their tribal relations, kingdoms, myths, fables, music, writing, industries, arts, religion and modern conditions." The course on "The Negro in American History" made a detailed study of Slavery, Emancipation, Reconstruction and Present Conditions of Negro Life." The contribution of the Negro as a "force in the army and navy of the country received special attention and likewise the Negro church, the school, the Negro in business and in the general economic and industrial situation in America."

In all the courses listed above, Brawley's, *A Short History of the American Negro* and Cromwell's, *The Negro in American History* were used as texts. Only Howard University, Tuskegee Institute, Atlanta University and Wilberforce University issued a bibliography or a selected list of books.

That interest might be created and opinions, methods and material exchanged, the author launched, in 1920, in Chicago, *The Up-Reach Magazine*, A Journal of Education and Social Work. This publication was intended for social workers, teachers in general, with a special department for those who were attempting to teach African history. He was assisted in this project by Professor Charles S. Johnson; Professor John H. Purnell, and Mr. Arthur A. Schomburg.

However, the *Journal of Negro Education* launched in April, 1932, by Dr. Charles H. Thompson, of Howard University, has carried out in detail the survey of the status of African history in the schools, which *The Up-reach Magazine* slightly checked in 1920.

Volume II, Number I, January, 1933, of *The Journal of Negro Education,* under the chief editorship of Dr. Thompson, contains an article, *The Teaching of Negro Life and History in Relation to Some Views of Educators on Race Adjustment.* It brings the situation down to date and is indispensable, especially, for the teacher. It was written by Mr. Irwin V. Shannon, research assistant in the department of sociology, Vanderbilt

STATEMENT OF COURSES IN SCHOOLS 147

University, Nashville, Tennessee and formerly assistant professor of sociology, in the University of Kentucky. Excerpts from
the article follow:

This project, in brief outline, involved investigation of
(1) administrative policies regarding the emphasis given to the
dissemination of information about Negroes; (2) the extent
of formal courses of study in Negro history, literature, art,
music, etc.; (3) the part played by the library programs and
extra-curricular activities in stimulating an interest in Negro
life and history; (4) the opinions and views of faculty members
on this phase of Negro education and on questions of race adjustment; (5) the extent to which college teachers regularly
stress the study of Negro life in all of their classes; (6) the
amount and kind of information that Negro students have concerning their race. This report however, is concerned only with
the results obtained from a questionnaire study of opinions
and practices of teachers on Negro college faculties.

METHOD OF PROCEDURE

A specially devised questionnaire, in the form of a check-
list, was employed in obtaining the data for this study. The
questionnaire used consisted of one section (See Section A)
made up of thirty-five statements representing various shades
of opinion in regard to the efforts made by Negro colleges to
teach students about their race. A second section (See Section
C) contains thirty additional statements of opinion relative to
various questions which have a bearing on the adjustment of
the Negro to American life.

In all, 129 part-courses in which definite attention is given
to the study of the Negro are reported by 86 teachers, or
39.63 per cent, and a total of 240 courses giving incidental
emphasis are indicated by 128 teachers, or 58.98 per cent. Out
of this entire group of 217 faculty members, there are 167 or
76.96 per cent who are engaged in giving instruction about the
Negro either through special courses, through courses partly
devoted to this purpose, or by means of incidental treatment.

The marked extent to which the study of the Negro is
emphasized by this group of teachers also appears from other
data supplied. Forty teachers, or about 18 per cent, use a total
of 52 books about the Negro as class texts. Reference books
dealing with the Negro are used for collateral reading purposes
by 94 of the respondents, or 43 per cent. In answer to the
question: "Do you assign term papers or projects on the
Negro?" 9.21 per cent of the group indicate that they do so
very frequently; 25.80 per cent. frequently; 24.88 per cent, seldom; and 17.51 per cent, never. No information on this point
is given by 22.58 per cent.

Mr. Shannon concludes:

The development of race consciousness among Negroes is viewed with favor. More than two-thirds think that Negroes succeed in their struggle for equal rights and opportunities without a strong race consciousness, and an equal number reject the idea that the development of race consciousness would only delay satisfactory adjustment of inter-racial relations. Only 40 per cent of the group, however, believe that the race should magnify the significance of anything that is distinctly Negro in order to attain recognition.

TALLADEGA COLLEGE, Talladega, Alabama. In a course in "Sociology and Economics" this institution made a part of it "a discussion of modern social problems . . . with particular emphasis on the Negro phase of these problems."

GENERAL SUMMARY

Taken as a whole, the views thus expressed create the definite impression, that no development for the Negro race along lines from whatever may be the main course pursued by other groups, is either desired or contemplated. In other words, there is no apparent tendency here on the part of these educators to identify the needs, interests, or future of the Negro as fundamentally different from what may be the common lot of all groups participating in American life. The only exception is that they seem to favor the development of race consciousness. Further research may or may not confirm this interpretation of the results. Tentatively, however, it is possible to infer a considerable disparity between the educational stress laid on teaching students about their race and the professed views of teachers concerning what they apparently expect of want the future status of the Negro to be.

It would appear from the results of this study that teachers are making numerous efforts to develop race conscious attitudes through the inculcation of knowledge of Negro life and history at the same time that they hold views about the status of the Negro seemingly unrelated to, if not inconsistent with such efforts. This, of course, is a matter that might well be given further study.

Groundwork for Teachers

AT THE OUTSET it will be necessary to grasp certain general principles. Those who attempt to teach in this field, will be constantly, queried, not only by the earnest seeker after truth, but more scathingly by the avowed scoffer. In order to be able to justify the work and to enhance its value:

1. Content and subject matter should be definitely planned. This can be done by keeping in constant touch with the libraries and Collections mentioned in the preface.
2. Teachers must have a knowledge of the bases and guardians of civilization;
3. Some facility in the use of internal and external criticism;
4. An understanding that there is, scientifically, no such thing as "race", and least of all a "pure race"; but at the same time have a table of the shifting in the so-called "race classifications".
5. Teachers must keep abreast of the arguments for and against the influence of geographic environment and have,
6. A critical attitude to the modern social order with,
7. Definite grounding in international relations.
8. A stand must be taken, sooner or later, on the use or the non use of the word "Negro".
9. None of the above will be of much avail unless the teacher pursues the work with courage and vision.
10. The task is to keep faith with the writers on Africans at home and abroad. We owe them that co-operation which will lead to the creation of a great, active reader-public; people who will buy and read, more than they will borrow and read.

A suggestive plan is set forth on page 162, and needs but little mention here, except to say that it has been possible to work out such a plan because of abundant material in New York City.

In general, civilization is based on property, home and family, education, appreciation and tolerance, religion, security under organized government, labor and trade.

The elementary guardians of civilization are faithful trustees i.e., efficient and unselfish leadership; the skill of the competent i.e., contented, trained, self-sustaining workers; and the virtue of the brave i.e., armies. If it appears that the states which Africans have created, do not square with these tenets, there need be neither shame nor alarm. Every black tyrant who has painted a trail of blood in Africa, will be over-matched by the merchants of death in Western Europe; for every black absolutist who has squelched the liberties of the people and blocked the road to progress, the history of Western Europe abounds with numerous counterparts. In situations such as these there is small comfort for any one. The positive core in the growth and development of a people is their way of life. It is yet to be proven that a way of life, suitable in one geographic area must be identical with that in another.

TERMINOLOGY

Those who come to a serious reading and study of African history, for the first time, will experience considerable difficulty in terminology. This will be true whether the area is West, Central, South or East Africa. There will be special difficulty with Ancient Ethiopia, Arabia, the Nile Valley and Egypt.

The involution of the names of rulers, varies but little, if any, from that in *standard* ancient history texts. The difference is that the field is considered *new,* the sound of the names is strange and the spelling, apparently, awkward.

For example, Aahmes (1700) B. C. is also called Amasis, Queen Nefertari is often called Nofrete, Nefertiti; Thothmes III is often labelled Thothmosis or Tahutmes; Akhnaton is likely to appear as Iknaton, Khu-Aten, Chuenaten or Amenophis; Zerak, the Ethiopian (Usarkon) is often Osarcon; likewise Shishak is Sheshenk or Sheshonk.

Queen Hatshepsut is Hatasu or Hashop and the Queen of Sheba is Saba, Makeda or Balkis. Tirhakah is Taharqua! Worst of all, Shabaka, may be Sabacon, Shaba, Saba, Sibe, Sua or So. Native usage tempered with Greek, Assyrian and other languages have made these variations.

The Land of Punt is Pewent. Arabia Patraea, is the stony

area, Arabia Deserta, the desert proper and Arabia Felix is *happy* Arabia, i.e., better watered and with more flora.

A check should be made in (Baldwin, 63-66) of the old *Dwipa* division of the world, noting carefully *Cusha-dwipa without* and *Cusha-dwipa within*, a good exercise in geography. Ethiopian rulers may have one name because of some incidental statement made to them or about them, as in American history, we have The Strenuous One (T. R. Roosevelt), Old Hickory (Jackson), or Honest Abe (Lincoln). For example, the great Theodore II—Ethiopia 1868—was formerly Lidj Kasa. This name means *Recompense* or *Little Child*. When he came to the throne, he chose for his name the regal, Theodore, and ordered that he be so called.

The Fulani on the West Coast today, may appear as Fulans, Fula, Fellani, Fellata or Fulbe.

Many people have lost interest in this field because they were unwilling to plow through this confusion in terminology. However, in the maze of it are hidden many significant African peoples.

Even in current literature certain writers have been bold enough to assert, that Kelly Miller, Roland Hayes and Paul Robeson, are not to be *exactly* classed with the black race. Doubtless Jack Johnson, has been recorded and will be read of in the distant future, as an *"Aryan Colossus"* that bestrode America in the opening quarter of the Twentieth Century!

Happily, confusion in terminology will soon be partially clarified. Experts in pre-historic and proto-historic science are now at work devising common rules, with the same measuring rods and the same dictionary. The chaos in the *"time"* element will also be slightly cleared. There, probably cannot be absolute uniformity in terminology because the range of human and pre-human history is too great. The terms, for example, Neanderthal, Piltdown or Grimaldi (Negroid) man, are actually meaningless. They have grown out of some rock, plain or cliff near the spot where the discovery was made.

The same thing is true in modern history. The Battle of Bunker Hill was not fought at Bunker Hill nor was the Battle of Waterloo fought at Waterloo. The clash labelled by the former was more properly fought at Breed's Hill and that which the latter covers, centered largely at Brian le Liew.

Be prepared, at the very beginning of the Theme on the Ancient East, to motivate the topics definitely, in order that terminology will not become a bore and a bugaboo. This properly done, the pupil will be less likely to drop the subject. If he elects to carry on, he will pursue the work with less of the ordinary listlessness, common in history classes.

A critical attitude toward the present social order will be difficult to set up and maintain without a definite grounding in modern international relations. Africans are a part of a world problem and program. Their history is only one phase of world history and if it is to be studied aright it must be viewed in its world relationships.

The causes, occasions and conditions which operate in history must be examined in relation to historical development and continuity. With special reference to America, it is well to realize that the blacks, of all units in American life, are in the best position to criticize it. Their racial memory and the diverse strains in their blood, aid them to understand America better than others. Their criticism can be actual because it is based upon clearer understanding. Being spiritually deeper in Americanism than the rest they can see more of its hypocrisy; being spiritually closer to the foundations of American democracy than others, they can the better see its cracks and rents.

When they criticize they speak not for abortive revolution and violence; they speak to heal and correct—not to destroy.

A troubled Gentile, doubtless perturbed over the matchless heritage of the Hebrew and his leavening influence in civilization, was moved to write, "How Odd, Of God, To Choose, The Jew." He will have to write again on the "strange" choice made of the black man, as the testing instrument for America as she works out the social program which destiny has entrusted to her, namely, that of dealing justly and fairly with the larg est number and the most diverse of races ever assembled in a single area and under a single social control.

The history of Africa, rightly envisioned is a thrilling story. Children need it. They cannot fully understand the world, as it affects them without knowing something, indeed a great deal, of what Africans were in the past and how they have come to their present condition. They cannot be fully intelligent American citizens, unless they add to what they know of modern governments and social institutions, a wider knowledge of governments and institutions which Africans have created and in which they were dominant actors.

The time when America will regard the blacks as members, in full and regular standing in its industrial and cultural society, is far distant. But the blacks cannot, they dare not, continue to remain indifferent to their own cultural heritage, in the well nigh vain hope of it being grafted into that of another.

The presence in this country of black folk has created a. multifarious psychic and economic situation which will, more and more, tax the hand and soul of the American people. The complexes which arise in the minds of the majority people in America on the question of color is a little less than sheer insanity. Their practical reaction flows, not so much from a color complex as it does from the paradoxical fact that they have created for the blacks a sub-human life; a sub-human economic status, and at the same time demand that the blacks enter into competition with the whites in merciless struggles for bread.

This situation is irreconcilable so long as the whites are unwilling to face the reality of the facts. For more than half a century scholars have been marshalling these facts for popular use. These facts, properly understood will enable all Americans to face modern problems armed with strength in the new knowledge of the victories and achievements when Africans were in sovereign groups. Black folk must find a new faith in themselves through this new strength. Crises will be overcome only and always by appeals to that which is within.

The black man in America can capitalize that which is within him if he will take the modicum of finance and economic opportunity which he has in this country, use it singly and pool it co-operatively, for mutual well-being and that of the nation.

As progress is made in this study, specialization should not be undertaken too quickly. A vision of the broad outlines of the early non-white world, guided by reliable data, is necessary. Such a panorama will help to clear away hidden doubt and active misgiving. The progress of this non-white world should be checked through the ages, with emphasis upon that part of it which is African and finally relating it to the status of black folk in America in the great business of living and making a living.

Constituting, as black men do, the last real spiritual reserve in this country, their duty is to glorify that spirituality not to emasculate it. The rift between the church and the people, especially so with the educated classes, must be mended. The job is to re-educate them. It will do a little good to rail at the church or fret because of an ill-prepared clergy. More and more should it be clear, that success in the job which must be done, depends on the joined hands of trained, conscientious teachers and minsters. It matters little how one may feel about it, the minister, be he charlatan or saint, has the people. Work with him so that with him and through him a better people and a better clergy can be made.

Business men would be doing a much more creditable job if the classroom and the pew backed their projects. Black actors are getting a message over the footlights, in many ways, highly beneficial and the artist is telling a finer story with his brush. A heartier, economically more sound and socially more satisfying life would be created, if black men would muster the forces which they have in an endeavor to stop the people from apologizing for their African blood; from self-abasement; from being communal cure-alls and know-alls; from apologizing for or making a mockery of religion; from dragging or trying to drag the church down to the level of a club house; from wanton squandering of means, the tenth part of which would stretch businesses from sea to sea.

The classroom, the pew, the stage, and the vigor of the press, are the basic agencies which must be used in reshaping individual and racial life.

That Word "Negro" — (negro)

DISCUSSION of the word "negro" proceeds apace. It is an old, old story. Honorable George W. Williams in his *History of the Negro Race in America*, 1882, objected much to the word, apparently accepted it and insisted that it be capitalized. Nothing new is said about it here. Rather a brief summary of attitudes for the guidance of young people who have become conscious and inquisitive of the trend up to now and for teachers who must face the question, again and again.

Many people are unalterably opposed to it; a still larger number are quiet, though secretly annoyed over its wide use and general acceptance. All register a decided shrink when the word *negress* is applied to black women. Attempts have been made to allay feeling over the latter term by parading actress, duchess, and princess as co-ordinates. The consideration remains, however, that it is with the word *tigress* that *negress* is meant to be coordinate. Though there are such words as *negrito* and *negrillo*, yet we have not seen their feminine counterparts. Often the word *Jewess* is cited in order to validate the situation, but such a mediator fails for several reasons. First of all *Jew* is a noun and is capitalized, along with its feminine counterpart wherever it appears, while *negro* is an adjective and need not be capitalized except when it begins a sentence. On the other hand it is not clear whether the word *Jew* is a racial or a religious designation. If it be religious, then it has no more to do with color designation than the words, Catholic, Mormon, or Mohammedan. If the word *Jew* be racial, ethnic, or biological, then it involves explanations, unnecessary to be entered into here.

The chief vexation over the word *negro* appears to be the the fact that it has been made to perform the double function of pointing out color and also that of assuming to signify ethnic or biologic origin. Let us pause for a moment for a word from Mr. Berthold Laufer, Curator of the Department of Anthropology, Field Museum of Natural History, Chicago. On page 4, of Leaflet Number 30 issued by that institution in 1933, we read:

> Much harm has been done by the general confusion of the terms race, nationality, language, and culture, all of which are entirely distinct. The best known school example illustrating the application of these terms is presented by our Negroes in America. As a biological type our Negroes belong to the African or "black" race and will always remain within this division; even intermarriage with whites will not modify their racial characteristics to any marked degree.

Here the Curator approaches the heart of the issue but offers no media for remedies or adjustments. Note too, the expression, "our Negroes," doubtless signifying the "genial ownership," in which the whites hold the Africans in America, seventy years after "emancipation," a subjective hang-over from slavery. The Curator continues on page 5:

> We cannot speak of a Negro nationality in America as the Negroes do not form a political unit, but live sporadically scattered in the white communities. It is chiefly social and legal restriction and segregation that keeps their race consciousness alive.

This is a challenge, unconsciously made; one which is baffling; one which has been ineffectively answered.

The vexation over the word *negro* extends to more than the facts mentioned above. It covers the devolution of the word, as misleading as it is, into its worst form still more despicable. In its ultimate objective, the word restricts African culture to a small, shut-in, so-called *true negro* group in the heart of Central Africa. This done and popularly accepted, African culture stands practically as nothing in the equation of world culture.

This sort of ethnographical legerdemain must be constantly challenged. The culture of the mountain whites in the fastnesses of Dixie, is neither the outer limit of the culture of America nor even of the whites in the South itself. Similarly, we must reject the so-called *true negro* as the outer limit of the culture of peoples of African descent in Africa itself, or abroad.

Neither do Mongolian, Malay, Indian, or Caucasian necessarily indicate skin-color, nor do they have Latin or Spanish words which tend to supplant them altogether. Yet Soudanese, Zulu, Basuto, and Bantu are superseded, or at least qualified, by the word, *negro*.

The Naturalization Act, 1875, ignores the word, altogether. It reads:

> (Section 2169)   The provisions of this title shall apply to aliens being free white persons; and to aliens of African nativity and to persons of African descent, (R.S. 1878, p380; 1 Comp. Stat. 1901, p1333.)

Another unique aspect of this Act is the fact that it provides for *free white persons* and at the same time lays the foundation for the exclusion of Hindus, a people uniformly set down as *white* in all *race classifications*. Manifestly then, in the scheme of American writers—and foreign ones who agree with them—peoples are *white* only when they can be so, advantageously. For example, Hindus are *white* as far as their art, architecture, literature, and philosophy are concerned, but *non-white*, for whatever else is considered hideous. Likewise the Ethiopians and Nubians are *white* in terms of their military prowess and the glory of their ancient line of rules, but black (negro) in terms of slaveholders or eaters of raw meat directly from the quivering carcass of a freshly killed cow.

The word, Ethiopian, in classical tradition, meant a *black or burnt-faced* man. If a color term is to be used, then Ethiopian is preferable because it has a long and respectable lineage. Those people of African blood who are not black, should be labelled for what they are, quadroon, octoroon, or under the general term, mulatto.

The native Indian races in this country are predominantly *red* men, although some of them, the Utes, for example, are quite black while others are quite white. No one thinks of speaking of an Iroquois as an *Iroquois rojo*, or if you will, of a Dane as a *Danish blanco,* yet it is the common practice to speak of a Senegalese, a Zulu, or a Mashona as a Senegalese *negro,* etc. Indeed so warped is the mind of the whites, especially, writers, publishers, and historians that they will capitalize the names of native African tribes and use a small letter for *negro* (American). They will do this even when discussing, in the same paragraph, all of these people as a single racial group. Let it be said, in all fairness, that white people, in general, mean neither scorn or ridicule when they use the word, unless they use the more corrupt form. They are unthinking in this matter, merely following custom. For example, years ago, the writer taught in a Chicago public school in a district which was just beginning to "turn black." The principal, became alarmed as the influx increased. On one occasion she whispered to him, "what are we going to do with all these negro children coming here?" She became conscious of the situation, and apologies continued for two years. Often white speakers will inquire what term to use in order to avoid being challenged when addressing meetings. The *New York Daily News* at its inception, inquired, in Harlem, for a designation of race. The word *colored* was advised. This it has consistently followed. The African Methodist Episcopal Church, and its later off-shoots, the A.M.E.Z. and the C.M.E. Churches, avoided the word, *negro;* likewise the National Association for the Advancement of Colored People. Even the organ of the latter organization is *A Record of the Darker Races.* More recently the National Negro Urban League has become simply the National Urban League. Add to these the Association for the Study of Negro Life and History, and the newest publication, the Journal of Negro Education, the cycle is completed, confusing but understandable. Strangest of all is the fact that the most rabid and uncompromising protagonist for Africa and things African, set up his organization as the *Universal Negro Improvement Association.*

All black authors use "Negro" except Dean Kelly Miller, in whose earlier works the word was never capitalized. All black editors use the word, capitalized, with the single excep-

tion of the *Chicago Defender* which has substituted for it the
word *Race*. The white press is gradually swinging into line
with a capital *N*.

Biblical literature has not a single reference to black men
as *negroes*, although black men figure repeatedly in Bible lore.
The literature of the middle ages with few exceptions used the
word *moor* or *blackamoor*, seldom *negro*.

When the Dutch traders brought *twenty negars* to the New
World, it is apparent that such reference to those Africans as
negars was solely a color designation without any relation to
breed or ethnic origin. Indeed those traders were not out on
an expedition to study ethnology or anthropology. They were
pious Christians, who had come over on *The Good Ship Jesus*
bringing human cargo to sell, for profit, in the marts of the
New World. It could not be expected that they would bother
to know whether they had Mandingoes, Woloffs, Krus, Fulani,
or any other combination of West Coast people.

Again, we do not find that there is a single African people
who call themselves *negro* as a tribal name. The fact that this
word has spread and has become more or less crystallized, furnishes no valid reason why it should be accepted.

If not strange, it is at least unique, that American-born
Africans become *negroes,* in common parlance, while American born Europeans or Asiatics, remain Italians, Poles, Koreans,
or Thibetans. Despite the fact that it is too late, indeed impossible, for American blacks to trace their lineage to any particular tribe, yet for all that they remain African, Afro-American, Ethiopian, Ethiopic, or again, if you will Hamitic. Instead
of *Afro-American,* Dr. James Weldon Johnson suggests *Afra-
merican,* a term which is slowly getting wider vogue.

Of course any of these terms can, and probably would, be
corrupted because of the general attitude of the white press.
The Japanese, for example, in order to rid themselves of the
term *Japs,* are beginning to turn to the word *Nippon* as the
official name of their country. This will do them no good, in
this country, because they will run directly into the terms, *Nips*
or *Nippies.*

Recently Chief Tschekedi, of Bechuanaland, South Africa ordered an Englishman flogged for the latter's alleged immorality with the women of that area. He was banished by the local representative of the British Government. At the instance of the Chief's mother, the British Crown ordered the suspension annulled and the Chief restored to his people. During the flare-up over this ruler's action, the word *negro* was not used in a single news-dispatch in either the British or American press. In each release this modern, upstanding African ruler was referred to as *Chief Tschekedi of the Bamangwato* and his mother as *Dowager Queen of the Bamangwato*.

When *smart writers*, in America, occasionally use the expression, *Senegambian in the wood pile*, they tend to run true on ethnology, but nevertheless they heighten the connotation which it is desired that the African at home and abroad, escape.

The word *negro*, strictly speaking and for the purposes to which it is put, is a betrayal of science and ethnic ideology; a misnomer which studied pressure keeps alive in the popular mind. For example, the French are gradually dropping the word *noir* for the word *negre* and the Germans are substituting the word *neger* for the word *schwartze*.

"What's in a name? A rose under any other name would smell as sweet? People of African descent, by whatever name they are called will be ill-treated just the same? Dignify the black race thus glorify the word and let the matter drop?" Well, these are alternatives which may be considered. Indeed a great deal could be done in regard to the latter alternative, if the word, in its vilest form, were not so current among the blacks themselves. Many of them broadcast it everywhere and on the slightest and most needless occasions, and then pretend to be angry when it is turned against them, even by white people who know that it is an abortive term. Let us note the way the world uses ridicule and scorn. The critics of the Germans today, for example, even among America's highest intellectuals, are referring to the Germans as *bosch, pagan, barbaric, savage*. They know that the things happening in Germany today are none too strange from the things happening at their very door here in

America. They know, too, that the culture of the Germans, which the world eagerly relished yesterday and in which it takes pride, even today, is not necessarily sullied by the present phase of German life. The world will not throw over German culture, tomorrow, any more than it has thrown over Greek, Roman, or modern French culture because unhappy breakdowns came after these cultures had been built. There is joy in the world, in some quarters, that Germany today, appears to a great disadvantage; fear and dread in other quarters that she may right herself and regain a commanding place in the world. Both attitudes are sharpened, quickened, by ridicule and boycott, deadly forces which scourge the hardiest individual or nation. The whole sordid business is largely a family fight, as of 1914, and more strictly so today. Its implications, lessons, and by-products, however, are not without meaning and interest to the black race.

Finally, the word *"Negro"* at its best is generally, a succinct way of expressing the popular concept of black folk in America. In spite of whatever opprobrium that it carries, there is, undoubtedly wrapped up in it, a record of achievement of which black men need not be ashamed. The word, at its worst, can be whatever is willed.

Basically, what is needed is education; unbiased instruction, that will lead to the recognition of peoples for what they are. This will require the honest preparation of simple texts in ethnology, ethnography and anthropology, and their findings placed in the schools and used by pulpit, press and platform. This can best be done by the exclusion of besetting or befogging talk about any utopian brotherhood of man.

Early Traces in the Ancient East

THIS theme will cover Southern Asia, especially India and Arabia; Southern Europe, Northern Africa, Egypt, Nubia, "Ethiopia," and the Sudan. The "true location of Cush and Ethiopia" and the number of such areas should be checked, preferably, in the following texts:

AZIKIWE, B. N. — "The Negro in Greek Myth", THE CRISIS, March, 1934
BALDWIN, JOHN D. — "Pre-Historic Nations", 1873, pp. 57-66, 306-334
BOAS, FRANZ — "Mind of Primitive Man", 1911
Question of Racial Purity—AMERICAN MERCURY, October, 1924
BUDGE, E. A. W. — "Annals of Nubian Kings", 1928 (see Piankhi, xliv)
BUDGE, WALLIS, SIR — "History of Ethiopia, etc.", 1928, Vol. I, Preface viii-xxiii
CUNARD, NANCY — "Negro", 1934
DELAFOSSE, M. — "Negroes of Africa", 1931, (Tr. by F. Fligelman) pp. 1-41
DUBOIS, W. E. B. — "The Negro", 1915, pp. 9-46, 245-246
ECKENSTEIN, L. — "Tutankh-Aten", 1924
FROBENIUS, LEO — "Voice of Africa", 1913, (Tr. by Gent)
GOBINEAU, COUNT DE — "Inequality of the Human Race", (See Baldwin, 316-322)
HADDON, A. C. — "Races of Man", 1925, pp. 37-58
"History of Anthropology", 1925, pp. 2-14, 138-139 (Thinkers Library)
HEEREN, — "African Researches"
"Bible", and any good Biblical Commentary
Specific Works for "Early Traces"
HIGGINS, GODFREY — "The Anacalypsis", 1834
HOLLINGSWORTH, F. N. — "Ethiopian Pyramids Give Up Ancient History", DEARBORN INDEPENDENT, July 8, 1922
JACOBI, H. M. — "Imperial Abyssinia" (ALL NATIONS MAGAZINE, January, 1933)
JOHNSTON, H. H. — "Backward Peoples, etc.", 1920, pp. 12-17 (chiefly India)
"Opening Up of Africa", viii, pp. 9-63, 38-94 (India)
LENORMANT, F. and E. CHEVALIER — Ancient History of the

East, 1870, Vol. II, pp. 64-101, 280-349
Here, will pass in review, the Adites, Joktanites, Jorham-
ites,Sabaens, etc., of Southern Arabia. Blacks were in
this area as early as 1500 B. C., intermingling freely
with the Arabs.
Records of this are shown in "Funeral Rituals" dated
in the XIXth Egyptian Lynasty. The hero of the ante-
Islamic Arabian romance, Antar, was a mulatto. (see p.
349)
LUDOLPHEUS, HIOB — "History of Ethiopia", 1682
MacCREAGH, GORDON — "Last of Free Africa", 1928
MAGOFFIN, R. V. D. — "Pyramids and Glory of Nubian Kings",
N. Y. TRIBUNE, January 19, 1930
"Was the Queen of Sheba a Negress?"
"Queen of Sheba Not an Ethiopian?" (Files of Sunday
editions, N. Y. AMERICAN, 1921 and 1928
"Abyssinia and King Theodore", ATLANTIC MONTHLY,
Vol. I, No. 138, June 25, 1933
"Nefertiti", N. Y. TIMES, June 25, 1933
"Face of the Sphinx", N. Y. AMERICAN, January 28, 1927
"African Popes?" (Souvenir Program, p. 16), Federated
Colored Catholics, Detroit, August, 1930
"St. Augustine, A Negro?" Catholic Weekly, AMERICA,
February 12, 1921, (Letters to the Editor)
"African Civilization", CRISIS, 1911
McKEE, OLIVER — "Abyssinia, An African Sovereign State",
CURRENT HISTORY, May, 1930
NORDEN, HERMANN — "Africa's Last Empire", 1930
NOTT and GLIDDON — "Types of Mankind"
PARKER, G. W. — "African Origin of Grecian Civilization",
JOURNAL OF NEGRO HISTORY, Vol. II
RAWLINSON, GEO. — "History of Egypt"
"Seven Great Monarchies", 1885, Vol. III, p. 28-41
ROGERS, J. A. — "World's Greatest Men of African Descent",
1931, pp. 1-17
SANDFORD, ARTHUR — "Making of Modern Abyssinia", CUR-
RENT HISTORY, February, 1924
SAYCE, A. H. — "Races of the Old Testament", 1925, pp. 51-60,
83-99, 126-150
SCHOLES, T. E. S. — "Glimpses of the Ages", 1905, pp. 223-235
SELIGMAN, C. G. — "Races of Africa", 1930, pp. 9-23, 52-95
(the "true negro")
VOLNEY, — "Ruins of Empire"
WEIGAL, ARTHUR — "Akhnaton, Pharaoh of Egypt", 1923

WENDEL, F. C. H. — "History of Egypt", pp. 66-106
WILLIAMS, G. W. — "History of the Negro Race", 1882, pp. 1-25, 443-460
WOODSON, C. G. — "Negro in Our History", 1922, pp. 1-14
ZINCKLE, F. B. — "Egypt of the Pharaohs", 1873, pp. 25-41, 168-169

Other works on the early traces can be checked up in the bibliographies of the authors cited above, especially DuBois, Woodson, Haddon, Budge, Johnston, Seligman, Delafosse. Note carefully what Dr. DuBois says in the Preface to "The Negro" and also his comment on standard writers, page 245. The untranslated work of L. J. Morié, Histoire de L'Ethiope (Nubie et Abyssinie), Depuis les temps les plus recules jusqu'a nos jours, 1904, is excellent parallel reading with the Work of Budge. More significant is the untranslated work of Frobenius, mentioned in the preface to this monograph. His Erlebte Erdteile and Das Unbekannte Afrika published in 1925 and the latest work, Kulturgeschichte Afrikas published in 1934.

Much periodical literature has permanent value. For example, the files of the National Geographic Magazine, Current History Magazine, Journal of Negro History, Crisis Magazine, Hammerton's Wonders of the Past in serial form, museum publications and scientific magazines dealing with race and civilization.

Teachers, especially, should immediately provide themselves with a copy of The Journal of Race Development, vol. I, April, 1911, for an article by A. F. Chamberlain, on The Contribution of the Negro to Human Civilization; a copy of Howard University Studies in History, November 1930, for an article by William L. Hansberry, on The Sources for the Study of Ethiopian History; and a copy of the Crisis, Magazine, July 1933, for an article by Alfred E. Smith on An Outline of the World History of the Negro in a Thousand Words, with "time line" Charts.

The historical novel, Dido, written in 1929 by Gertrude Atherton, plays up Iarbas, the Black King of Libya, whom Elissa (Dido) out-witted in the famous oxhide incident. "Iarbas," is probably, "Japon, King of the Zavecians," who gave to Libya the name, Zeugitana. The book is an excellent piece of light reading for this period.

Lacking a general history in this field, attention and interest can be best developed by centering upon pivotal events and great personalities, as, for example: Khafra, Amenemhat I and III, Usertesen I, Ra-Nehesi, Aahmes I, Nefertari, Thothmes III, and Hatshepsut, Akhnaton, Zerakh (Usarkon I), Shishak, and later Libyan kings; the Ethiopian kings: Kashta, Piankhi, Shabaka, Shabakata, Taharqua, Tanut-Amen; the Candaces of Meroe, the "Negroes of Pun," the Black Battalions of Una, during the Sixth Dynasty under Pepi I; the Joktanite and Jorhamite rule in Arabia. While stressing the magnificence of the personalities mentioned above also face directly, the smash of Ethiopian ascendancy by Usertesen III and the final failure of the later Ethiopian rulers of Egypt when they faced the Assyrian hosts, led by Sargon, Essarhaddon and Asshurbanipal. Likewise show how the rulers of Ethiopia, since Menelik II, weakened themselves and finally fell under the Italian yoke.

A SUGGESTION

Touch the high points that have been developed in the Ethiopia. Use the works of Morié and Budge mentioned elsewhere. Suggested topics on Ethiopia are as follows;

Transfer of power from Meroë to Aksum—4th Century A. D., 56-98

EZANA (Abreha I) — "Constantine of Ethiopia", 242-258

JOHN I, 1275 A. D., — First to use the title, "King of Kings of Ethiopia"—but in name only. 285

THEODORE II, — 1855-1868; 492-519; Herald of Modern Ethiopia

JOHN IV, — 1868-1889; 520 et seq.

MENELIK II, — 1889-1913; 528-542, the first, "King of Kings of Ethiopia" in fact and name; creator of Ethiopia The nominal rule of Lidj Iasu, 1908-1915

RAS TAFARI and QUEEN ZAWDITU, — "co-rulers", 1916-1931

RAS TAFARI, — crowned "Haille Selassie I, Emperor of Ethiopia, 1932, ruling today.

Mulatto Egypt would be re-conquered by the blacks to the

South, but for the strength of the "Great Powers," who, themselves, not content with the destruction of 1914 have schemed and are ready today, for a better and bigger Armageddon.

(Supplementary Book List)

BREUIL, ABBE H. — L'Afrique Prehistorique, 1930
BURKITT, M. C. — South Africa's Past in Stone and Paint, 1928
BOAS, FRANZ — Anthropology and Modern Life, 1928
FIELD, HENRY — Races of Mankind, Leaflet No. 30, Field Museum, Chicago, 1933
FROBENIUS, LEO — Early African Culture as an Indication of Present Potentialities, Annals of the American Academy of Political Sciences (tr. by Becker) November 1928, Vol. CXXXX, 153-165
GOLDENWEISER, A. A. — Early Civilization, An Introduction to Anthropology, 1922
History, Psychology and Culture, 1933
GOODWIN, A. J. H. and VAN RIET LOWE — Stone Age Culture in South Africa, Annals of the South African Museum, XXVII, 1929
HARLAN, H. V. — A Caravan Journey Through Abyssinia, National Geographic, June 1915
HOOTON, E. A. — Up from the Ape, 1931 (Reviewed in the CRISIS, November, 1932
HOUSTON, DRUSILLA D. — Wonderful Ethiopians, 1925
JOHNSON, E. A. — Adam Versus Ape-Man and Ethiopia, 1932
KEITH, SIR ARTHUR — The Antiquity of Man, 1915
Certain Factors Concerned in the Evolution of Human Races, Journal Royal Anthropological Institute, 1916, Vol. XLVI, 10
Differentiation of Mankind into Racial Types, Reports of the British Asso. (Bournemouth)
Reports of the British Asso. 1919, P/275
Reports of the British Asso. (Lancet, 1919, Vol. II, 553)
Race and Nationality From an Anthropoligist's Point of View, 1919
Adaptational Machinery Concerned in the Evolution of Man's Body, NATURE, 1923, Vol. CXII, 252
Ethos, The Problem of Race Considered from a New Point of View, 1930
The Evolution of Human Races, Journal, Royal Anthropological Institute, Vol. LVIII, 305
Place of Prejudice in Modern Civilization, 1931
Races of Mankind, Leaflet No. 30, 1933, Field Museum of Natural History, Chicago. (See also Leaflet No. 26 on the Early History of Man.) Both Leaflets have excellent bibliographies.

LAUFER, BERTHOLD — Races of Mankind, Leaflet No. 30, Field
Museum, Chicago

LEAKY, L. S. B. *et al* — Stone Age Cultures of Kenya Colony,
1933
Leaky's book raised great discussion last year. It con-
firmed the findings of Dr. Hans Reck in the Oldoway
district in Kenya in 1913. This "Oldoway" man—(Negroid?) was hailed as the most "modern" of "homo
sapiens" much to the disgust of Sir Arthur Keith. Sir
Arthur denied the "negroid" assertion on the ground that
the "Oldoway Man" was too "intellectual" to be a
Negro. (See NEW YORK TIMES: 3-24-32; 4-19-32; 8-3-
32; 8-7-32; 7-25-33)

McLEAN, M. D. — African Civilization, CRISIS, 1911

MOORE, W. R. — Coronation Days in Addis Ababa, NATIONAL·
GEOGRAPHIC MAGAZINE, June, 1931

NORDEN, HERMAN — The Black Jews of Abyssinia, TRAVEL
MAGAZINE, January, 1930

OSBORNE, H. F. — Men of the Old Stone Age, 1916

OSGOOD, W. H. — Nature and Man in Ethiopia, NATIONAL
GEOGRAPHIC MAGAZINE, August, 1928

PERINGUEY, L. — The Stone Ages of South Africa, Annals of
the South African Museum, VIII, 1912

REISNER, G. H. — Expeditions, Harvard University Publications

SOUTHARD, A. E. — Modern Ethiopia, NATIONAL GEOGRAPHIC
MAGAZINE, 1931

SMITH, G. ELIOT — Search for Man's Ancestors, 1931

Summary of Native States

THIS PERIOD is a fruitful field for orientation in relation to the principles used by native leaders in the process of nation and empire-building.

Definite drill should be done in connection with the Empire of Ghana, the Almoravide Movement, the Kingdoms of Benin, Diara and Soso, the Empires of the Songhoy (Songhois, Sanghai) the Mandingo, (Mende, Mali, Mande) and the Mossi.

Personalities in these struggles should be cast in high relief, for example, Yussof, 1087, Mansa-Musa, 1213, Gongo-Musa (Kankan- Musa) 1325, Sonni Ali, 1468, Mohammed Askia, 1493, down through the centuries to Samory (Samori Touré), who, in 1898, was made prisoner by the French, after he had held the West Coast against them for twenty years, 1878 to 1898.

In July, 1934, there were in London, two Missions of native rulers, the one headed by the Hon. Nana Sir Ofori Atta, Paramount Chief (Omanhene) of Akim Abuakwa, Gold Coast, and the other by Sultan Hassan, of Sokoto, Abdullah Bayaro dan Abbas, Emir of Kano and Usaman, Emir of Gwando. This Mission was from Northern Nigeria and represents the Arab influence of the Eleventh Century. The British press represented them as not being of the same "race" as the Mission from the Gold Coast.

The Gold Coast Delegation placed before Parliament its grievances against administrative abuses, lack of popular representation, the Sedition Bill, which makes the bare possession of alleged seditious literature a crime. It also protested against the delay in constructing the water works system and the shamefully low prices of the economic products of the people.

The Mohammedan Delegation was chiefly interested in

trade, the development of waterways in its area and the processes by which the British, fashion native products into finished goods or foodstuffs.

Though the members of the Delegation were housed and
sumptuously fed in London's best hotels and served teas with
strawberries and cream, sweet cakes and kola nuts, the British
did not overlook the "little matter" of taking them to Portsmouth where they could see giant Dreadnaughts, symbols of
the might and power of Britain.

The choice of 1878, as a typical turning point, is made for
several reasons. World politics and international relations were
at fever heat. The distracted nations in Europe, caught in these
complications, sought to ease their pains by stretching themselves out in the African Sun.

Germany, inept and never secure in Africa, was in (1878)
flushed with her victory over France, 1870-71. She forced an
international conference and the treaty-making powers, to meet
in Berlin. The "Aryan" Bismarck, singing "Deutschland, Uber
Alles" and dreaming of "Der Tag," scorned "non-Aryan"
whites and balked at taking colonies of blacks who were still,
"lesser breeds without the law." But the hands of the German
Colonial Society and those of Dr. Nachtigal, bent the "Iron
Chancellor" and seized black morsels in Africa which later,
1914-18, turned into wormwood and gall.

Within a brief span, 1878-1884, England and France
came to grips over control in Egypt. France snatched Tunis
from Italy and gave the latter an excuse to seize Tripoli and
later enter the Triple Alliance with Germany and Austria.

Leopold I, of Belgium, stood in the offing ready to put
over his infamous deal in the Congo through the Berlin and
Brussels Conferences 1878 and 1884. The rape of Africa
was on.

Turmoil in the Sudan under the "Mahdi" and the Ashanti
Wars on the West Coast had quieted down, to the advantage
of England and France. Meanwhile disorders increased in
Ethiopia due to the defeat of Theodore II, 1868, and the weak-
ness of John IV, 1868-1889. Out of the turmoil in West

Africa, the Sudan, and the intrigue in the Nile Valley, stepped the incomparable Menelik II, who halted the despoilers of his land and saved Ethiopia as the leading, free native government ruled by black men in Africa.

South Africa had long lain in the shadows. Moshesh, Khama, Chaka, Lobengula, Dingaan and Cetywayo had done their best and their worst. All had passed on save Khama, who lingered until 1923 in Bechuanaland and Lobengula who made his last stand against white penetration in 1893.

The chief aids in dealing with this Theme are:

ARON, ROBERT — "France's Treatment of Her Negroes", CURRENT HISTORY, February, 1924

BLYDEN, E. W. — "Christianity, Islam and the Negro"

BROOKES, E. H. — "Color-Bar in South Africa", CURRENT HISTORY, July, 1932

BRYCE, J. — "Impressions of South Africa", 1900

DAVIS, ROBERT — "Tshaka, The Great Zulu", 1934

DELAFOSSE, M. — "Negroes of Africa", 42-140 (Foundation of this Theme)

DUBOIS, W. E. B. — "The Negro", 47-78, 79-102; Bib. 246-249

ELLIS, A. B. — "Tshi-Speaking People, etc."
"Ewe-Speaking People, etc."
"Yoruba-Speaking People, etc."
(G. W. Ellis is especially valuable for an understanding of the "Vai" people, who have developed an alphabet with written language and literature; A. B. Ellis, not related to the former, has done the same thing for the Yorubas and the Ewes. Both of these books work well with Delafosse.)

ELLIS, G. W. — "Negro Culture in West Africa", (Footnotes, 21-25)

GIDE, ANDRE — "Travels in the Congo,etc.", 1929
"Message from the King of Buganda", CRISIS, June, 1932
"Khama, The Enlightened King, etc.", N. Y. TIMES, May 6, 1923
"Publications of The Phelps-Stokes Foundation, New York

GOLLOCK, G. A. — "Sons of Africa", (Brief Biographies)

HADDON, A. C. — "Races of Man", 37-58

HARDY, GEO. — "Les Religions Fetichistes de L'Afrique Noire" LA REVUE DE PARIS, July, 1933

HARRIS, J. C. — "Khama, The Great African Chief" (Bechuanaland) 1922
"The South African Native" (by The South African Native Races Com.) 1909

HOFMEYER, JAN H. — "South Africa", 1932

SUMMARY OF NATIVE STATES   171

JOHNSTON, H. H. — "Opening Up for Africa", 1928, 115-136,
    152-191 (White penetration)
    "Story of My Life"
KENWORTHY, J. M. — "Africa, World Tinder-Box", N. Y.
    TIMES, May 22, 1932
LEWIS, W. — "The Blue Sultan of Africa", N. Y. TRIBUNE,
    January 17, 1932
LOVELL, R. I. — "The Struggle for South Africa", 1934
MAUE, D. R. — "The Basutos, etc.", CURRENT HISTORY, August,
    1927
MILLIN, GERTRUDE — "The South Africans", 1927
    "God's Step-Children"
MOFOLO, THOS. — "Chaka", 1931
MORRIS, N. — "The Riddle of Mkawa-Mkawa's Skull", N. Y.
    WORLD MAGAZINE, December 14, 1930
    NOTE: A special provision of the Versailles Treaty—Art.
    246—ordered the Germans to return the skull to the
    Wahehes, Tanganyika, East Africa, of whom Mkawa
    was Paramount Chief.
RATTRAY, R. S. — "Ashanti"
ROGERS, J. A. — "World's Greatest Men of African Descent",
    25-34
STAFFORD, A. O. — "Tarikh-es-Soudan", JOURNAL OF NEGRO
    HISTORY, Vol. II
STAFFORD, A. C. — "Antar, etc.", JOURNAL OF NEGRO HISTORY,
    Vol. I
SELIGMAN, C. G. — "Races of Africa", ("True Negro", 52-95)
    (Bantu, 181-232)
WILLIAMS, G. W. — "History of the Negro Race" (26-49,
    250-269)
WILLIAMS, S. J. & JOSEPH, J. — "Hebrewism in West Africa"
WOODSON, C. G. — "Negro in Our History", 6-12; (Foot-
    notes, 1-14)

With *Sons of Africa* by Gollock and *World's Greatest
Men of African Descent* by Rogers as a foundation, a larger list
of intellectuals, statesmen, and warriors can be made by careful selection from DuBois, Delafosse, Budge and George W.
Williams. The most compact presentation of Native States will
be found in Delafosse, 42-140.

Pupils should become familiar with the meaning of such
terms as, Monomotapa, Zymbabwe, Table of the Sun, Bantu,
aggry beads, fetisches, maribout, griots, Tarik-el-Sudan. Considerable interest can be developed by devoting some time to
the origin, involution and meaning of certain place names and
tribal names.

An examination of the book-lists issued by the *Crisis Magazine* and by Dr. Woodson will indicate works with an abundance of folk-lore, myths, fables, and tradition. Wherever incursion of blood from the East and North have over-laid Africa, it is more than likely that much of it was blood that had once been carried from Africa to those areas, flowing back to its original base. For example, when the recent Virginia Race Purity Law was about to be logically carried out, it was found that many outstanding "whites" would be caught in the net. Quietly the whole matter was dropped. Pupils should be shown how similar practices have shorn African peoples of cultural appendages.

Classes should be provided with large wall maps of Africa issued by French, American and English publishers; usually the French map will best serve, in many cases. Maps of ancient and mediaeval native states should be on hand. Students, as a rule, will be glad to make them. When all the native states have been covered, stress the organization of the peoples of Uganda, Swaziland, and Basutoland as modern native types that might well be admitted into the family of nations.

Liberia and Sierra Leone

SINCE the founding of Liberia was a sort of gesture at "repatriation," it would be well to partially cover the question of slavery and the slave trade before dealing with Liberia proper. Such partial treatment would include slavery from the advent of the Portuguese in the Fifteenth Century to the founding of Liberia in 1821. Also show the Mohammedan phase of slavery.

Emphasis should be placed upon areas from which the slaves were chiefly drawn, centers in Europe to which they were chiefly carried, and the enormity of the traffic to the new world. To native revolts on the West Coast should be added the successful revolt of the Haitians at the end of the Eighteenth Century. Types of "slavery," "pawning," and "indentured service," current in Africa today, should be aptly reviewed at this point.

The major discussion of slavery should be reserved for the Theme on the United States and Latin America.

References:

DuBois, W. E. B. — "Suppression of the African Slave Trade" "The Negro", 69-72; Bib. 246-247
HALLGREN, M. A. — "Liberia in Shackles", NATION, August 16, 1933
JOHNSTON, H. H. — "Liberia", (2 vols.) 1906 "Backward Peoples", 1920
JONES, W. N. — "Liberia Today and Tomorrow", BALTIMORE AFRO-AMERICAN, December 30, 1933 to March 17, 1934. (It is hoped that this serial will appear in pamphlet form. It is needed for the present scene.)
His Excellency, Honorable Edwin Barclay, President of Liberia, "The Case of Libera'. Abstract from his original message to the Liberian Legislature, October 25, 1933. (CRISIS MAGAZINE, February, 1934)
MacPERSON, T. H. T. — "History of Liberia"
SCHUYLER, GEORGE — "Slaves Today", 1932 "Is Liberia a Slave State?" (Serial in the NEW YORK EVENING POST, June 27, 1931, etc.)

STARR, F. — "Liberia", 1913
WALTON, L. — "Liberia", N. Y. TRIBUNE, December 3, 1933
WOODSON, C. G. — "Negro in Our History", Chapter II
    League of Nations Reports on Liberia:—
        Geneva, January 26, 1932
        Geneva, May 17, 1932
        Geneva, August 6, 1932
        Geneva, September 12, 1932
        Geneva, September 24, 1932
        Geneva, September 27, 1932 (in French)

International Relations

(*Protectorates and Mandates Since* 1878)

IN THE preceding section a thumb-nail sketch was given of international relations as they focused themselves around 1878. Data for this section will be found chiefly in an assortment of "standard" works on Modern European History, and the proceedings and publications of the League of Nations and the World Court. These can be secured from the League of Nations Association, New York.

References:

ARAQUISTAN, LUIS — "La Angonia Antillana", 1928

BUELL, RAYMOND LESLIE — "Backward" Peoples Under the Mandate System. CURRENT HISTORY MAGAZINE, June, 1924
Black and White in South Africa, Annals of the Am. Acad. of Polit. and So. Sci., November, 1928, Vol. CXXXX, 299-316
West Africa, ibid, 319-331

BUNCHE, R. J. — French Colonial Adm. In Togoland and Dahomey Tappan Prize, Harvard, 1934

CHATER, M. — Under the South African Union, NAT. GEOG. MAGAZINE, April, 1931

FERRIS, W. H. — "The African Abroad", 1913

JOHNSON, CHAS. S. — "The Negro in American Civilization", 1930, p. 3-15

JOHNSTON, H. H. — "Backward Peoples", etc., 1920
"Negro in the World War", 1910
"Opening Up of Africa", 1911, 142-252
"Story of My Life", 1923

KEITH, SIR ARTHUR — "Place of Prejudice in Modern Civilization", 1931

LOGAN, RAYFORD — "Anglo-Egyptian Sudan, A Problem in International Relations (JOURNAL OF NEGRO HISTORY, Vol. XVI)

LOGAN — "Operation of Mandate System in Africa", (JOURNAL OF NEGRO HISTORY, Vol. XIII)

MATTHEWS, BASIL — "The Clash of Color", 1924

MOON, T. P. — Syllabus on International Relations, 1925.
(Study carefully, Part Three, "Imperialism and World
Politics", 37-73, as follows:
    Central Africa, 43-44
    South Africa, 45-46
    Abyssinia and the Sudan, 46
    North Africa, 46-48
    In the Pacific, 55-57
    Latin America, 57-61
    Review of the Colonial Policies of the Chief Imperialist
        Nations, 61-67)
PERHAM, MARGERY — "The Future of East Africa", LONDON
TIMES, (Serial) August 13, 1931
WHITE, WALTER — "Color Line in Europe" (Annals, American
Academy of Political and Social Science, Vol. CXXXX,
November, 1928. pp. 331-337)
ZIMMERN, ALFRED — "Study of International Relations", 1931
Congress and Treaty of Berlin, 1878
Berlin and Brussels Conferences, 1884
Anglo-German Agreement, 1890
Fashoda Affair, 1898
Belgian Annexation, 1908
Algeciras Conference, 1906
Agadir Incident, 1911
Present proposals to placate Germany by "relieving" Portugal
of Angola and giving that to Germany; an outright "gift"
of Liberia to Germany or the "restoration" of certain
areas formerly held by Germany.
League of Nations Publications:
    Official Journal, Minutes of the Sixth Committee, Supple-
        ment No. 19, September 1923 (Entry of Ethiopia into
        the League sponsored by Italy)
    Official Journal, No. 11, November 1926 (British and
        Italian Interests in Abyssinia)
    Dispute Between Abyssinia and Italy. No. C 49 M 22 VII.
        January 17, 1935
    Dispute Between Ethiopia and Italy. No. C 230 M 114 VII.
        June 12, 1935
    Dispute Between Ethiopia and Italy. No. C 340 M 171 VII.
        September 11, 1935 (Memorandum by the Italian Govern-
        ment on the Situation in Ethiopia)
    Dispuae Between Ethiopia and Italy. Official Journal,
        Supplement No. 145. October 11, 1935 (Co-ordination
        Committee)
    Dispute Between Ethiopia and Italy. No. C 225 M 137 VII.
        May 12, 1936
    Dispute Between Ethiopia and Italy. No. 125 Co-ordina-
        tion Committee. June 2, 1936

Royal Institute of International Affairs. (London) Information
Paper No. 16. July, 1935. "Abyssinia and Italy"
These League Publications may be secured from the League of
Nations Bureau, 8 West 40th Street, New York. These
with allied information will furnish invaluable data for term
reports or thesisses baseed on Ethiopia.

In July, 1934 notice was given in the press that 200,000
"lost" natives (black) had been discovered in New Guinea,
probably "hidden" there for upwards of 5,000 years. They are
said to be of "Semitic Origin."

Mr. E. W. P. Chinnery, British Anthropologist, described
them as follows, *New York Times*, July 31,—

> There is little doubt that some civilized race lived in these
> uplands centuries ago and passed on. We found stone mortars
> such as the ancient Egyptians used for crushing grain, but the
> present day natives did not know how to use them. We found
> the natives using ornamented clay whistles unlike anything ever
> seen in New Guinea, but strangely similar to those found in
> South America.*****
> Physically they are fine healthy blacks not unlike their
> neighbors in other parts of the island, but much stronger and
> sturdier.*****
> It is a pretty big responsibility to add 200,000 natives to the
> British Empire and make sure they won't be exploited.***
> I don't expect any trouble unless gold is found in the new
> lands. Then prospectors will pour in and it will be difficult to
> keep the country for the natives.

Of course these people will be robbed. This will not be a
new problem for the Mandates Commission is under the aegis of
"White Australia." A missionary has entered a plea that these
"new" people be not clothed lest they lose their "simplicity of
outlook" and develop, "vice and immorality."

Finally, students should become familiar with the theory
of "A," "B," and "C," Mandates. Thus from the Covenant of
the League of Nations:-

"A" MANDATES
(Palestine, Syria and Mesopotamia (Irak))

Communities which have reached a stage of development
where their existence as independent nations can be provisionally recognized subject to the rendering advice and assistance
by a Mandatory until they are able to stand alone.

NOTE: Irak has been permitted by England to join the League.

"B" MANDATES

(Former German Colonies in Central Africa, Togoland in West Africa and German East Africa). These are reputed to be areas in which:

. . . it is recognized that self-government is impossible and that the Mandatories must carry on their administration to certain safeguards in the interest of the native population, and to guarantees of economic equality to nationals of all States Members of the League.

NOTE: Theoretically no land can be taken from them.

"C" MANDATES

(South West Africa and the former German Possessions in the Pacific)

These areas:

. . . are subject to the same safe-guards for interest of the indigenous populations as the "B" territories, but can best be administered,—states the Covenant of the League of Nations —as integral portions of the territory of the Mandatory.

NOTE: The Constitution (Covenant) of the League of Nations provides for the wholesale seizure and transfer of these lands.

Raymond Leslie Buell, in his article, *"Backward" Peoples Under the Mandate System,* Current History Magazine, June, 1924 shows that 17,500,000 people have been caught in this mandate-web, 11,000,000 of whom are native Africans.

Africans in Latin America

A MORE careful study of these areas is needed because they have assumed greated importance. The new policy of *"The Good Neighbor"* of the present Roosevelt administration, is beginning to heal old wounds in Pan-American Relations. In 1917, a gesture of citizenship was extended to Puerto Rico. Since 1929 Santo Domingo has been on the way to stabilization. Cuba, still in the shadows of revolution and the Platt Amendment, is striving for internal adjustment and accord with the United States. Haiti is ready to go on her own. Within the welter of conflict in these areas, we have an interest, historic and present. For example, Colonel Fulgencia Batista, the mulatto military leader in the Cuban Revolution of 1933 has echoed the mightier work of Antonio Maceo of an earlier day.

Among the leaders in the arts of peace in Cuba was Don Guilberto Gomez-Ferrer, editor and publisher, whose death March, 1933, at 78, removed a steadying hand in the internal affairs of that republic.

Among the influence that tend to create rifts among the people in these communities is the book, *La Agonia Antillana* (*Agony of the Antilles"*) by Luis Araquistain, widely reviewed in 1928 in the American press under the caption, *"Black Blood Simmers in the Caribbean Melting Pot."*

The book was acclaimed in Spain but condemned in Cuba by conservatives and many liberals. It is prohibited in the latter by government edict. This means, naturally, that copies smuggled in will bring a higher price and will be read with avidity. The Latin-American press and popular opinion generally appeared about equally divided in regard to the book. Senor Araquistain hangs his argument on the following pegs:

. . . the work of political and social decadence initiated in this archipelago (the Antilles) by different European nations, —with the exception of Spain, the only one which in its colonies maintained the predominance of the white race—is being completed by the United States. Spain Europeanized her possessions, while France, England, Holland and Denmark—and now the North American Republic—Africanized theirs; destroying the germs of nationality and white civilization which the earliest colonizers bore from Europe.

. . . There came a time when Cuba ran the risk of becoming Africanized like Barbados, like the other black Antilles. It was when in 1762 Havana fell into the hands of the English. During the months of British control it is calculated that more than 10,000 African negroes entered the island.

With Cuba restored to Spain the importation of slaves continued, but not to such an extent as for them radically to replace white labor as in the other Antilles, but only to supply the scarcity of hands. There was, nevertheless, a period during which the negroes outnumbered the whites—an 1827 census enumerates a total population of 704,487; consisting of 311,057 whites and 393,436 negroes, slave and free.

Though Araquistain's attacks on the colonial methods of the Great Powers especially on what he calls *"Yankee Imperialism,"* brought glee in Spain, his assertion that the population (Cuban) is not absolutely pure white, aroused feeling that caused it to be banned by the Government.

ARAQUISTAN, LUIS — "La Angonia Antillana", 1928

BEALS, CARLTON — "The Crime of Cuba", 1933

BERNARD, L. L. & J. S. — The Negro in Relation to Other Races in Latin-America, Annals of the American Academy of Political Science, Vol. CXXXX, Nov. 1928, pp. 316-317

CLEVEN, N. A. N. — Convention between Spain and Holland regulating the Return of Deserters and Fugitive Slaves, etc., Vol. XIV

Plans for Colonizing Liberated Slaves in Hispanic America, Vol. XI

"Thee Negro in Cuba in the 17th Century", Vol.XIII

COCHIN, M. — "Results of Emancipation", 1864

DuBois, W. E. B. — "The Negro", 1915, 160-182; Bib. 249-250

FERRIS, W. H. — "The African Abroad", 2 Vols., 1913

JOHNSON, CHAS. S. — "Negro in American Civilization", 1930, p. 3-15

"The Negro in American Civilization", 1930

JOHNSON, H. H. — " Negro in the New World", 1910

"Backward Peoples, etc.", 1920

"Story of My Life", 1923

LOGAN, RAYFORD — "The Cuban Revolution", 1933 Baltimore
Afro-American (serial) August 16, 1933
MARTIN, MARGARET R. — "The Last Word in Cuba", CRISIS,
May, 1933. THE JOURNAL OF NEGRO HISTORY
MOON, P. T. — "Syllabus on International Relations", 57-61
SHOTWELL, J. T. — "Whither Latin-America", 1934
VANDERCOOK, JOHN W. — "Black Majesty" (See special bib.
204-207)
WRIGHT, I. A. — Digest of Documents in the Archives of the
Indies, Seville, Spain, bearing on the Negroes of Cuba, etc.,
Vol. XIV
Indies, Seville, Spain, bearing on the Negroes of Cuba, etc.,
"Horrors of Santo Domingo", ATLANTIC MONTHLY, August,
1862 (serial) Chap. III, pp. 212-223
NOTE: This article will furnish leads to important books,
notably the works of Herrara and Oviedo. It will also
help to clarify thee true relation of Father Las Casas
and Bishop Ximenes to the slavee trade in Latin-America.
Additional information can be gained on this point from
the Public Library, 135th Street, (Harlem) New York.
(Works of Thatcher and Helps.)
Dawes Commission Report on Santo Domingo, 1929
Publications of the Foreign Policy Association, New York
(Raymond Leslie Buell, Director)
Publications of the Pan-American Union, Washington, D. C.

SOUTH AMERICA

A.—(Exclusive of Brazil)

B.—Brazil

A.

The free intermingling of the races in South America
largely obscures definite traces of the African.

The black wave, faintest perhaps in Chili, rises appreciably
in Venezuela and Colombia and comes to high tide in Brazil.
To mention Latin America and Brazil should instantly bring
to mind, Bolivar, the great patriot who used blacks and mulattoes to help him in the establishment of independence in Bo-
livia. Bolivar himself was once a refugee in Haiti; St. Peter
Claver in Cartagena, *"Slave of Slaves Forever,"* who gave his
life for the blacks in that old town in Colombia and Palmares,
the Negro Numantia, in Brazil. In South America we find the
Bush Negroes — Djukas, Dutch Maroons — who rebelled

against their Dutch Masters in Guiana, fled into the hinterland and set up a government for themselves. High up on the honor roll of great men, from this area, is the Right Reverend Francisco Xavier de Luna Victoria y Castro (Bishop Luna Victoria), the first great Churchman of African descent to wear the mitre in the western world, 1751-1760. Indeed it is probable that he was the first Catholic bishop, white or black, to be so honored in the Americas. Ante-dating Bishop Victoria by about two centuries was the Blessed Martin de Porras, of Peru, a contemporary of St. Rose of Lima.

Again on this honor roll is the Right Reverend Sylveria Gomez Pimentar, who was raised to the Bishopric in Marianno, Brazil in 1902. In Latin American annals Africa can claim the *"Negro, Stephen Dorantes (Estavanico)"* the guide and scout of Father Marcos of Nizza. Estavanico was a companion of Cabeza de Vaca, in the journey across the continent, 1528-1536, and is the discoverer of *"The Seven Cities of Cibola,"* the area known today as New Mexico.

Much is yet to be done by the research student to bring Latin-American sources into bolder relief.

B.—BRAZIL

Only one additional statement need be added to the above foreword in order to get the proper setting for Brazil.

The population of that country is a little more than half African and Indian. In the city of Bahia, capital of the State of Bahia, there are about 300,000 inhabitants, nearly 250,000 of whom are of African descent.

Such a proportion holds good for the rest of the State of Bahia. Such preponderance is due to the fact that Bahia was a distributing point for the Portuguese slave trade.

References:

BANDELIER, FANNY — "Journey of Alvar Numez Cabeza de Vaca", 1905
BOYCE, W. D. — "South America", 1912
    NOTE: Boyce, always inimical to our interests, neverthe-
    less, this travel book of his is valuable for his occasional

hint, suggestions and sometimes solid facts in which we are interested.

In a 640 page work treating all South America, he devotes little less than one-sixth (443-546) to Brazil, and 17 pages (547-564) to "Three Guianas", the region made famous by the Bust Negroes—Djukas, Dutch Maroons—of whom Vandercook wrote in 1926, Khan in 1931 and Herschkovitz, this year, 1934.

DuBois, W. E. B. — "The Negro", 160-182; bib. 248-249
Herschkovitz, Melville — "Rebel Destiny", 1934
Journal of Negro History: —
    Adams, Jane E. — "Brazilian Slave Trade", Vol. X
    Alexander, H. B. — "Brazilian and United States Slavery, etc.", Vol. VII
    Chapman, Chas. P. — "Palmares, the Negro Numantia", Vol. V
    Kunst, Karl — "Negroes of Guatemala During the 17th Century", Vol. I
    Rippy, J. F. — "Negro Colonization Project in Mexico", 1895, Vol. VI
Kahn, M. C. — "Djuka" (People of Dutch Guiana) 1931
McEntire, W. F. — "An American Negro Catholic Bishop, The Lamp", Graymoor, N. Y. March 15, 1915 (Bishop Luna Victoria)
Tomlinson, Edward — "Brazil, Land of Contrasts", Current History, December, 1930
Vandercook, J. W. — "Tom Tom", 1926
Woodson, C. G. — "Negro in Our History", 1922, 28-33
Publications of the Pan American Union, Washington, L. C.
Publications of the Foreign Policy Society, N. Y.

HAITI

Unique in the annals of history is the Haitian Republic. It is the sole example of an enslaved people, who rose against their masters, drove them out and set up an independent government of their own.

The careers of Louverture, Dessalines and Christophe, represent a re-birth, in the new world, of the spirit of the ancient Ethiopian kings; of Samory, Behanzin, the Askias, and other builders of empire in West Africa; of Theodore II and Menelek II in Abyssinia (modern Ethiopia), of Moshesh-we, Dingaan, Chaka, Lobengula, and Khama in South Africa.

The Citadel of Christophe at Milot, three thousand feet above the sea, is but a flash of the black man's urge for massive building as shown in certain ruins in the Nile Valley, the West Coast and the Zymbabwe in South Africa.

When Dessalines tore the "white" out of the tri-color of France, he not only signalized the spirit and power of the new Haiti, but he represented a faint echo of the might of Piankhi, who subdued twenty rebellious princes and set up Ethiopian rulers as Kings of Upper and Lower Egypt.

The successful revolt in Haiti had beneficial results for America. Had Napoleon subdued the island, the whole of the Mississippi Valley would have been endangered, a fact which Thomas Jefferson was not slow to see. On the other hand, when in 1822 the Panama Congress was to have met in Washington, Congress yielded to pleas that the sessions be rejected, lest the blacks in Washington see representatives of their victorious kinsmen in Haiti being received as equals, at the White House and riding in state through the streets of the National Capitol. (See Muzzy, D. S., American History, unrevised ed., 176-177)

By this action Pan-American good-will, never much at best, was delayed until 1886 until a sort of drowsy gesture under Blaine revived the situation. The American occupation of Haiti, 1915-1934, created suspicion, was a source of irritation and a standing threat to all Latin-America. The withdrawal of troops from Haiti —July-August 1934 —may tend to maintain the theory of the "Good Neighbor."

BELLEGARDE, DANTES — "L'Occupation Americaine D'Haiti Ses Consequences Morales et Economiques", 1929
"Un Haitien Parle", 1934
"Pour Une Haiti Heureuse", 1929
DENNY, H. N. — "Proud Haiti, etc.", N. Y. TIMES, Oct. 9, 1932
DORSAINVIL, J. C. — "Manuel D'Histoire D'Haiti"
"Quelque Vues Politiques et Morales" (Questions Haitiennes) 1934
"Vodou et Névrose" (Médico Sociolgie) 1931
DuBois, H. E. W. — "The Negro", 1915, 169-178, bib. 249-250
FERRIS, W. H. — "The African Abroad", 2 Vols., 1913
HUGGINS, WILLIS N. — "Haiti in Transition", (Report of the Haitian Afro-American Chamber of Commerce)
JOHNSON, CHAS. S. — "The Negro in American Civilization", 1930, p. 3-15
LOGAN, RAYFORD — "Education in Haiti", 1933

AFRICANS IN LATIN AMERICA   185

SIMPSON, G. R. — "Touissant Louverture", (Biography in French,
    1933
VANDERCOOK, JOHN — "Black Majesty", 1928 (bib. 204-207)
WAXMAN, PERCY — "The Black Napoleon", 1931
WHITTIER, J. G. — Poetical Works—Touissant Louverture p. 53-56
JOURNAL OF NEGRO HISTORY:—
BROWN, G. W. — "Haiti and the United States", Vol. VIII
CLEVEN, N. A. N. — "The First Panama Mission and Congress
    of the United States", Vol. XIII
JOHNSTON, H. H. — "Backward Peoples, etc.", 1920
    "The Negro in the New World", 1910
LOKKE, CARL L. — "The LeClerc Instructions", Vol. X
MARSHALL, HARRIET G. — "The Story of Haiti"
RIDDELL, W. R. — "Notes on the Slave in Nouvelle, France",
    Vol. VIII
WESLEY, C. H. — "Struggle of Haiti and Liberia for Recog-
    nition", Vol. II
Publications of the League of Nations, Geneva, and New York
Publication of the Pan-American Union, Washington, D. C.
Publications of the Foreign Policy Association, New York
Report of the Forbes Commission
Report of the United States Commission on Education in Haiti.
    (Moton Commission) 1931

Information of Martinique and Guadeloupe may be secured
from the French Colonial Office. The peoples in these areas
send representatives to the Chamber of Deputies in Paris. Additional interest (in Martinique) rests in the controversy concerning Josephine, considered a mulatto, who became the first wife
of the great Napoleon, first Consul and Emperor of France,
1804-1815.

THE BRITISH WEST INDIES

Though the blacks in the British West Indies did not
achieve independence nor rise to the heights of military glory
as was done in Haiti, nevertheless they fill, with distinction,
many positions of honor and trust in the civil, political and
judicial life in all the islands.

The black British West Indian Regiment, long the pride
of whites and blacks alike, in recent years, has been disbanded.
A white regiment has been substituted for it. Fear of revolt by
the blacks on any large scale, at this late day, was probably no
great consideration at all in this action. West Indian blacks were

recruited for service in the World War, but promptly disbanded when the war was over. The permanent dissolution of the original Regiment is due very likely to unpleasant experiences it had abroad in the post-war interim before it returned home. Local disturbances thereafter hastened the final order to disband.

The West Indian, though check-mated in his own islands, has been active in all the movements for freedom from the Bahamas to South America. Too much credit cannot be given to them and to the Haitians for aid extended in the fight for abolition in the United States. West Indians, at home and abroad, have added glory to racial literature and classical scholarship, strength and direction to political struggles, force, character and sturdiness to business and commercial life.

It was the great West Indian, Dr. Edwin Wilmot Blyden, who, with the immortal Frederick Douglass, placed before the bar of public opinion in England and Europe, the case of black men in the Americas. The role they have played in the United States is a long and distinguished one. Denmark Vesey, memorable in his militancy for abolition was a signal for our Nat Turner. The Honorable Marcus Garvey, charlatan or statesman, as you will, can be laughed out of court not at all. Booker T. Washington paved the way for West Indians to enter the United States in larger numbers and also aided them in securing work in the Canal Zone.

In the light of past loyalty, each to each, it is incumbent upon American blacks and West Indians in America, under common oppression, to create and maintain a united front, whether the latter be scattered here and yon throughout the nation, or dwell in large numbers on the Atlantic seabord.

COCHIN, A. — "Results of Emancipation", 1864
CUNEY-HARE, MAUD — "Song in the Virgin Islands", CRISIS, April-May, 1933
DuBois, W. E. B. — "The Negro", 1915; 160-182; bib. 249-50
EDWARDS, BRYAN — "British West Indies", Vols. II-V, 1793-1819
FERRIS, W. H. — "The African Abroad", 2 Vols. 1913 .
JOHNSON, CHAS. S. — "The Negro in American Civilization", 1930, p. 3-15
JOHNSTON, H. H. — "Backward Peoples, etc.", 1920

"The Negro in the New World", 1910
"The Story of My Life", 1923
JOURNAL OF NEGRO HISTORY:—
PITTMAN, F. W. — "Slavery on the British West Indie Plantations, etc.", Vol. XI
WESLEY, CHAS. S. — "Emancipation in Great Britain", Vol. XVII
"Negro in the West Indies", Vol. XVII
WESTERGAARD, WALDEMAR — "The Negro Rebellion on St. Croix, Danish West Indies", Vol. XI
WILLIAMS, MARY W. — "Negro Slaves in the British Em pire", Vol. XV
LUCAS, SIR CHAS. — "The West Indies", 1900-05
WILLIAMS, S. J., JOSEPH J. — "The Black Irish of Jamaica", 1933
WOODSON, C. G. — "The Negro in our History", 1922, 22-30

Africans in Oceania

A N UNBIASED treatment of the blacks in the islands of the
Seven Seas, would be an ambition worthy of the boldest
literary and historical navigator. Research would carry the seeker
after truth back to the controversial Lemuria, Atlantis, Mu
and Gonwandaland.

The Easter Islands, mysterious and challenging, are doubtless sectors of some "lost" continent, that long ago was the
habitat of African peoples.

There is, no doubt, however, of the trail of the blacks
which are seen in Australia, Indo-Maylasia and Melanesia.

On these areas, Sir H. H. Johnston remarks in his "Backward Peoples, etc." (p. 14-15);

> The Burmese seem to be an ancient mixture of Tibetan,
> Siamese and Negrito.
> The term Negrito means an Asiatic Negro rather short in
> stature. Negrito tribes still linger in the forests of Southern
> India. They are found almost pure in race in the Andaman
> Islands.
> They are not quite extirpated yet from the Malay Penin-
> sula, Sumatra and the Philippine Islands and though—curiously
> enough—they seem to be absent from Java and Borneo with-
> out leaving a trace, they crop out again in the Islands of the
> Celebes and in the interior of many of the other big eastern
> islands of the Malay Archipelago. . . . In former times this
> Asiatic Negro spread, we can scarcely explain how, unless the
> land connections of those days were more extended, through
> Eastern Australia to Tasmania and from the Solomon Islands
> to New Caledonia and even New Zealand, to Fiji and Hawaii.
> The Negroid element in Burma and Annam is, therefore, easily
> to be explained by supposing that in ancient times Southern
> Asia had a Negro population ranging from the Persian Gulf
> to Indo-China and the Malay Archipelago.

Along this wise, it is strikingly significant that in July,
1934 announcements were made which showed that 200,000

lost blacks had been *found* in New Guinea, *hidden* there perhaps for centuries.

Before reading the article we anticipated that the old stereotype would be placed on them, namely, stub-nosed cannibals in blood rituals and orgies of human sacrifices. Strangely, they were reported to be a peaceful people, with orderly laid out fields, which, with other gifts of nature, supplied their simple needs. Yet the might of Britain will go there to *establish law and order.* These people will be dispossessed from their lands, confined in clothes and indoctrinated with 57 brands of *christianity* to their utter unhappiness, ruin and decay.

In reading the article the stereotype was not wholly missing. We got the obverse side. An additional announcement on this "find" stated that the people were "Semitic" that they had mortars such as the ancient Egyptians used, but did not know what to do with them.

This section on Oceania can best be approached by the use of Sir H. H. Johnston's *Opening Up of Africa,* chapter I, 9-37 along with Dr. DuBois' *"The Negro" chapter* I, 9-19.

Selections made from the reference list below will amplify or counter statements made by these authorities.

The citations in the list below deal with the controversy in regard to the *"Lost Continent Theory"* of Churchward, Spence and Thevenin. In general, these men are greeted with guffaws, if not with actual guile, when their works appear.

It is well for us to know all sides of the story, winnowing it for what it is worth. Lewis Spence is a Scotsman, not likely to trouble publishers on fruitless literary or historical ventures. Churchward is as devout as Spence, while, to some extent, Thevenin is an exhibitionist, though in the main his work is solid and dependable.

LOST CONTINENT THEORY

CHURCHWARD, JAMES — The Lost Continent of Mu, 1931
    The Children of Mu, 1931
    The Sacred Symbols of Mu, 1931

GONWANDALAND — Report of the John Murray Expidition of
HELL, HEINZ — The Mysterious Easter Islands, (NEW YORK
TRIBUNE, February 26, 1933)
HOGGAN, F. — Prehistoric Negroids and Their Contributions
to Civilization (CRISIS, February, 1920)
INTERNATIONAL GEOLOGICAL CONGRESS, Washington, July, 1933:
Report of A. L. du Toit of Johannesburg, South Africa,
on Gonwandaland.
Report of Sir Arthur Smith Woodward, on Africa the
Birthplace of Modern Man. (This address was countered
by Dr. Fred Morris, of Massachusetts Institute of
Technology, who held to the theory of Asian origin.)
NEWTON, BISHOP HENRY — In Far New Guinea, 1914 (out of
print)
POTTER, R. D. — Prehistoric Land
RIVERS, W. H. R. — History of Melanesian Society (2 Vols.,
1914)
SPENCE, LEWIS — The Problem of Lemuria, 1933
Atlantis
SWETTENHAM, FRANK — British Malaya, 1907
THEVENIN, RENE — Lemuria Chapter IX (serial) AMERICAN
WEEKLY, January 10, 1932. (This series was begun in the
magazine section of the SUNDAY NEW YORK AMERICAN,
November 15, 1931)
Bridges Across the Oceans, (N. Y. TRIBUNE, Section II,
August 6, 1933)

African Art

BRIEF HISTORICAL SETTING

ANY DISCUSSION of African art may well proceed from the accolades given to it by M. Brugsch-Bey and Count de Gobineau.

As early as 1858 M. Brugsch-Bey had surveyed the Nile Valley. He returned to Germany and enriched the Berlin Museum with antiquities from Thebes.

In his *History of Egypt Under the Pharaohs,* he deals at length with the art of the Northern tributary peoples. Then with a show of boldness—albeit, streaked with trepidation—he turned his attention to the Southern peoples in the lands of *burnt faced* men.

We pause for the story of Brugsch-Bey:

> If it may be allowed us, on the other hand, with equal certainty, to pass a judgment on the condition of culture, and of handicraft in the lands of the negroes in the fifteenth century B. C., from the colored representations of these sepulchral chambers, a knowledge of which was acquired to science from the Prussian expidition to Egypt under Lepsius, it becomes evident that here also—in spite of peculiar direction of taste which is seen, among other things, in furnishing the tips of the horns of the oxen with ornaments like the hands of men—a certain artistic spirit is observable in the composition and in the execution of the outward forms of the utensils.
>
> Passing over for a moment the costly golden vessels, set with precious stones, the manifold utensils of domestic life, the chariots, the ships, the weapons, and all the articles which the queen brings to Thebes, all these exhibit an unmistakable development of artistic power, which must without a doubt be ascribed on the one hand to Egyptian influence, and on the other to the natural position of the so-called savage tribes, and to their powers of imitation.
>
> Even at this day, the prejudice that the negro is, both in taste and in art, an unprogressive son of Adam, can be refuted by hundreds of facts which prove the direct contrary in an

incontrovertible manner in favor of our colored brethren. As the representative of modern Egypt at the two universal exhibitions at Vienna in 1873, and at Philadelphia in 1876, I had the much desired opportunity of exhibiting the most wonderful works in gold and silver, as the examples of the finished artistic skill of the peoples of the Sudan, and of receiving prizes for black artists.

We pass without comment to de Gobineau, a contemporary of Brugsch-Bey. The setting in which we find de Gobineau was one, on the face of which, he should have been constrained to keep quiet. Namely that about excellences which Africans possessed, for, in the middle of the Nineteenth Century, de Gobineau had to set out to prove racial superiority. Accordingly he wrote a work, *Sur L'Inegalité des Races Humaines* (*Upon the Inequality of the Human Races*), largely because he wanted to see France of the mid-Nineteenth Century turned back to the France of the mid-Eighteenth Century. The way to get the backward motion started, as he saw it, was to prove that only royalty, noblemen and courtiers deserved palladium and that, through the sweat, labor and blood of peasants, serfs and slaves. His writing was a masterly defense of the ruling classes, first, in the Old Regime in France, and, secondly, royalty everywhere except the native ruling classes in Africa.

Taking a cue from de Gobineau, the ruling classes in Germany today—and for some time past—are set to *prove* that among the white races only the *Aryans* are superior and only *Nordics* can live, proudly, in a society of *equals* among *unequals*.

Count de Gobineau maintains that, in the great civilizations of antiquity, the inspiration of poetry and art came from the black race. The white race organized those civilizations and established their laws and governments; but

> the source from which their art issued was foreign to the instincts of the organizing civilizers; it lay in the blood of the blacks. That universal power of imagination which we see enveloping and penetrating the primordial civilizations, came entirely from the ever increasing infusion of blood from the black race into the whites.
> The negro possesses in a higher degree, the faculty of

emotion from the senses, without which art is not possible. It will be said that I am placing a beautiful crown upon the deformed head of the negro, and doing him a very great honor by associating him with the harmonious choir of the Muses.
. But the honor is not so great. I have not associated him with the highest, thoe in whom reflection is superior to passion. Certainly the black element is indispensable to the development of artistic in a race.

It should be noted here that de Gobineau remains faithful to *Aryan-Nordicism,* for although he did associate the African, *with the harmonious choir of the Muses,* he did not associate him, *with the highest, in whom reflection is superior to passion.* Note, also his sadistic by-play, on the *deformed head* of the African.

Some day it will be manifest and understood, that, eternal sunshine in the eyes and soul of the African, and surrounded as he is by profuse and variegated flora, massive and cunning fauna, could not but produce an imagery, a rhythm and an imagination in him which could not possibly come to early man in the frozen North, amidst his bleak forests and his ice-covered plains.

Where is the art of the Eskimo, where is his laughter, his song and his dance! Why has not his fund of exuberance, in these fields, gone out to enrich the souls and quicken the pace of mankind!

Even the *neo-Aryans* in the chilly regions in Northern Europe have bequeathed to their *moderns* a stolidity of temperament, carried out in German art today. Stroll—or ride—leisurely, through the Boulevards, streets and parks of Paris, for example, and then, repeat the process in the city of Berlin; the rigid, masculine, and generally, undecorative art of the latter, will be seen, in sharp contrast, with the soft, easy and graceful lines in the art of the former. Italy is still further South.

The views of de Gobineau are challenging. They disturbed Baldwin, generally unfriendly to Africa, and led that great historian to remark:

Wonderful force to attack, subdue and sway other peoples, distinguishes the faculty of our race (Aryan)—

But is this the highest and most admirable development of human nature? We cannot reflect seriously without feeling that something is nobler, something more beautiful, something more richly fraught with blessing that increases the possibilities and heightens the charm of existence, something that must necessarily revise our ideal of what is superior in people and races.

It was not our own proud Aryan race that created the great civilizations of Arabia, Chaldea and the Old Monarchy of Egypt. Our race was preceded in development by others, and it was in times quite modern that our own family of the race took its place among the foremost.

See Baldwin "Prehistoric Nations", p. 321.

A striking example of how force and might, today, operate in ignoring world co-operation in order to save that which is best and noble in the fine arts and in the arts of peace, is shown in the open, unashamed and merciless treatment of the Jews in *Aryan* Germany and the suggestive exhibits of the English before the black potentates from Central and Western Sudan. After a hearty, civil reception and extremely courteous entertainment, these natural rulers from Africa were carried to Portsmouth to look into the muzzles of gruesome guns mounted on British battleships. That sight, doubtless, was the real message that Britian has for Africa.

MODERN INFLUENCE AND APPLICATION

Except for the ripple in American art circles, caused by Brugsch-Bey, when he exhibited art works from the Sudan at the Philadelphia Centennial Exposition, 1876, very little was said of the artistic genius of the blacks until 1900.

Men who knew the truth, as early as 1850 kept their lips sealed. Slavery must be upheld and *justified;* the missionary racket from *Christian* America had to be developed in order to *save the souls of the heathen,* and black men, heirs of great civilizations, must be snatched more and more from their freedom in Africa, to labor in order that a *culture* might be developed in the Southland for the heirs of many who had come to these shores, from the damp, murky confines of Old Bailey, in England.

As a slave in America, the African had no time for weaving, for pottery, for carving or sculpture, but he could sing and sing he did.

His song boiled up out of the unplumbed depths of his artistic soul, without compulsion, restraint or direction; it came out of an inner necessity, which he, its own creator, cannot wholly harness or understand. Thus he gave to America a new art/form in music, indeed the only genuine folk-stuff that America has today.

His music and song, as art expressions, caused wonderment, from the triumphal pilgrimage of the Fisk Jubilee Singers 1873 to Hayes, Robeson, and Bledsoe; Jarboro, Anderson and Mitchell; Lillian Evanti and Charlotte Murray, all leaders in the brilliant galaxy of artists today.

However, in 1905 popular acclaim for genuine African art, in other forms, began. In that year Picasso's, Vlaminck's and Derain's enthusiasm for this material, spread it into the orbit of post-impressionistic circles. By 1912 the vogue increased because the *Fauves* in Paris, the *red wing* in the modern movement, set up the black African artist as a sort of idol. This was approved by Martisse. These so-called ultra-modernists have been accepted as solid citizens of contemporary French art. But they went to fetiches and masks for the qualities of direct expressiveness, of naiveté, of non-realistic formalization, which they were advocating as the keys to the saving of European art.

Though the name of the African artist and the exact period in which he worked is not known, the *standard* histories of art have been discreetly silent, even on the existence of an art form which had been known, to an inner circle, for nearly a hundred years.

Prior to 1912, however, the founding of special museums of African art in several European centers and the later opening of African wings in some of the less conservative museums, elsewhere, have added official recognition after much personal discovery and appreciation. The George de Zayas exhibitions in 1916, set the vogue, more or less firmly in America.

When the war broke out in 1914 the devotees of modernism were just beginning to study the *new* art. Books were being written on the natives, their religious customs, tribal laws, fetiches and their practices in mysticism and magic. The dust-laden African antiques in the basements and on the top-shelves of art shops, disappeared speedily. Profiteers and despoilers hastened to the heart of Africa and returned, with bag and baggage bulging, with trinkets, beads, idols and fetiches, with which they swelled the coffers of the art dealers and enriched the designs of the modernists. They followed the routes of the lawless slaver of a hundred years ago and that of the ivory hunter of today. This time the *connoisseurs,* snatched the soul-stuff from the hands of the African, just as their forebears, the slave raider had wrenched the African's body from the land in those fateful days. It was not until 1922 that the African art began to assume large proportions as regards its leadership in the *modernist* movement. In 1925, a four-inch African statue, picked up in the Latin Quarter in Paris, for 25 francs, was sold for 60,000 francs. This gives an idea of fortunes made in the first flush of the vogue.

In 1926, Paul Guillaume and Dr. Thomas Munro, published their work on *Primitive Negro Sculpture,* probably anticipating the work of Dr. Albert C. Barnes of Philadelphia, who has the largest collection in America.

Even though El Greco, Chardin, Gaugin and Cezanne did distort, for the sake of achievement, a rhythmic design, long before African art was generally known and recognized, it still remains true that the discovery of these primitive statues gave artists a new urge in the direction, away from *realism,* and toward newer design.

It is evident that the modernists, Modigliani, Soutine, Picasso, in painting, have used the African rhythm and Archipenko, Brancusi, Lipschitz, Lembruch and Epstein, have used it in sculpture.

Sheldon Cheney writing on African art in 1927 sums up its principles as follows:—

The virtues of African art are neither in a skillful imitation of nature nor in prettification, in sentimental idealization of natural objects. They lie rather in the skill, the appropriateness of the craftsmanship and in direct emotional expressiveness; in a stern formalization of nature that lifts the individual pieces out of the realm of mere likeness and into a realm of creative and imaginative expression. It is here that the parallel to modernist art comes in.
**—The art of the African is always an art that fills some definite place in his tribal or religious life.

While Sheldon Cheney, Gertrude Benson, John F. Hanscom, Arthur Strawn, George de Zayas, Paul Guillaume, Dr. Thomas Munro and Dr. Albert C. Barnes were hailing the *discovery* of African art, other critics were labelling the black artist as *primitive, instinctive, ingenuous, wayward, lacking in originality* and *lacking in abilty to create organic wholes.* Such criticism is natural and, honestly, should be made. However, Dr. Schouteden and Dr. Maes, directors of the Tervueren Museum—Brussels—along with Henry Lavachery and Prof. Leo Frobenius, of the Frankfort Institute, Germany, were firm, as late as 1930, in their assertions of the uniform high quality of their classified collections.

One of the greatest exhibits of African art in modern times was that of La Société Auxiliare des Expositions, in the Palais des Beaux-Arts, Brussels, 1930. There were 800 exhibits, 500 of which were from Tervueren and 150 from the private collections of Vlaminck, Lhote, Derain, and Braque, to mention only a few of the co-operators. On hand, too, were reproductions of African murals by Boschimann who accompanied Frobenius, on the latter's African Expedition 1928-1930.

As late as May 1933, the exhibition of African art at the Lefevre Galleries in London, bore more witness to its genuine worth. The editor of the Illustrated London News, May 13, 1933 commented on this exhibit thus:

> Whether it be deemed a cause for rejoicing or for regret, there is no doubt that primative African sculpture of the type now on view—has inspired a number of our most modern painters and sculptors—since artists such as Picasso, Matisse, Modigliani, Derain and Epstein first began to get excited about it thirty years ago, the interest in Negro sculpture has steadily

increased.—Negro sculpture played a great part in the birth of cubism, and has had a powerful influence on all contemporary painting and sculpture. It has helped the artist to realize the intrinsic emotional significance of shapes as distinct from their representational values.

The finest examples of sculpture come from the Ivory Coast, Gabun-by-the-Sea, from the back-country regions of the Southwestern Sudan, the newly *"found"* Pahouins, the upper and lower Congo. Other impressive art work comes from French Guinea, Dahomey, Benin and the Cameroons. Lest the reader too tardily, get a copy of *Primitive Negro Sculpture* by Paul Guillaume and Dr. Thomas Munro, we venture an excerpt from their work here. Says Guillaume:

"People who know realize that Adam was black and that Eve was black, and that our primitives started the arts just as they started everything else," he argues. "Then the blacks captured the white barbarians and infused black blood into them. Thousands of years passed and the regenerated whites conquered their masters and forced them to flee to the unknown regions of the earth to escape slavery. The blacks have left the ethnic traces of their presence in the north and in the east of Africa in the form of the Semites an dthe Chamites. The ages have split these peoples up into divisions and tribes and forced them into settled localities. In the northwest of Africa we now find the population of the Nigers, the Bobo-Dioulasso, the Aigui, the Gouros, the Dan and many others. Below the equator an din the southwest are the M'Fangs, the most beautiful of the Pahouins, who are almost as fair as the Anglo-Saxons. On the equator, but at a distance from the coast, are the pastoral races of the Bushongos, the Bambulas, the Gwembis, the Bakele, the Yunga and the Bangonga.

"Each of these tribes has built up an art peculiar to its religion and customs. To classify the work, both as regards ages and tribes, it is necessary to combine a knowledge of African folk lore and fetish legends with the technical data that have been gathered by the explorers. Not the least important of the technical accounts is the manuscript written by the Portuguese adventurers who penetrated into the heart of the Benin country in the fourteenth century. This manuscript was only discovered in 1922, but it has already proved of capital importance in the identification work."

Dr. Munro, co-author with Guillaume concludes:

By two main contributions negro sculpture has thrown a ferment into modern plastic art that must inevitably go on

working. These are * * * a general method of building up a
design fro mthe dissociated parts of a natural object, and the
array of actual designs it achieved by this method. Potentially
the general method is more important than any particular designs. This has helped to liberate the artist from Renaissance
traditions, yet given him a concrete basis to build upon.
If African art does that it does more than to give the
modern artist the courage of the primitive negro's convictions.
It opens a new vista of art.

The struggle of African art for recognition, has had a circuitous and a tortuous road from Brugsch-Bey and de Gobineau
to Frobenius, the Modernists, Dr. Albert C. Barnes, Dr. Thomas
Munro and Paul Guillaume. These men have fought the battle
for Africa. They have spent money. Plenty of it. We must begin
now, to share the burden with funds. Some of Frobenius' works
are still untranslated, particularly, his Das Unbekannte Afrikas,
a work packed with information. His latest work, Kulturgeschichte Afrika will probably be in English, soon; in the German edition it costs $40.00. As late as 1935 Charles Rattoon,
of The Librairie des Arts Decoratifs, Paris, placed on exhibition, in the Museum of Modern Art, New York, his collection
of "Masques Africains" and additional works in textiles, wood,
iron and bronze.

In 1937, in The Museum of Modern Art, the great Dr.
Leo Frobenius exhibited selections from his "Prehistoric Rock
Pictures in Europe and Africa" which he brought to New York
from his "Research Institute for the Morphology of Civilization," which he founded at Frankfort-am-Main, Germany, in
1923. The researches of Dr. Frobenius, in Africa, have continued, with increasing vigor and convincingness, for the past
33 years.

Miss Nancy Cunard's work, in English—$15.00—a copy
will, on the art side, suffice until the work of Frobenius is available, in English. Other aids for the proper presentation of
African art are set down below.

References:

BARNES, ALBERT C. — Primitive Negro Sculpture, etc. (OPPOR-
TUNITY MAGAZINE—Reprint)

BENSON, GERTRUDE — African Art Displayed in Brussels, December 28, 1930
BRUGSCH-BEY — History of Egypt under the Pharohs
CHENEY, SHELDON — Darkest Africa Sends Us Art, NEW YORK TIMES, February 13, 1927
CUNARD, NANCY — Negro 1934, p. 656-733, p. 93-194
EINSTEIN, VON CARL — Negerplastik, 1920
FAURE, ELIE — Form in Art
FROBENIUS, LEO — Das Unbekannte Afrikas, 1925
    Kulturgeschichte Africa, 1934
FUHRMANN, VON ERNST — Afrika, 1922
FUHRMANN, VON ERNST — Afrika, 1922
GUILLAUME, PAUL and MUNRO, THOS. — Primitive Negro Sculpture, 1926
HASCOM, JOHN F. — Newest Art Chaze is Black African, NEW YORK TRIBUNE, January 31, 1926 (Sunday Magazine)
LOCKE, ALAIN — A Collection of Congo Art. ARTS MAGAZINE, February, 1927
PITT-RIVERS, LIEUT. — Antique works of Art from Benin, 1900
RATTRAY, R. S. — Ashanti Proverbs, 1916
    Ashanti, 1923
    et al, Religion and Art in Ashanti, 1927
STRAWN, ARTHUR — Black Art in Bizarre Carven Masks, etc., NEW YORK TIMES, June 6, 1926 (Sunday Magazine)
VERNEAU, R. DR. — L'Homme, Races, et Coutumes, 1931 (Larousse, Paris, Fasc. 1-14)

    (With Einstein, Fuhrmann, Rattray, Pitt-Rivers and Verneau all of which contain numerous illustrations of art, a good beginning could be made until the work of Cunard—$15.00—and Frobenius—$40.00—could be secured.)

LE MONDE COLONIALE ILLUSTRE, 1931 — (Official publication Of the French Colonial Exposition, Paris, 1931)
LONDON ILLUSTRATED NEWS — Native Architecture in Central Africa, January 15, 1927
    Rhodesian Rock Paintings, December 10, 1927
    Did Pharaoh Necho's Minstrels Visit South Africa, December 10, 1927
    Types of Mangbetou Women, January 28, 1928
    West African Art, January 21, 1928
    The Art of the Head-Hunters—New Guinea and Admirality, September 12, 1931
    Prehistoric Art in the Fezzan Desert (Frobenius) November 10, 1932
    Postage Stamp Reproduction of Native Types, December 10, 1932
    Art Affinities of Fezzan Rock Drawings and New Found Masterpieces of African Prehistoric Art (Frebenius,

November 19, 1932)
Nefertiti, Akhnaton and the Tel Armarna Finds, May
6, 1933
Primitive African Culture, Influencers of Ultra-Modern
Artists, May 13, 1933
South Africa's Prehistoric Academy, April 29, 1933
Did The Ancient Egyptians Visit South Africa? April 29,
1933
NEW YORK AMERICAN — Files for 1931, 1932 and 1933 (Sunday
Edition)
Wierd Works of Savage Art, 1931
Masterpieces of Prehistoric (Bushman) Art, February
2, 1932
Tracing Africa's Races Through their Paintings, 1932
Sculptors and Painters (African), etc., 1932
Humanity's Earliest Art, August 13, 1933
Prehistoric African Art, April 22, 1934
REPRODUCTION OF MALVINA HOFFMAN'S ART : —
NEW YORK HERALD TRIBUNE, June 4 and August 13, 1933
NEW YORK TIMES, May 21, 1933

References:

BLYDEN, EDWIN W. — "Islam and the Negro"
DELAFOSSE, M. — "Negroes of Africa, The Almoravide Move-
ment", p. 48-59
DORSEY, GEORGE A. — "Man's Own Show: Civilization", pp.
640-653
DRAPER, J. W. — "History of the Intellectual Development of
Europe", Vol. II, Chapter 2.
DuBois, W. E. B. — "The Negro", Chapters 4 and 8
ENCYCLOPEDIA BRITTANICA — Vol. 21,p. 128 (14th edition)
GIBBON, EDWARD — "History of the Decline and Fall of the
Roman Empire", Chapter 52
ROBINSON, JAMES HARVEY — "The Ordeal of Civilization",
pp. 72-81, 261-263
SPRATLIN, V. B. — "Juan Lation, Slave and Humanist",
CRISIS, September, 1932
"The Negro in Spanish Literature", JOURNAL OF NEGRO
HISTORY, January, 1934
THOMPSON, JAMES W. — "An Economic and Social History
of the Middle Ages", Chapters 7, 15 and 22
WELLS, H. G. — "The New and Revised Outline of History",
Chapter 30

Africans in the United States

ERE the teacher's program is simplified. In fact Dr. Dubois, Dr. Woodson, Dr. Brawley, and Professor Charles S. Johnson have laid out the program. A suggestion for a minimum teacher library would range about as follows for the initial groundwork:

BOAS, FRANZ — "Mind of Primitive Man"
BRAWLEY, B. G. — "Short History of the American"
BROWN, STERLING — "Outline for the Study of Negro Poetry"
CALVERTON, V. F. — "Anthology of Negro Literature"
CROMWELL, JOHN W. — "The Negro in American History"
DELAFOSSE, M. — "Negroes of Africa"
DuBois, W. E. B. — "The Negro" (for general view from prehistoric times to the present)
FERRIS, *W. H.* — "The African Abroad", 2 Vols.
JOHNSON, CHAS. S. — "The Negro in American Civilization"
JOHNSON, JAMES, W. — "The Book of American Negro Poetry"
JOHNSTON, H. H. — "The Negro in the New World"
LOGGINS, VERNON — "The Negro Author" (His Development in America)
ROGERS, J. A. — "World's Greatest Men of African Descent"
SCHUYLER, GEORGE — "Black no More" and "Slaves Today"
TURNER, LORENZA *D.* — "Readings from Negro Authors"
CROMWELL, OTELIA
DYKES, EVA
WOODSON, C. G. — "Negro Makers of History" (for the grades)
"The Negro in Our History"
"Story of the Negro Retold" (for Jr.-Sr. High Schools)
YOUNG, DONALD — "Race and Cultural Contacts in the United States" (Racial Minorities)
(See book list under theme, "African Art")

SUGGESTIVE PERIODICAL LITERATURE
Should be purchased or checked in libraries

Publications of the American Negro Academy
Hindu Stories in American Negro Folklore, ASIA, August, 1921
The Negro Digs Up His Past, A. A. Schomburg, Survey, March 1925

Annals of the American Academy of Political and Social
Science, Vol. CXXXX, November, 1924:
Bases of Race Prejudice, p. 10-20, R. E. Park
Progress of the American Negro in Slavery, p. 116-122,
R. F. Nichols
The Church and Negro Progress, 264-272, G. E. Haynes
The Negro in America, Alain Locke (Am. Library Asso.
Pam. 68)
America's Greatest Race Experiment, Sir Arthur Keith,
NEW YORK TIMES, January 24, 1932
My Trip to Cuba in Quest of Negro Books, A. A. Schom-
burg, Opp. February, 1933
Footnote to the History of Negro Slaving, M. J. and F. S.
Hershovitz, OPPORTUNITY, June, 1933
Races of Mankind (Anthropology) Leaflet No. 30, Field
Museum, Chicago
Sources for the Study of Ethiopian History, W. L. Hans-
berry, Howard University Studies in History, November,
1930, 21-41
We Turn to Prose, Alain Locke, OPPORTUNITY, February,
1932
The Browsing Reader, CRISIS, February, 1932 (The CRISIS
for August, 1934, publishes a list of available back-num-
bers, 1911-1934. p. 248)
The Asociated Publishers issue a battery of pamphlets.
(Ask for a copy of Valuable Books on the Negro, which
volume, from Volume I to Volume XVIII)
The Color Line Within the Race, A. N. Fields, ABBOTT'S
MAGAZINE, July, 1933
Thousand Words, Alfred E. Smith. CRISIS July, 1933.
An Outline of the World History of the Negro in a
On Being Ashamed of Ourselves, Dr. W. E. B. DuBois,
CRISIS, September, 1933
Files of Journal of Negro Education, Howard University,
Washington, D. C. (since April, 1922)
Annual Reports (25) of The N. A. A. C. P., constitute a
library of practical, dynamic civics and history. These
reports should be studied given as assigned reading which
require the student to report.
Bibliography of the Negro in Africa and America, and the
Negro Year Book both by M. W. Work, should be in
the school library.

Summary and Conclusion

THE MORE the story of the African is studied, the more wonderful his place in the world scheme is found to be. Indeed the place of the African in world history is comparable to the place of rivers in the scheme of nature.

For example, rivers, as they wend their way to the sea, wash along some share of the waste of the land. They work untiringly.

Mountains may tower aloft, where the crust of the earth has been upheaved by irresistible forces from within; the weather attacks them; clouds gather around their summits; rain and snow fall upon them and the streams and rivers bear off their wastes as they are worn away.

Only when all the hills are worn down, can rivers rest from their labors. Even then, if the lands are again uplifted, the rivers, will, at once, resume their labors.

Thus like a river, African stock has swept through India, Babylonia and Assyria; the land of the Hittites, the land of Canaan and the land of the Midianites. It became tributary to the civilizations of the Tigris and Euphrates and found itself, at flood tide, in the valley of the Nile.

Southward, in Africa, Bantus carried indigenous culture to the Cape. Rounding the Cape and heading northward through ancient Ethiopia and Monomotapa, native culture reached Benin, in the bend of the Niger.

But already great empires had stretched themselves from the Mellestine in the West, straightaway across Central Africa, once more to Nubia and modern Ethiopia in the East.

But ere these cultures had come to full flower, the hand of the slave raider had gripped the West Coast, and turned the black stream across the seas, through the Middle Passage, to the shores of the new western world.

The African has known rivers; the Indus, the Ganges, the Tigris and Euphrates; the Jordan and the Nile; the Niger and the Congo; the Amazon, the Hudson and the Mississippi. Here, in America, for more than three centuries, the black horde from Africa, like a mighty river, has borne away the wastes of American labor; has added to the spiritual side of American culture and is now washing the mountain sides of American prejudice.

Inarticulate, like "ole Man River," the African in America says very little effectively, but he does know something definitely.

He knows that in this modern age, no national problem in America can be settled until it is honestly and humanly settled with him in the equation; he knows that international relations cannot be settled humanly right until the rape of Africa, India and China has been stopped and atonement made; he knows that true culture, true enlightenment, true civilization and true religion, in this modern age will remain muzzled as long as he is muzzled.

To aid in the achievement of the objectives set down next above, the "black river" in America must alter and change its course toward:

1. Respect for the purity of womanhood and the sacredness of childhood as the twin creators and preservers of the race,
2. Co-operation, which means the dropping of intra-racial wrangling in his religious, political and social life, needlessly going on now;
3. Valuation of his glorious past and his present opportunity.
4. Clear thinking and the power to "follow through" with clear thinking.

As a guide in this new field we must needs give a last summary caution. The field has been lightly sketched. Inquisitors will counter with the assertion that deterioration and decline mark every spot where Africans have trod. They will repair to

Heeren, Nott, Gliddon, Knox, Hunt, Carroll, Dixon, Grant and
Stoddard, *Aryan* spear-heads in a *christian* phalanx against the
claims of worth, honor and virtue, by people whom they consider, *"lesser breeds without the law."*

That which passes for christianity in the modern world is
rank poison to western civilization. The principles of real
Christianity are foreign to the Occidental mind. Indeed they
are little known and less still used. Assuming, for sake of presentation, that the non-white races are the feminine element in
human-kind, we see their prostrate forms, torn, bleeding, despoiled, all in the name of wealth, power, *Christianity.* From
these non-whites, have come the bases of the arts, sciences,
philosophies and religions; things if rightly used, would create
a world in which all men could have bread and peace of mind.

The masculine (white) nations have developed the gifts
of the non-whites, but have turned the strength of these gifts
to abuse, ignoring, in large measure, their spirit. Armed with
this strength the Great Powers today are eyeing each other—if
at all, they can see eye-to-eye—over the prostrate forms of Arabia, Africa, India and China. They are carrying out bigger, and
more *Christian* stealth, protected by fiat and mandate of the
Covenant of the League of Nations.

To give color to the *righteousness of their cause,* they and
their ghost writers, hurl maledictions upon the heads of the
conquered. Slavery and indentured service as the labor force
in America, have largely passed away. Today the American
workers repeatedly defy onslaught upon the fruits of their brain
and brawn. They refuse to be robbed as of yore. In the non-
white world, at large, claims are staked out around land and
labor. No other Great Power may enter. All of them now must
start anew to rob each other. This has begun.

The Four Horsemen are ready to ride again, as they did
1914 to 1918, mangling the form of Western Civilization be-
neath the rough-shod hoofs of steeds of its own making.

As for the gory, bone-strewn paths of Ghengis Khan.
Tamerlane, the Mahdi, Mehemet Ali, Dingaan, Chaka and
Lobengula, their ancient "heathen" caravans have rattled and

shambled down the corridor, far into the night. These moderns have laid them in a deeper shade. As for Civilization and the War of the Great Powers tomorrow, who can tell! "Being a member of a superior race, is trying business," says Broun, "for to them there comes no rest."—Being a member of a race conscious of its faults, modest about its excellencies, willing and ready to appreciate, use and preserve the talents and virtues in others, is pleasant business.

Superior races, *Aryans, Nordics,* have little time for the larger justice, the nobler love and the more prudent reflection. Their job is to carry the *White Man's Burden* and be Dominant.

THE END

General Bibliography

AFRICANUS, LEO — History and Description of Africa, 3 Vol.
ATLANTA UNIVERSITY PUBLICATIONS — 1896-1915, Atlanta, Ga.
AMERICAN COLONIZATION SOCIETY — The Reports of 1818-1867.
AMERICAN ANTI-SLAVERY SOCIETY — Reports and Proceedings, 1834-1861
ALLEN, RICHARD — Doctrine and Disciple of the A. M. E. Church, 1819

BASSETT, JOHN S. — History of Slavery in North Carolina, 1899
BALCH, EMILY G. — Occupied Hayti, 1925
BEARDSLEY, G. H. — The Negro in Greek and Roman Civilization, Phila.
BEASLEY, DELILAH L. — Negro Trail Blazers, Los Angeles, 1922
BRAWLEY, BENJAMIN J. — Short History of the American Negro, Atlanta
    Negro in Literature and Art, Atlanta
BLYDEN, EDWIN WILMOT — Christianity, Islam and the Negro, London 1888
    Negro in Ancient History
    Washington 18
BENEZET, ANTHONY — Inquiry into the Rise and Progress of the Slave
    Trade, Philadelphia, 1771
    Notes on the Slave Trade, 1780
BLAKE, W. O. — History of Slavery and the Slave Trade, Columbus 1859
BRACKETT, J. R. — Notes on the Progress of the Colored People of Mary-
    land since the War, Baltimore, 1890
BOAS, FRANZ — Mind of Primitive Man, The — New York, 1911
    The Real Race Problem, CRISIS MAGAZINE, D. 12, 1919
    Human Faculty as Determined by Race,—Proceedings of the American
        Asso. for the Advancement of Science, Vol. 43—301—327, 1924
    Old African Civilization, Atlanta University, 1906
BALDWIN, JOHN D. — Prehistoric Nations, An Inquiry Concerning Ancient
    Negro Civilization in Africa and of the Ethiopians, Boston, 1875
BAKER, RAY STANNARD — Following the Color Line, New York, 1908
BANDELIER, FANNY — Journey of Alver Nunez Cabeza de Vaca; Mendoza
    and Estavanico in the Discovery of the Seven Cities of Cobola, 1528-36,
    Philadelphia, 1905

CHAMBERLAIN, A. F. — Contribution of the Negro to Human Civilization,
    Journal of Race Development, Vol. 1 and 4, 1911
CRUMMEL, ALEXANDER — The Future of Africa, Washington, 1862
    Africa and America, Washington, 1891
CROMWELL, JOHN W. — Negro in American History, The, Washington,
    1915
CHATELAIN, H. — Some Causes of the Retardation of African Progress,
    Journal of American Folklore, Vol. 20, 8; 177-184, 1895
CABLE, GEO. W. — The Silent South, New York, 1885

DALTON, O. M. — READ, C. H. — Antiquities from the City of Benin, 1899
DENIKER, J. — The Races of Man, New York, 1904
DETT, DR. NATHANIEL — Religious Folk Songs of the Negro, Hampton, Va.
DETWILER, F. T. — The Negro Press in the U. S., Pittsburgh, 1926
DELAFOSSE, M. — Negroes in Africa; Their History and Civilization, Paris,
    1929, (Translated by F. Fligelman)
DOUGLASS, FREDERICK — My Bondage and My Freedom, New York, 1855
    Narrative by and of Frederick Douglass, New York, B 45
    Claims of the Negro Ethnologically Considered, New York, 1854
    Life and Times of Frederick Douglass
DOWD, JEROME — The Negro Races, 1907
DUNBAR, PAUL LAWRENCE—(Complete Works), Doubleday Co., New York
DuBOIS, W. E. B. — Suppression of the African Slave Trade, N. Y., 1896
    Bibliography of the American Negro, Atlanta, 1905
    Philadelphia Negro, Philadelphia, 1890
    Souls of Black Folk, New York, 1903
    Gift of Black Folk, The — New York
    The Negro (Home University Library Series No. 91) New York, 1915

ELLIS, GEORGE W. — Negro Culture in West Africa, New York, 1915
EDWARDS, BRYAN — History of the British West Indies, Vols. 2 and 4

FORD COLLECTION — (Slavery Controversy), New York Public Library
FREEDMEN'S BUREAU REPORTS — 1862-1877
FLEMING, J. T. — Slavery and the Race Problem in the South
FLEMING, WALTER L. — Freedmen's Savings Bank
FERRIS, WILLIAM H. — The African Abroad, New Haven, 1913
FINOT, JEAN — Race Prejudice, (Trans. by Wade Evans), N. Y., 1907
FROBENIUS, LEO. — The Voice of Africa, (Trans. by Blind), 1913
FLIPPER, HENRY O. Colored Cadet at West Point, New York, 1878
FLEETWOOD, G. A. — The Negro as a Soldier, Washington, D. C., 1895

GREEN, LORENZO J. — The Negro Wage Earner
GREEN, ELIZABETH LAY — The Negro in Contemporary Literature
GREGOIRE, H. — An Inquiry Concerning the Intellectual and Moral Faculties
    and Literature of Negroes, (Trans. by Warden), Brooklyn, 1910
GUGGISBERG and FRASER — Future of the Negro, New York, 1929

HARMON, J. H. — The Negro as a Business Man, Washington, D. C., 1928
HAYNES, GEORGE E. — Negro at Work in New York, New York, 1909
    The Trend of the Races (Published under the auspices of the Federal
    Council of Churches of America)
HERSKOVITZ, MELVILLE — The American Negro (Evolving a New Racial
    Type), New York, 1928
HELPER, HINTON ROWAN — Impending Crisis, New York, 1860
HUGGINS, WILLIS N. — Educating a Community, A Year of Social Service
    Work in Huntsville, Alabama, 1918

INGLE, EDWARD — The Negro in the District of Columbia, Baltimore, 1893
JAY, WILLIAM — An Inquiry into the Character and Tendency of the
    American Colonization Society, New York, 1837.
JOHNSON, EDWARD A. — School History of the Negro Race, Raleigh, 1893
    History of the Negro Soldier in the Spanish American War, N. Y., 1899

JOHNSON, JAMES WELDON — American Negro Poetry
    Autobiography of an ex-Colored Man
    The Book of American Negro Spirituals
JOHNSON, CHARLES S. — Recent Gains in American Civilization, 1930
JOHNSTON, SIR HARRY H. — The Opening Up of Africa
    History of the Colonization of Africa by Alien Races
    The Negro in the New World

KING, W. J. — The Negro in American Life
KINGSLEY, M. H. — West African Studies, 1904
KRIEHBEL, J. S. — The Partition of Africa, 1895

LEIPER, H. S. — Blind Spots of Self-Cure for Race Prejudice
LIVERMORE, GEORGE — Historical Research Respecting Negroes as Slaves,
    Citizens and Soldiers, 1862
LIVINGSTON, DAVID — Missionary Travels in Africa, 1857
LEGER, J. N. — Haiti and her Detractors, 1907
LOCKE, DR. ALAIN L. — The New Negro
LOEB, JACQUES — Inter-Racial Problems, CRISIS MAGAZINE, Vols. 8-9
LYNCH, JOHN R. — Facts of Reconstruction, 1913
LUDOLPHUS, JOB — A New History of Ethiopia, (Trans. by Ghent), 1862

MARYLAND ABOLITION SOCIETY — Records of Baltimore, 1792
MAYER, BRANTZ — Emancipation Problem in Maryland
MATTHEWS, BASIL — The Clash of Color, London, 1924
MATTHIESON, W. L. — British Slavery and its Abolition
MORRIAN, G. S. — The Negro and the Nation, 1906
MILLER, KELLY — Race Adjustment, 1908
    Out of the House of Bondage, 1914
    Disgrace of Democracy, 1917
MCCARTHY — Lincoln's Plan of Reconstruction
MOTON, ROBERT R. — What the Negro Thinks, 1929

NEGROES IN THE UNITED STATES — Bulletin 129, Bureau of Census
NEGRO COLLEGES AND UNIVERSITIES, A SURVEY OF — U. S. Bureau of
    Education, Bulletin 19, 1926; No. 27, 1919; No. 7, 1928; No. 12, 1928;
    Chapter 38, Report of the U. S. Commissioner of Education, 1910
NEARING, SCOTT — Black America
NILES REGISTER — (Edited by Nathaniel Niles, 75 Vols.)

OLDHAM, J. H. — Christianity and the Race Problem
ODUM, HOWARD W. — Negro and His Songs
OLIVIER, LORD — White Capital and Coloured Labor

PICKENS, WILLIAM — Bursting Bonds
PHILLIPS, U. B. — Life and Labor in the Old South

RATZEL, P. — History of Mankind, (Trans. by Butler), 3 Cols., 1902
ROYCE, JOSIAH — Race Questions, 1908
REINACH, P. S. — Negro Race and European Civilization, American Journal
    Society, Vol. 11, 1905
REUTER, EDWIN B. — The Tragedy of the Mulatto
    The American Race Problem
ROGERS, J. A. — How Fares the Negro in Catholic France? N. Y., 1928

BIBLIOGRAPHY 211

SCHOMBURG COLLECTION — (On Negro History), New York Public Library, 42nd St. & 5th Ave.; 135th St. & Lenox Ave.
SINCLAIR, WILLIAM A. — The Aftermath of Slavery, Boston, 1915
SELIGMAN, HERBERT — The Negro Faces America
SIMPSON, G. R. — Touissant L'Overture, A Biography
SMITH, E. W. — Aggrey of Africa
STILL, WILLIAM — The Underground Railroad, Philadelphia, 1871
SIMMONS, W. J. — Men of Mark, 1887
STOWE, HARRIET BEECHER — Uncle Tom's Cabin
STARR, FREDERICK — Liberia, 1913
TAYLOR, A. A. — The Negro in the Reconstruction of Virginia
The Negro in South Carolina during Reconstruction
TURNER, LORENZO W. — Anti-Slavery Sentiment in American Literature
Prior to 1865
WASHINGTON, BOOKER T. — Up From Slavery
Story of the Negro
My Larger Education
WALKER'S APPEAL — Radical Negro Journal, 1827
WESLEY, CHARLES J. — Negro Labor in the United States
WHITE — The Development of Africa, 1892
WILLIAMS, GEORGE W. — History of the Negro Race in America, 1882
WILSON, HENRY — The Rise and Fall of the Slave Power in America
WILSON, J. T. — The Black Phalanx
WOODSON, CARTER GODWIN — Education of the Negro Prior to 1861
History of the Negro Church
The Negro in Our History
A Century of Negro Migration
Negro Makers of History
Negro Orators and their Orations
Free Negro Owners of Slaves in U. S., 1830
Free Negro Heads of Families in U. S., 1830
(Associated Publishers, Washington, D. C.)
Journal of Negro History (Editor)
WORK, MONROE N. — Bibliography of the Negro in Africa and America
(Issued annually from Tuskegee Institute, Alabama)

MAGAZINES, PAMPHLETS AND NEWSPAPERS

AMERICAN NEGRO EVOLVING A NEW PHYSICAL TYPE — CURRENT HISTORY,
September, 1926, Melville J. Herskovits
AMERICAN NEGRO ACADEMY, PAPERS OF — December, 1915
Message of San Domingo to African Race, Steward
Free Negroes Prior to 1860, L. M. Hershaw
Economic Contribution of Negroes to U. S.
Schomburg
The Free Negro, 1860-70, Pickens
BLACK BLOOD IN THE CARIBBEAN MELTING POT — N. Y. TIMES, July 29,
1928, Muna Lee

BLACK VIRGIN, THE — Carrie W. Clifford, CRISIS MAGAZINE, April, 1916, (La Vierge Noire de Notre Dame DuPuy)

BALTIMORE LITERARY AND RELIGIOUS MAGAZINES — Condition of the Colored People of Baltimore, 1838, Vol. 4, April 1838

BLACK BELT FADING?, IS THE — LITERARY DIGEST, February 22, 1925 (Ed.)

CONTROL OF RACE RELATIONS IN THE COMMUNITY, THE — OPPORTUNITY MAGAZINE, July, 1929, Norman M. Kastler

COLORED RURAL CHURCH — Thelma Taylor, Baltimore AFRO-AMERICAN, March 5, 1930

CHURCH TODAY, THE — Editoral AMSTERDAM NEWS, N. Y., Sept. 22, 1926

CHURCH AND SOCIETY — Vol. 1, No. 3, February 1929
Church and Race Relations
Unfinished Task of the Church
Practical Task of the Church (Ed. by Bruno Lasker)

COLOR LINE AND THE CHURCH, THE — Editorial, CRISIS, November, 1929

COLOR BAR IN CHURCHES — CHRISTIAN CENTURY, May, 28, 1930

CRUX OF NEGRO-WHITE RELATIONS — WORLD TOMORROW, May, 1923

COLOR LINE IN THE CHURCH — H. H. Proctor, AMSTERDAM NEWS, N. Y.

EUGENICS, EUTHENICS, AND RACE — Thomas R. Garth, OPPORTUNITY, July, 1930

FARM TENANCY IN THE SOUTH — Scott Nearing, OPPORTUNITY, 1928

HAITI, ITS RELATIONS WITH U. S. AND THE CHURCH — AMERICA, September 1930

FORGOTTEN SLAVERY OF COLONIAL DAYS — M. W. Jernegan, HARPERS

HARLEM, THE DEVIL'S PLAYGROUND — Edgar M. Grey, AMSTERDAM NEWS, New York

INTELLECTUAL PROGRESS IN THE SOUTH — Edwin Mims, AMERICAN REVIEW OF R — INTER-RACIAL BRIDGE BUILDING — E. C. Bye, OPPORTUNITY, April, 1926

KING COTTON — E. F. Frazer, OPPORTUNITY, February, 1926

LET US PRAY — Ira De Reid, OPPORTUNITY

LIFE, DEATH AND THE NEGRO — L. I. Dublin, AMERICAN MERCURY, September, 1929

NEGRO HARMONY, A STUDY IN — P. R. Kirby, MUS. QUARTERLY, August, 1930

NEGRO LABOR'S QUARREL WITH WHITE WORKMEN — A. F. Harris, CURRENT HISTORY, September, 1926

POINT DE SAIBLE, JEAN BAPTISTE — Augustus Grignon, JOURNAL OF THE WISCONSIN HISTORICAL SOCIETY, Vol. 8

PEOPLE OF COLOR IN LOUISIANA — Alice Dunbar Nelson, JOURNAL OF NEGRO HISTORY, October, 1916

RACE VALUE IN AFRO-AMERICAN MUSIC — P. F. Laubenstein, MUSICAL QUARTERLY, August, 1930

RELIGIOUS INSTRUCTION OF NEGROES — Report of Charleston, 1845

SLAVE DAYS IN NEW YORK — N. Y. TIMES, July 3, 1927

WALL STREET AND ITS SLAVES OF OTHER DAYS—N. Y. SUN, March 14, 1915

SPECIAL BIBLIOGRAPHY

(Chiefly, French, German and Italian)

ABYSSINIA, PEACE HANDBOOK No. 129 — British Foreign Office, 1936
ABYSSINIA AND ITALY — Bulletin No. 16, Royal Institute of International
    Affairs, London, 1935
    Abyssinia, Great Britain and Italy, Survey of International Affairs.
ALLEN, MARCUS — The Gold Coast, London, 1874
ASHMEAD, B. E. — Passing of the Shereefian Empire, New York, 1910

BADOGLIO, PIETRO — The Ethiopian War, Rome, 1936
BARAVELLI, G. C. — The Last Stronghold of Slavery, Rome, 1935
BARRATTA, MARIO — Atlante Delle Colonie Italiani, Rome, 1928
BARBUSSE, HENRI — La Guerre en Ethiopie, Paris, 1935
BARNES, HARRY ELMER — Ploetz' Epitome of History, New York, 1925
BARROWS, DAVID P. — Berbers and Blacks, New York, 1927
BARROWS, R. H. — Slavery in the Roman Empire, New York, 1928
BARTH, HENRY — Travels in North and Central Africa, New York, 1857
BASSET, RÈNE — Études sur l'Histoire d'Ethiopie, Paris, 1882
    Études Nord-Africaines et Orientales, Paris, 1923-25
    Melanges Africains et Orientaux, Paris, 1915
BEER, GEORGE L. — African Questions at the Paris Peace Conference,
    Paris, 1923
BEER, MAX — Social Struggles in Antiquity, New York, 1929
BELLAVITA, EMILIO — Adua, I Precendente, La Battaglia, Le Conseguenze,
    Rome, 1931
BEKE, CHARLES T. — Abyssinia, (Journal of the Royal Anthropological
    Society, London, 1884)
BELEK, WALTHER — Zeitschrift fur Ethnologie, Berlin, 1907
BELLEGARDE, DANTES — Un Haitien Parle, Port-au-Prince, Haiti, 1934
    Haiti et Ses Problemes, San Juan, Puerto Rico, 1936
BENDA, OSCAR — The Teaching of History and Geography, Geneva, 1936
    (Bulletin of League of Nations Teaching No. 3)
BENT, J. T. — The Sacred City of the Ethiopians, London, 1893
BERGFELD, EWALD — Franzoischen Mandatsgebiete, Berlin, 1935
BERNASCONI, G. — Le Guerre É la Politica Dell'Italia Nell'Africa Orientale,
    Rome, 1935
BERTHELOT, ANDRÈ — L'Afrique Saharienne et Soudanaise, Paris, 1927
BERDIAFF, NICOLAS — De la Dignité du Christianisme et de l'Indignité des
    Chrétiens, Paris, 1931
BOAS, FRANZ — Anthropology and Modern Life, New York, 1928
BREASTED, JAMES H. — Ancient Times, Boston, 1916
    Conquest of Civilization, New York, 1926
BRODEUR, ARTHUR G. — The Pageant of Civilization, New York, 1931
BRUCE, JAMES — Travels to Discover the Source of the Nile, Edinburgh,
    1804

BRUGSCH-BEY, HENRY — Exodus of Israel, Boston, 1880

BRYCE, JAMES — Impressions of South Africa, New York, 1900

BUDGE, E. A. WALLIS — Annals of Nubian Kings, London, 1912; Egypt, New York, 1925

BUELL, RAYMOND LESLIE — The Native Problem in Africa, New York, 1928

BUXTON, A. — The Four Winds of Ethiopia, New York, 1935

CALVERTON, V. F. — The Making of Man, (with Boas et al), New York, 1931

CASSERLY, GORDON — Africa Today, New Castle-on-Tyne

CELARIE, HENRIETTE — Ethiopie, Paris, 1934

CLEMENT, C. E. — Egypt, Boston, 1880

CLELAND, HERDMAN F. — Our Prehistoric Ancestors, New York, 1928

COHEN, CHAPMAN — Spain and the Church, London, 1936

CONTI-ROSSINI — La Storia Della Scioa (Enciclopedia Italiano Treccano)

CONTI-ROSSINI, CARLO — L'Abissinia, Rome, 1929

COON, CARLETON S. — Measuring Ethiopia, 1935

COSTES, A. — Germany and Portuguese East Africa, (Documents Diplomatiques Francais, 1871-1914), Paris 1935

COTY, FRANCOIS — Sauvons nos Colonies, "Le Péril Rouge en Pays Noir," Paris, 1935

CUST, ROBERT N. — Modern Languages of Africa, London, 1883

DE BONO, EMILIO — The Preparation and the First Operations, Rome, 1936

DE CARD, E. ROURARD — L'Éthiopie au Point de Vue du Droit International, Paris, 1929

D'ESME, JEAN — A Travers l'Empire de Menelik, Paris, 1928

DE MONFRIED, HENRY — Vers Les Terres Hostiles de l'Éthiopie, Paris, 1933

Le Lepreux, Paris, 1935

Le Drame Ethiopien, Paris, 1936

Le Masque d'Or, ou Le Dernier Negus, Paris, 1936

L'Avion Noir, Paris, 1936

DIGGS, MARGARET — Catholic Negro Education in the United States, 1937

DIXON, ROLAND — Racial History of Man, New York, 1923

Building of Cultures, New York, 1928

DONNELLY, IGNATIUS — Atlantis, The Antediluvian World, New York, 1882

DORSAINVIL, J. C. — Manuel D'Histoire D'Haiti, Port-au-Prince, 1925

Vodou et Névrose (Medico-sociologie), Bibliothéque Haitienne, Port-au-Prince, 1931

Lectures Historiques, Port-au-Prince, 1931

Quelques Vues Politiques et Morales, (Questions Haitiennes,) Port-au-Prince, 1934

DORSEY, GEORGE A. — Man's Own Show; Civilization, New York, 1931

ELGOOD, P. G. — Egypt, 1935

EINSTEIN, CARL — Negerplastik, Munich, 1920

EL-CADER, CHIHAD EDDIN AHMED BEN — Histoire de la Conquete de l'Abyssinie, Paris, 1909

FAITLOVITCH, JACQUES — The Falashas, Philadelphia, 1920
FARRAGO, LADISLAS — Abyssinia on the Eve, New York, 1935
FAURE, ELIE — History of Art
FORBES, ROSITA — From the Red Sea to the Blue Nile, 1935
FRASER, JAMES G. — Folklore in the Old Testament, New York, 1927
FROBENIUS, LEO — Prehistoric Rock Pictures in Europe and Africa, New
    York
FIRMIN, M. A. — Haiti, Au Poit de Vue Politique, Administratif et Éco-
    nomie
    L'Egalité des Races Humaines

GAFFAREL, P. — La Conquete de L'Afrique, Paris, 1892
GARVEY, MARCUS — Haille Selassie, (Files of the Black Man), London,
    1936-37
GILLARD, S. J., JOHN T. — The Catholic Church and the American Negro
GINESTORE and HACHETTE, RENE — Djibouti, et les Possessions Francaises
    de l'Inde, Paris, 1930
GLANVILLE, JAMES L. — Colonialism in the New Italy, 1934
GEORGE, EUGEN — The Adventure of Mankind, New York, 1931
GOLDENWEISER, ALEXANDER A. — Early Civilization, New York, 1926
GRIAULE, MARCEL — Abyssinian Journey, London, 1935
GSELL, STEPHEN — Histoire Ancienne de l'Afrique du Nord, Paris, 1921

HADDON, A. C. — The Races of Man, New York, 1925
    History of Anthropology, London, 1934
HANKINS, FRANK H. — Racial Basis of Civilization, New York, 1926
HANKINS, G. T. — The Teaching of History and Geography, Geneva, 1936,
    (League of Nations Bulletin No. 3)
HARDY, GEORGE — L'Art Nègre, Paris, 1927
HAYTCR, FRANK — In Quest of Sheba's Mines, 1935
HAITI — American Nation Series, (Pan-American Union,) No. 11, 1931
HAITI ET LES PROBLÈMES PANAMÈRICAINS — L'Assaut, No. 3, Port-au-Prince,
    1936
Haiti, Education in — Report of United States Commission, 1931
HEBREN, A. H. L. — African Nations, Oxford, 1832
HERTZ, F. — Race and Civilization, New York, 1928
HIGGINS, GODFREY — Anacalypsis, New York, 1927
HINDE, SIDNEY L. — The Last of the Masai, London, 1901
HUGGINS, WILLIS N. — A Guide to the Study of African History, New
    York, 1934

Italy and Abyssinia, (Documents) — Royal Institute of International Affairs,
    London, 1935
Italy, Great Britain and the League — New York, 1935
Italy, Great Britain and the League — New York, 1935
    Italo-Ethiopian Conflict: Italian Point of View as Set Forth by H. E.
        Daniele Varé and Ugo V. D'Annubzio
International Conciliation — Carnegie Foundation for International Peace,
    No. 314, November, 1935, New York
    Background of the Italy and Ethiopia Dispute; Secretary Cordell Hull's

Statement; Sir Samuel Hoare's Address to the League of Nations' Assembly; M. Pierre Laval's Address to the League of Nations and Abstract of Report on Italy's Aggression

JABAVU, JOHN TENGO — The South African Natives, (In Collaboration with The South African Native Committee,) New York, 1909
JANSEN, WERNER — The Light of Egypt, New York, 1928
JASPERT, WILLEM — Das Geheimnis Des Schwartzen Erdteils, Berlin, 1931
JOHNSON, SAMUEL — History of the Yorubas, London, 1921
JONES, A. H. M. and MONROE, ELIZABETH — History of Abyssinia, New York, 1936
JONES, THOMAS JESSE — Education in Africa, New York, 1922
JOHNSTON, H. H. — The Story of My Life, New York, 1923

KEANE, A. H. — Africa, London, 1895
Man, Past and Present, Cambridge, 1920
KETELS, ROBERT — Le Culte de la Race Blanche, (Le Racisme Pan-Europene) Paris, 1935

LAING, S. — Human Origins, London, 1913
LEARNED, ARTHUR — Morocco and the Moors, London, 1891
LEAGUE Documents on Ethiopia, 1923-1936
LEBEL, ROLAND — Le Livre du Pays Noir, Paris, 1928
LE HERISSE, A. — L'Ancienne Royaume de Dahomey, Paris, 1911
LEUTHOLF, JOB — Historia Aethiopica, Frankfort, 1881
LOWIE, ROBERT H. — Culture and Ethnology, New York, 1916
Primitive Society, New York, 1919
Primitive Religion, New York, 1924
LUCAS, CHARLES P. — Partition and Colonization of Africa, Oxford, 1922
LUGARD, LADY — Tropical Dependency, London, 1905
LUNN, ARNOLD — St. Peter Claver; A Saint in the Slave Trade, New York, 1935

MADIOU, THOMAS — Histoire D'Haiti, Annees 1492-1799; 1799-1803, Port-au-Prince, 1922
McCABE, J. — The Social Record of Christianity, London 1935
Splendours of Moorish Spain, London, 1935
MACCALLUM, E. P. — Rivalries in Ethiopia, New York, 1935
MACFIE, W. S. — An Ethiopian Diary, Liverpool, 1936
MACCREAGH, GORDON — The Last of Free Africa, New York, 1935
MACKENZIE, DONALD — Ancient Civilizations, London, 1927
MACLEAN, DONALD — John Hoy of Ethiopia, Toronto, 1936
MACMICHAEL, H. — The Anglo-Egyptian Sudan, London, 1934
MALLIZZA, NICOLA — L'Africa Orientale, Rome, 1935
MANGIN, EUGENE — Les Mossi, Paris, 1921
MARETT, R. R. — Anthropology, New York, 1911
MARTY, PAUL — L'Islam en Mauritanie et Senegal, Paris, 1915-16
Les Tribus de l'Haute Mauritanes, Paris, 1915
Etudes sur l'Islam au Senegal, Paris, 1917
L'Islam en Guinee, Paris, 1921

Etudes sur l'Islam en Cote d'Ivorie, Paris, 1922
Etudes sur l'Islam au Dahomey, Paris, 1926
Etudes Senegalaises, Paris, 1927
MAYARD, CONSTANTIN — Haiti, (L'Action intellectuelle), Port-au-Prince, 1934
MASSEY, GERALD — Book of Beginnings, 1896
MAZZUCCONI, RIDOLFO — La Giornata di Adua, Rome, 1935
MONCEAUX, PAUL — Histoire litteraire de l'Afrique Chrétienne depuis les Originies jusqu'a a l'Envasion Arabe, Paris, 1901
Paiens Judaisante, Paris, 1902
Les Colonie Juives dans l'Afrique Romaine, Paris, 1902
MORET, ALEXANDER — In the Times of the Pharaohs, New York, 1911
Kings and Gods of Egypt, New York, 1912
The Nile and Egyptian Civilization, London, 1927
MORIÈ, L. J. — Histoire de L'Ethiopie (Nubie et Abyssinie) Depuis les Temps les plus recules jusqu'a nos jours, Paris, 1904
MYRES, J. L. — The Dawn of History, New York, 1911

NANNI, UGO — Che Cosa e l'Etiopia, Rome, 1935
NESBIT, L. M. — Hell Hole of Creation, New York, 1935
NORDEN, HERMANN — En Abyssinie, Le Dernier Empire Africain, Paris, 1930
White and Black in East Africa, Boston, 1924
NYABONGO, AKIKI — Africa Answers Back, London, 1936

OGILBY, JOHN — Africa, London, 1679
OLDHAM, J. H. — Christianity and the Race Problem
OLIVIER, LORD — Jamaica
O'ROURKE, VERNON — The Juristic Status of Egypt and the Sudan, London, 1935

PADMORE, GEORGE — How Britain Rules Africa, London, 1936
PEAKE, HAROLD — The Flood, New York, 1930
PEARSON, DREW and BROWN, CONSTANTINE — The American Diplomatic Game, New York, 1935
Mussolini Moves to Abyssinia, New York, 1935
PENDLEBURY, J. D. S. — Tell-el-Armana, London, 1935
PETRIE, FLINDERS — Egypt and Israel, New York, 1925
PIERRE-'ALYPE, L. M. — L'Empire de Negus, de la Reine de Saba a la Societé des Nations, Paris, 1925
L'Ethiopie et Les Convoitises Allemands, (La Politique Anglo-Franco-Italienne,) Paris, 1917
PINON, RENE — Au Max Maroc, Paris, 1935
PITTARD, EUGENE — Les Races et L'Histoire, Paris, 1924
PITT-RIVERS, GENERAL — Antique Works of Art from Benin, London, 1900
PORY, JOHN — Geographical History of Africa, London, 1800
POLLERA, ALBERTO — Lo Stato Etiopica E La Sua Chiesa, Rome, 1926
Storie, Leggende E Favole Del Paese dell Negus, 1935
PROROK, BYRON K. — Digging for Lost African Gods, New York, 1926

218 AN INTRODUCTION TO AFRICAN CIVILIZATIONS

RAWLINSON, GEORGE — The Seven Great Monarchies, New York, 1885
History of Phoenicia, London, 1889
READE, WINWOOD — The Martyrdom of Man, London, 1932
RECLUS, E. — Africa and Its Inhabitants, London, 1878
REIN, G. K. — Abessinien, Berlin, 1918
REY, C. F. — The Real Abyssinia, London, 1935
Unconquered Abyssinia as It is Today, London, 1923
RIDLEY, F. A. — Mussolini Over Africa, 1935
ROCCHI, A. — Etiopia é Etiopi, Rome, 1935

SAYCE, A. H. — Races of the Old Testament, London, 1925
SCARFOGLIO, EDOARDO — Abissinia, Naples, 1888
SCHAPERA, I. — Western Civilization and the Natives of South Africa,
London, 1934 (In Collaboration with John Jabavu et al)
SCHOMBURGH, GEHRTS — Negertypen Des Schwartzen Erdteils, Zurich, 1930
SCHNOEKEL, PAUL — Die Weltpolitische, Lage Unter Kolonien Geschichts-
punkten, Leipzig, 1935
SCHOFIELD, J. F. — Zimbabwe, London, 1926
SCHREIBER, JOACHIM H. — Die Deutschen Kolonien, Berlin, 1935
SELLASSIE, GUEBRE — Chronique du Regne de Menelik II, Paris, 1930
SELIGMAN, G. C. — The Races of Africa, London, 1930
SHAW, JOHN H. — (Consul General of Ethiopia), New York, 1936
SHOBERL, F. — Africa, (4 vols.,) London, 1866
SHOLES, T. E. S. — Glimpses of the Ages, London, 1905
SMITH, G. ELIOT — In the Beginning, London, 1932
SOUTTAR, ROBINSON — Short History of Ancient People, London, 1904
STANLEY, HENRY M. — Magdala, London, 1896
STEER, G. L — Caesar in Abyssinia, London, 1936
STERN, H. A. — The Falashas in Abyssinia, London, 1802
SUMNER, WILLIAM G. — Folkways, Boston, 1906
SWEENEY, JAMES J. — African Negro Art, New York, 1935
SYLVAIN, SUZANNE — Le Creole Haitien, (Morphologie et Syntaxe,) Port-
au-Prince, 1936

TELLEZ, BALTHAZAR — Travels of the Jesuits in Ethiopia, London, 1710
THOMSON and RANDALL MACIVER — Ancient Races of the Thebaid, Oxford,
1905
TORDAY, E. — On the Trail of the Bushongo, Paris, 1920
TOUTAIN, J. — Les Cultes Paiens dans l'Empire Roman, Paris, 1920
TYLOR, E. B. — Anthropology, (2 vols.,) London, 1930

VERNEAUX, M. — L'Homme, Races et Coutumes, (Larousse,) Paris, 1931
VILLARI, LUIGI — The Expansion of Italy, Rome, 1930
VINCENT, STENIO — (President de la Republique Haitien) — Discours,
prononcé á Cap-Haitien, sur la Politique Exterieure du Gouvernement,
Octobre, 1933.
VON REITZENSTEIN — Das Weib Bei Den Naturvolkern, Berlin, 1930
VANDERCOOK, J. W. — Black Majesty, New York, 1928

WAUGH, EVELYN — Waugh in Abyssinia, New York, 1937
WEIGAL, ARTHUR — Akhnaton, Pharaoh of Egypt, New York, 1923
WENCKLER, FRIERICH — Abessinien, Das Pulverfass Afrikas, Wildberg, 1935
WERLEIGH, CHRISTIAN — Le Palmiste dans L'Ouragan, Port-au-Prince, 1933
WILLIAMS, J. J. — Whence the Black Irish of Jamaica? New York, 1932
WISSLER, CLARK — Man and Culture, New York, 1923
WILLOUGHBY, W. C. — Race Problems in the New Africa, Oxford, 1923
    The Soul of the Bantu, New York, 1928
WOOD, CLEMENT — History of the World, New York, 1935
    Outline of Man's Knowledge, New York, 1930
WOODSON, CARTER G. — The African Background Outlined, Washington, D. C., 1936
WOOLF, LEONARD — Empire and Commerce in Africa, London, 1919
WORK, ERNEST — Ethiopia, Pawn in European Diplomacy, New York, 1935

SPECIAL PERIODICAL LITERATURE
(Chiefly French, German and Italian)

ADDO, AKUFO — African Thoughts on African Education, West Africa, October, 1936
AFRICAN NATIONALIST — (Files), Monrovia, Liberia
AFRICAN SOCIETY — Journal of, (Files), London
ANZANI, PAOLO — Motherhood and Infancy in Ethiopia, ATLANTICA, November, 1936
APPELIUS, MARIO — Future of Italian Ethiopia, ATLANTICA, September 1936

BARAVELLI, G. C. — A Century of Italian Explorations into Ethiopia, ATLANTICA, September, 1936
BEJEAN, F. — Wie Lidsch Jassu ermordet wurde, DIE WOCHE, April, 1937
BRUCHHAUSEN, P. — Southwest Africa, JOURNAL OF GEOGRAPHY, May, 1936
BARCLAY, EDWIN — (President of the Republic of Liberia), His Policy, WEST AFRICA MAGAZINE, (Files, 1936)
BLANCHET, JULES — La Releve, Politique-Litteraire, Port-au-Prince
BREASTED, J. H. — History and Social Idealism, RATIONALIST ANNUAL, London, 1936

CATHOLIC WORLD (June 1936) — The Ethiopian Fiasco and After (July, 1936), Catholic Journalism and Race Prejudice

CHAUMEIX, ANDRÈ — L'Europe et le Drame Ethiopien, REVUE DES DEUX MONDES, October, 1935

CANU, JEAN and DRAILMIERE, PAUL — L'Opinion Anglo-Saxonne et l'Ethiopie, L'EUROPE NOUVELLE, August, 1935

CIPRIANUS — Francesi Contro Inglesi in Abissinia nel 1859 (Files of Il Progresso Italo-Americano, 1935)

DEAN, VERA MICHELES — The League and the Italo-Ethiopian Crisis; The Quest for Ethiopian Peace, (Files of the Foreign Policy Association Reports, 1936)

DEWILDE, JOHN C. — Testing League Sanctions, Foreign Policy Association Reports, 1935

DICKINSON, LORD — The League on Trial, CONTEMPORARY REVIEW, London, 1935

DIEDERICH, BENNO — Kamehameha I, von Hawaii, Der Napoleon der Sudsee Atlantis, Berlin, 1936

DI A. B. — Haille Selassie, L'Ultimo Negus dell'Etiopia, (C) 1936

DI BALDI, ICILIO — Monaci, Monasteri è Culto Nell'Abissinia, (C) 1936

DI CIRO, S. — Sino a Quindici Anni fa gli Inglesi Erano Convinti che gli · Etiopi Fossero, Selvaggi, (C) 1936

DI DORICUS, S. — La Pingue Taitu nemica Giurata dell'Italia, (C) 1936 La Donna che Domino è Diresse Cinque Negus, (C) 1936

DI MAFFIO, MAFFII — Cinquemila Anni di Storia Dell'Africa Orientale, (C)

DI MARIO DEI GASLINI — Il Negus Neghesti alla Caccia di Schiavi Durante le Tragiche Spedizioni Zemeccia, (C) 1936

DI MENICUCCI, S. — Bambini d'Etiopia che Vanno già a Scuola, (C)

DI NAVARRA, MARGHERITA — Il Destino Romano di Addis Abeba Compiuto (C)

DI PAOLO, ZAPPA — L'Etiopia, un Paese Prodigiosamente Ricco ove Migli-aia di Gente Muore per la Fame, (C) 1936

DI SALA, M. — Cavour e L'Africa Orientale, (Il tratto 1859 una proposta Allettante l'errore del Ministro DaBormida), (P) 1936

DI VARINI, M. — L'Italia alla Redenzione del Popolo Galla, (C) 1936

DOCUMENTE — Dell'Avanzata su Dessie E Della Sotto Missioni Di Capi E Notabili Degli Uollo-Galla, L'ILLUSTRAZIONE ITALIANA, Vol. 63, No. 17, April 26, 1936, Roma

DuBois, W. E. B. — Inter-Racial Implications of the Ethiopian Crisis, FOREIGN AFFAIRS, October, 1935

FADISCO, N. A. — Stirring Up West Africa, (Files West Africa Magazine,) 1936

EKINS, H. R. — Meet the Ethiopians, CURRENT HISTORY, May, 1936

ERROL, F. J. — The Black Man Buys, GEOGRAPHICAL MAGAZINE, September, 1936

FEDERZONI, LUIGI — The Question of Mandates and Italian Colonial Rights, ATLANTICA, August, 1936

FUCHS, LOUIS — Abyssinian Realities, Files. National Review, London, 1935

FUHRMANN, ERNEST — Sakrakulte Vorgeschichte der Hieroglyphen, Atlantis, (Files) Berlin and Darmstadt, 1922

FRASER, A. G. — Is there a Future for the Educated Native African? The Educational System in British West Africa. (Files, West Africa Magazine, 1935-1936)

GARVEY, MARCUS — Files of "The Black Man," 2 Beaumont Crescent, Kensington, London, W.14. Especially the following:
Italy and Abyssinia—July, 1935
Italy's Conquest, July-August, 1936 and September-October, 1936
Fighting in Abyssinia, The Emperor Runs, January, 1937
More Light on Haille Selassie, January, 1937
Haille Selassie and Benito Mussolini, January, 1936

GLANVILLE, J. L. — Italy's Colonial Policy, Atlantica, February, 1935

HAUSER, ERNEST OTTO — The American Negro and the Dark World, Crisis Magazine, February, 1937

HARRIS, JOHN — Italy and Abyssinia, Contemporary Review, London, 1935

HICHENS, W. — Talking to the African, English Review, London, 1936

HOGAN, FRANCES — Prehistoric Negroes and Their Contribution to Civilization, Crisis, February, 1920

JACKSON, JOHN G. — The Sacred Monogram IHS, Truth Seeker, Vol. 64, No. 3, New York

KOREN, JR., WM. — Imperialist Rivalries in Ethiopia. Reports of the Foreign Policy Association, Files, 1935

LESOURD, PAUL — L'Annee Missionaire, Files (Especially, 1931-36), Paris

LOUKIANOFF, GR. — New Fragments of the Pianhki Stele, Ancient Egypt, September, 1926, Part III, Publication of the British School of Archaeology in Egypt

LUGARD, LORD — The Changing Problems of Africa, West Africa, 1936

LIBERIA — The Truth About It, Files, West Africa, 1936
Notes on Liberia, West Africa, 1936
Reform Program, West Africa, 1936

L'Oeuvre de la France en Afrique Occidentale. L'Illustration, February, 1936

La Voix de L'Ethiopie. Files, 1935-1936, Paris

LUDWIG, EMIL — Abyssinian Slavery and the League, English Review, 1935

MEYEROWITZ, H. V. — Basutoland. Geographical Magazine, September, 1936

MERS DU SUD. — Le Document. Juillet, 1935, Paris

MAIR, L. P. — Native Policies in Africa. West Africa, Files, 1936

MARTIAL, RENE — Les Problemes des Races. Les Nouvelles Litteraires, 1937

INDEX

010721-100-9-60W